Ninja Dual Zone Air Fryer Cookbook 2022 UK

1000 of the latest Ninja Dual Zone Air Fryer recipes, the number one choice for all beginners and advanced users

Pauline Foye

CONTENTS

Fish And Seafood....79

Snacks Appetizers And Sides....94

Ninja Foodi Dual Zone Air Fryer

Looking for a cooking appliance to enhance your existing lineup? Ninja's versatile offering may just be for you. Lavishing us with choice, the Ninja Dual Zone Air Fryer Cookbook 2022 UK joins Ninja's fast-growing kitchen appliance collection. Best known for its range of blenders and food processors that rival the likes of Nutribullet in terms of style and functionality, Ninja designs appliances to 'fit the lifestyles of busy people all over the world'. As well as blenders and food processors, the company offers an intuitive range of choppers, multi-cookers and health grills, all designed to create great tasting food, fast.

The Ninja Foodi Dual Zone Air Fryer is the latest model to join Ninja's range of dedicated air fryers and multi-cookers, boasting the most sleek finish and convenient features to date. It's unique in that it provides the ability to produce two separate dishes in record time. This is possible as a result of its Sync mode, which does the hard work for you by ensuring that the food you place inside meat in one compartment and veg in the other, for example are both ready at the same time.

The Ninja Foodi Dual Zone Air Fryer Cookbook 2022 UK offers all the health benefits of a decent air fryer in that it can cook up to 75 per cent faster than a fan oven, with little to no oil required. What's more, it has the ability to carry out five other tasks, including max crisp for cooking frozen foods such as nuggets and chips; roast, for vegetables and meats; reheat, which is great for leftovers; dehydrate, for making veggie crisps; and bake, for when you fancy something sweet.

Design and key features

Ninja's Foodi Dual Zone Air Fryer is unlike any other air fryer we've tried. As well as the ability to create healthy air-fried foods using little to no oil, it comes with a unique offering in that it can cook two separate foods at the same time and ensure they're ready to serve together.

Measuring an ample H31.5 x D35cm, it's quite a large appliance as countertop gadgets go, but its design is sleek and attractive, as well as functional. A sophisticated black and chrome finish means it's the kind of gadget you won't mind keeping out on your worktop provided you have the room for it.

The appliance feels ergonomic in hand and is luxuriously made. It features two independent cooking drawers that slide out easily to give you an overall capacity of 7.6 litres. Each compartment is deep enough to cook a decent amount of food be it a 500g batch of sweet potato fries, 1kg of chicken or up to 12 cupcakes, for example. The drawer handles feel comfortable and are easy to insert and take out.

Within each compartment is a crisper plate that helps to brown the food when you air-fry; it ensures that air can circulate around the food to remove excess moisture and ensure a crispy, golden finish. They also stop the food sticking to the base of each compartment. We found them easy to take out for simple cleaning, either by hand or in the dishwasher.

As well as air frying, the device has the ability to max crisp, roast, reheat, dehydrate and bake, too, and all these features are clearly marked on the digital control panel. The countdown timer also makes it easy for you to see how much cooking time remains in each section.

Performance

At 8.2 kg, lifting the Ninja Dual Zone Air Fryer Cookbook 2022 UK out of the box and positioning it on the worktop is the hardest part of handling the machine. It features clearly marked controls that light up stylishly as soon as you plug in the appliance and turn it on.

To get a feel for the six-in-one appliance, we used it to perform a number of tasks. Firstly, we air-fried some fresh pork sausages and frozen sweet potatoes. While each zone automatically suggests a set time and temperature, you can easily adjust these to your preference. The guide suggests cooking sausages for around 9 mins at 200 degrees, and the sweet potato fries for around 20 minutes at 190 degrees. Once you've programmed your zone, you can then press Sync to ensure the foods finish cooking at the same time, which is a feature we're most impressed by.

It's recommended that you check food mid-way through the cook, giving it a shake to ensure food is being cooked evenly but this almost defeats the whole USP of such a machine, whereby you're meant to be able to set it and wait for the end to work its magic. That said, trying to get the perfect finish takes some experimentation.

The Ninja Foodi Dual Zone Air Fryer is a powerful machine. Our sausages cooked in super-quick time; in fact, following the suggested time, they were a little overcooked. As mentioned, this will improve as you become familiar with the machine and cooking times, and you'll soon be creating flavoursome dishes in super-quick time.

We particularly like the fact that you can choose different settings for each compartment. For example, you can roast meat on one side, and bake on the other side. We tested its dual functionality by roasting chopped courgettes in one compartment and reheating lamb cutlets in the other. We were suitably happy with the results.

We also attempted to make a batch of halloumi fries and were impressed at how well the fries kept their structure while they cooked. We were able to enjoy crispy, melt-in-the-mouth halloumi fries in under five minutes.

Should I buy the Ninja Dual Zone Air Fryer Cookbook 2022 UK?

Buy it if You want flexibility in the kitchen. This device will give you six cooking settings in one, which you can access easily use it to cook roast chicken on one side, and dessert on the other.

You want to avoid deep-fat frying but love the taste. Use this and choose a healthier air-fry option to limit the amount of oil you serve on your food.

Turkey Burgers

Servings: 4
Cooking Time: 24 Minutes
Ingredients:

- 1 pound lean ground turkey breast
- 2 tablespoons bread crumbs
- 3 2 tablespoons barbecue sauce
- 4 ½ teaspoon garlic powder
- ½ teaspoon chili powder
- Salt and freshly ground black pepper to taste

Directions:

1. Combine all ingredients in a bowl, mixing well. Divide into 4 portions and shape into patties.
2. BROIL on a rack with a pan underneath for 20 minutes, or until the meat is browned and the juice runs clear when pierced with a fork.

Goat Cheese Rosemary Crostini With Roasted Garlic + Tomatoes

Servings: 20
Cooking Time: 25 Minutes
Ingredients:

- 4 to 5 large cloves garlic, trimmed, not peeled
- 1 ½ tablespoons olive oil
- 2 cups grape tomatoes
- Kosher salt and freshly ground black pepper
- 1 teaspoon balsamic or red wine vinegar
- 4 ounces soft, creamy goat cheese, softened (about ½ cup)
- 1 tablespoon minced fresh rosemary leaves
- 1 baguette loaf, cut into ½-inch-thick slices
- Fresh rosemary leaves or minced flat-leaf (Italian) parsley, for garnish (optional)

Directions:

1. Preheat the toaster oven to 400°F.
2. Place the garlic on an 8- to 12-inch square of aluminum foil and bring up the edges to make a shallow bowl. Drizzle the garlic with ½ tablespoon olive oil. Bring the foil over the garlic and fold the edges to make a sealed packet. Place the packet on one side of a 12 x 12-inch baking pan. (Note: Be sure to make the aluminum foil packet compact and place it on the pan but positioned so it is not near the heating element.)
3. Place the tomatoes in a medium bowl. Drizzle with the remaining tablespoon of olive oil and season with salt and pepper. Pour the tomatoes into a single layer on the other end of the baking pan. Roast, uncovered, for 20 to 25 minutes or until the edges of the tomatoes begin to brown and they are tender.
4. Remove the tomatoes and garlic from the oven and let cool slightly. Spoon the roasted tomatoes, with any collected liquid, into a medium bowl. When the garlic is cool enough to handle, gently squeeze the garlic into a small bowl and discard the garlic peels. Use the back of a spoon to mash the garlic. Stir the roasted garlic and vinegar into the tomatoes. Season with salt and pepper; set aside.
5. Stir the goat cheese and rosemary in a small bowl. Season it generously with pepper. Blend until smooth; set aside.
6. Toast the slices of the baguette in the toaster oven.
7. Distribute the goat cheese mixture evenly over the toasted bread slices. Top with a teaspoon of the roasted tomato-garlic mixture. If desired, garnish with fresh rosemary.

Cinnamon Rolls

Servings: 12
Cooking Time: 10 Minutes
Ingredients:

- Buttermilk Biscuit dough
- Cinnamon mixture:
- 3 tablespoons dark brown sugar
- 3 tablespoons chopped pecans
- 2 tablespoons margarine
- 1 teaspoon ground cinnamon
- Salt to taste
- Icing:
- 1 cup confectioners' sugar, sifted
- 1 tablespoon fat-free half-and-half
- ½ teaspoon vanilla extract
- Salt to taste

Directions:

1. Preheat the toaster oven to 400° F.
2. Make the buttermilk biscuit dough.
3. Roll out or pat the dough to ½ inch thick. In a small bowl, combine the cinnamon mixture ingredients. Spread the dough evenly with the cinnamon mixture and roll up like a jelly roll. With a sharp knife, cut the roll into 1-inch slices. Place on an oiled or nonstick 6½ × 10-inch baking sheet.
4. BAKE for 15 minutes, or until lightly browned. Let cool before frosting.
5. Combine the icing ingredients in a small bowl, adding more half-and-half or confectioners' sugar until the consistency is like thick cream. Drizzle over the tops of the cinnamon rolls and serve.

Breakfast Blueberry Peach Crisp

Servings: 8
Cooking Time: 60 Minutes
Ingredients:

- Filling Ingredients
- 4 cups blueberries, fresh or frozen
- 2 cups peaches, sliced
- 1 teaspoon vanilla extract
- 2 teaspoons lemon juice
- 4 tablespoons pure maple syrup
- 1½ tablespoons cornstarch
- A tiny pinch of salt
- Topping Ingredients

- 2½ cups rolled oats
- 5 tablespoons almond meal (or almond flour)
- 1 teaspoon cinnamon
- 5 tablespoons pure maple syrup
- 3 tablespoons coconut sugar (or brown sugar)
- 7 tablespoons coconut oil, melted
- 1 cup sliced almonds
- 1 cup chopped walnuts
- ¼ teaspoon salt

Directions:

1. Combine the blueberries, peaches, vanilla extract, lemon juice, maple syrup, cornstarch, and salt in a bowl and toss to combine. Pour mixture into the baking dish.
2. Combine all the topping ingredients in a separate bowl and stir until clumps form, then spread evenly over the fruit mixture.
3. Preheat the toaster Oven to 350°F.
4. Place the baking dish on the wire rack, then insert rack at low position in the preheated oven.
5. Select the Bake function, adjust time to 1 hour, then press
6. Start/Pause.
7. Remove crisp when golden on top and fruit is bubbly.
8. Serve with yogurt for breakfast or vanilla ice cream for dessert.

Buttermilk Biscuits

Servings: 6
Cooking Time: 15minutes
Ingredients:

- 2 cups unbleached flour
- 1 tablespoon baking powder
- ½ teaspoon baking soda
- Salt
- 3 tablespoons margarine, at room temperature
- 1 cup low-fat buttermilk
- Vegetable oil

Directions:

1. Preheat the toaster oven to 400° F.
2. Combine the flour, baking powder, baking soda, and salt to taste in a medium bowl.
3. Cut in the margarine with 2 knives or a pastry blender until the mixture is crumbly.
4. Stir in the buttermilk, adding just enough so the dough will stay together when pinched.
5. KNEAD the dough on a floured surface for one minute, then pat or roll out the dough to ¾ inch thick. Cut out biscuit rounds with a 2½-inch biscuit cutter. Place the rounds on an oiled or nonstick 6½ × 10inch baking sheet.
6. BAKE for 15 minutes, or until golden brown.

Tuna Tarragon Picnic Loaf

Servings: 4
Cooking Time: 10 Minutes
Ingredients:

- 1 French baguette, sliced in half lengthwise, then quartered
- Filling:
- 1 6-ounce can tuna in water, well drained
- 2 tablespoons chopped onion
- 2 tablespoons chopped Spanish olives with pimientos, drained
- 2 tablespoons chopped fresh parsley
- 2 tablespoons chopped bell pepper
- 1 teaspoon dried tarragon
- Salt and butcher's pepper to taste
- ½ cup shredded low-fat mozzarella cheese

Directions:

1. Remove enough bread from each quarter to make a small cavity for the sandwich filling.
2. Combine all the filling ingredients and spoon the mixture in equal portions into each of the bread quarter cavities. Sprinkle each quarter with equal portions of mozzarella cheese.
3. BROIL on a broiling rack with a pan underneath for 10 minutes, or until the bread is lightly browned and the cheese is melted. If your toaster oven cannot accommodate 4 French bread quarters, broil them in two batches. Slice and serve.

Onion And Cheese Buttermilk Biscuits

Servings: 4
Cooking Time: 15 Minutes
Ingredients:

- 2 cups unbleached flour
- 3 tablespoons margarine, at room temperature
- ¾ cup low-fat buttermilk
- 4 teaspoons baking powder
- 1 teaspoon garlic powder
- ¼ cup grated Parmesan cheese
- 3 tablespoons finely chopped onion
- 2 tablespoons chopped fresh parsley
- Salt to taste

Directions:

1. Preheat the toaster oven to 400° F.
2. Blend all the ingredients in a medium bowl with a fork, then press together to form a dough ball.
3. KNEAD the dough on a lightly floured surface just until smooth.
4. Roll the dough to ½-inch thickness and cut with a round 3-inch cookie cutter. Place on an oiled or nonstick 6½ × 10-inch baking sheet or in an oiled or nonstick 8½ × 8½ × 2-inch square baking (cake) pan.
5. BAKE for 15 minutes, or until lightly browned.

Coffee Cake

Servings: 6
Cooking Time: 40 Minutes
Ingredients:

- Cake:
- 2 cups unbleached flour
- 2 teaspoons baking powder
- 2 tablespoons vegetable oil
- 1 egg
- 1¼ cups skim milk
- Topping:

- ½ cup brown sugar
- 1 tablespoon margarine, at room temperature
- 1 teaspoon ground cinnamon
- ¼ teaspoon grated nutmeg
- ¼ cup chopped pecans
- Salt to taste

Directions:

1. Preheat the toaster oven to 375° F.
2. Combine the ingredients for the cake in a medium bowl and mix thoroughly. Pour the batter into an oiled or 8½ × 8½ × 2inch square baking (cake) pan and set aside.
3. Combine the topping ingredients in a small bowl, mashing the margarine into the dry ingredients with a fork until the mixture is crumbly. Sprinkle evenly on top of the batter.
4. BAKE for 40 minutes, or until a toothpick inserted in the center comes out clean. Cool and cut into squares.

Sam's Maple Raisin Bran Muffins

Servings: 12
Cooking Time: 15 Minutes

Ingredients:

- 2 cups oat bran
- 2 teaspoons baking powder
- 2 eggs
- 1¼ cups low-fat soy milk
- ¾ cup raisins
- 3 tablespoons maple syrup
- 2 tablespoons vegetable oil
- Pinch of salt (optional)

Directions:

1. Preheat toaster oven to 425° F.
2. Combine all the ingredients in a bowl and stir until well blended. In a six-muffin 7 × 10 × 1½-inch tin, brush the pans with vegetable oil or use baking cups. Fill the pans or cups three-fourths full with batter.
3. BAKE for 15 minutes, or until a toothpick inserted in the center of a muffin comes out clean.

Garlic-cheese Biscuits

Servings: 8
Cooking Time: 8 Minutes

Ingredients:

- 1 cup self-rising flour
- 1 teaspoon garlic powder
- 2 tablespoons butter, diced
- 2 ounces sharp Cheddar cheese, grated
- ½ cup milk
- cooking spray

Directions:

1. Preheat the toaster oven to 330°F.
2. Combine flour and garlic in a medium bowl and stir together.
3. Using a pastry blender or knives, cut butter into dry ingredients.
4. Stir in cheese.
5. Add milk and stir until stiff dough forms.
6. If dough is too sticky to handle, stir in 1 or 2 more tablespoons of self-rising flour before shaping. Biscuits should be firm enough to hold their shape. Otherwise, they'll stick to the air fryer oven.
7. Divide dough into 8 portions and shape into 2-inch biscuits about ¾-inch thick.
8. Spray air fryer oven with nonstick cooking spray.
9. Place all 8 biscuits in air fryer oven and air-fry at 330°F for 8 minutes.

Turkey And Tuna Melt

Servings: 2
Cooking Time: 4 Minutes

Ingredients:

- 4 slices multigrain bread Spicy brown mustard
- 1 6-ounce can tuna in water, drained well and crumbled
- ¼ pound thinly sliced turkey breast
- 4 slices low-fat Monterey Jack cheese
- 2 tablespoons finely chopped scallions
- Salt and freshly ground black pepper

Directions:

1. Spread one side of each bread slice with mustard and place on an oiled or nonstick
2. 6½ × 10-inch baking sheet.
3. Layer 2 slices with equal portions of tuna, turkey, cheese, and scallion. Season to taste with salt and pepper.
4. TOAST twice, or until the cheese is melted.

Mediterranean Egg Sandwich

Servings: 1
Cooking Time: 8 Minutes

Ingredients:

- 1 large egg
- 5 baby spinach leaves, chopped
- 1 tablespoon roasted bell pepper, chopped
- 1 English muffin
- 1 thin slice prosciutto or Canadian bacon

Directions:

1. Spray a ramekin with cooking spray or brush the inside with extra-virgin olive oil.
2. In a small bowl, whisk together the egg, baby spinach, and bell pepper.
3. Split the English muffin in half and spray the inside lightly with cooking spray or brush with extra-virgin olive oil.
4. Preheat the toaster oven to 350°F for 2 minutes. Place the egg ramekin and open English muffin into the air fryer oven, and air-fry at 350°F for 5 minutes. Open the air fryer oven and add the prosciutto or bacon; air-fry for an additional 1 minute.
5. To assemble the sandwich, place the egg on one half of the English muffin, top with prosciutto or bacon, and place the remaining piece of English muffin on top.

Green Onion Pancakes

Servings: 4
Cooking Time: 8 Minutes
Ingredients:

- 2 cup all-purpose flour
- ½ teaspoon salt
- ¾ cup hot water
- 1 tablespoon vegetable oil
- 1 tablespoon butter, melted
- 2 cups finely chopped green onions
- 1 tablespoon black sesame seeds, for garnish

Directions:

1. In a large bowl, whisk together the flour and salt. Make a well in the center and pour in the hot water. Quickly stir the flour mixture together until a dough forms. Knead the dough for 5 minutes; then cover with a warm, wet towel and set aside for 30 minutes to rest.
2. In a small bowl, mix together the vegetable oil and melted butter.
3. On a floured surface, place the dough and cut it into 8 pieces. Working with 1 piece of dough at a time, use a rolling pin to roll out the dough until it's ¼ inch thick; then brush the surface with the oil and butter mixture and sprinkle with green onions. Next, fold the dough in half and then in half again. Roll out the dough again until it's ¼ inch thick and brush with the oil and butter mixture and green onions. Fold the dough in half and then in half again and roll out one last time until it's ¼ inch thick. Repeat this technique with all 8 pieces.
4. Meanwhile, preheat the toaster oven to 400°F.
5. Place 1 or 2 pancakes into the air fryer oven (or as many as will fit in your fryer), and air-fry for 2 minutes or until crispy and golden brown. Repeat until all the pancakes are cooked. Top with black sesame seeds for garnish, if desired.

Garlic Cheese Pull-apart Bread

Servings: 6
Cooking Time: 26 Minutes
Ingredients:

- 1 (1-pound) loaf frozen white bread dough
- Canola or vegetable oil
- Nonstick cooking spray
- 6 tablespoons unsalted butter, melted
- 3 cloves garlic, finely minced
- 2 tablespoons minced fresh flat-leaf (Italian) parsley
- ¼ teaspoon table salt
- ¼ teaspoon freshly ground black pepper
- ⅔ cup shredded Parmesan cheese
- ¾ cup shredded mozzarella cheese

Directions:

1. Rub the frozen dough lightly with the oil. Place it in a zip-top bag and refrigerate overnight to thaw.
2. Spray a 9 x 5-inch loaf pan with nonstick cooking spray.
3. Stir the butter, garlic, parsley, salt, and pepper in a small bowl; set aside.
4. Place the thawed dough on a lightly floured board and roll into a 12-inch square. Brush about 3 tablespoons of the butter mixture over the top of the dough. Sprinkle evenly with about ½ cup Parmesan and ½ cup mozzarella. Roll the dough over the filling, jelly-roll style. Cut into rolls ½ to ¾ inch thick. Stand the rolls upright in the loaf pan, two across, with the cut side of the rolls facing the narrow end of the pan. (There will be two rows, side by side, with 8 to 10 rolls in each row.) Cover with a towel and let rise for about 1 hour.
5. Preheat the toaster oven to 350°F. Bake for 18 to 23 minutes, or until the loaf is golden brown. Drizzle with the remaining melted butter mixture. Sprinkle with the remaining 2 tablespoons Parmesan cheese and the remaining¼ cup mozzarella cheese. Bake for 2 to 3 minutes for the cheese to melt.
6. Place the pan on a wire rack and let stand for 5 minutes. Remove the loaf from the pan. Serve warm.

Mahi Mahi Tacos With Pineapple Salsa

Servings: 2
Cooking Time: 9 Minutes
Ingredients:

- Salsa Ingredients
- 1 cup pineapple, diced
- ½ lime, zested and juiced
- 1 small jalapeno, diced
- 1 avocado, diced
- ¼ red onion, diced
- 2 tablespoons cilantro, chopped
- A pinch of salt
- Mahi Mahi Ingredients
- 2 (6-ounce) filets of Mahi Mahi fish
- 1 tablespoon olive oil
- Salt & pepper, to taste
- Corn tortillas for serving

Directions:

1. Combine all the salsa ingredients in a bowl. Stir together and taste, then add additional salt if desired. Store salsa in the fridge until ready to serve.
2. Preheat the toaster Oven to 430°F.
3. Line the food tray with foil, then place mahi mahi on the tray. Drizzle with olive oil and season with salt and pepper.
4. Insert food tray at top position in the preheated oven.
5. Select the Air Fry function, adjust time to 9 minutes, and press Start/Pause.
6. Remove when the internal temperature of the mahi mahi reaches close to 145°F. Allow fish to rest for 5 minutes, then flake into large pieces.
7. Assemble tacos by placing pieces of mahi mahi onto warmed corn tortillas. Top with salsa and serve.

Portobello Burgers

Servings: 4
Cooking Time: 12 Minutes
Ingredients:

- 4 multigrain hamburger buns Dijon mustard
- 4 large portobello mushroom caps, stemmed and brushed clean
- 2 tablespoons olive oil
- Garlic powder
- Salt and butcher's pepper
- 4 thin onion slices

- 4 tomato slices

Directions:

1. TOAST the split hamburger buns and spread each slice with mustard. Set aside.
2. Brush both sides of the mushroom caps with olive oil and sprinkle with garlic powder and salt and pepper to taste.
3. BROIL the caps on a broiling rack with a pan underneath, ribbed side up, for 6 minutes. Turn the mushrooms carefully with tongs and broil again for 6 minutes, or until lightly browned. Place the mushroom caps on the bottom buns and layer each with an onion and tomato slice. Top with the remaining bun halves and serve.

Broiled Grapefruit With Cinnamon Brown Sugar

Servings: 4
Cooking Time: 7 Minutes

Ingredients:

- 2 large grapefruit, halved
- 1/4 cup packed light brown sugar
- 1/4 teaspoon ground cinnamon
- 1 tablespoon butter, softened
- 1/4 cup vanilla yogurt
- 2 tablespoons granola

Directions:

1. Preheat the toaster oven to 400°F. Place rack in upper position.
2. Remove all seeds from grapefruit and section with a paring knife. Cut a small slice from the bottom of each grapefruit half to prevent them from rocking. Place grapefruit halves on toaster oven baking pan.
3. In small bowl, mix brown sugar and cinnamon. Sprinkle evenly over top of grapefruit halves. Dot with butter.
4. Broil for 6 to 7 minutes or until brown sugar and butter is bubbly. Top each half with 1 tablespoon yogurt and 1/2 tablespoon granola.

Cinnamon Swirl Bread

Servings: 4
Cooking Time: 50 Minutes

Ingredients:

- 2 cups all-purpose flour
- 1 cup granulated sugar
- 1 teaspoon baking soda
- ½ teaspoon table salt
- 1 teaspoon cider vinegar
- 1 cup whole milk
- 1 large egg
- ¼ cup canola or vegetable oil
- FILLING
- ½ cup granulated sugar
- 1 tablespoon ground cinnamon
- GLAZE
- ¼ cup confectioners' sugar
- 2 teaspoons whole milk

Directions:

1. Preheat the toaster oven to 350 °F. Grease the bottom of a 9 x 5-inch loaf pan.
2. Combine the flour, granulated sugar, baking soda, and salt in a large bowl. Place the vinegar in a 1-cup liquid measuring cup and add the milk; stir to combine. Whisk the milk mixture, egg, and oil in a medium bowl. Stir into the flour mixture, blending until combined.
3. Make the filling: Combine the granulated sugar and cinnamon in a small bowl.
4. Pour half of the batter into the prepared pan. Sprinkle half the cinnamon-sugar mixture over the batter in the loaf pan. Top with the remaining batter and sprinkle with remaining cinnamon-sugar mixture. Using a butter knife, make deep swirls in the batter. Make sure most of the cinnamon-sugar mixture from the top is covered in batter.
5. Bake for 45 to 50 minutes, or until a wooden pick inserted into the center comes out clean. Cool on a wire rack for 10 minutes. Run a knife around the edges of the bread, then remove the bread from the pan. Cool for an additional 10 minutes.
6. Meanwhile, make the glaze: Whisk the confectioners' sugar and milk in a small bowl until smooth. Drizzle the glaze over the partially cooled loaf. Serve warm or at room temperature.

Sheet-pan Hash Browns

Servings: 2
Cooking Time: 60 Minutes

Ingredients:

- 1½ pounds Yukon Gold potatoes, unpeeled, shredded
- 3 tablespoons extra-virgin olive oil
- ½ teaspoon table salt
- ⅛ teaspoon pepper

Directions:

1. Adjust toaster oven rack to lowest position, select air-fry or convection function, and preheat the toaster oven to 450 degrees. Place potatoes in large bowl and cover with cold water. Let sit for 5 minutes.
2. Lift potatoes out of water, one handful at a time, and transfer to colander; discard water. Rinse and dry bowl. Place half of shredded potatoes in center of clean dish towel. Gather ends of towel and twist tightly to wring out excess moisture from potatoes. Transfer dried potatoes to now-empty bowl. Repeat with remaining potatoes.
3. Add oil, salt, and pepper to potatoes and toss to combine. Distribute potatoes in even layer on small rimmed baking sheet, but do not pack down. Cook until top of potatoes is spotty brown, 30 to 40 minutes, rotating sheet halfway through baking.
4. Remove sheet from oven. Using spatula, flip hash browns in sections. Return sheet to oven and continue to cook until spotty brown and dry, 10 to 15 minutes. Season with salt and pepper to taste. Serve.

Bread Boat Eggs

Servings: 4
Cooking Time: 10 Minutes

Ingredients:

- 4 pistolette rolls
- 1 teaspoon butter
- ¼ cup diced fresh mushrooms
- ½ teaspoon dried onion flakes

- 4 eggs
- ½ teaspoon salt
- ¼ teaspoon dried dill weed
- ¼ teaspoon dried parsley
- 1 tablespoon milk

Directions:

1. Cut a rectangle in the top of each roll and scoop out center, leaving ½-inch shell on the sides and bottom.
2. Place butter, mushrooms, and dried onion in air fryer oven baking pan and air-fry for 1 minute. Stir and cook 3 more minutes.
3. In a medium bowl, beat together the eggs, salt, dill, parsley, and milk. Pour mixture into pan with mushrooms.
4. Air-fry at 390°F for 2 minutes. Stir. Continue cooking for 3 or 4 minutes, stirring every minute, until eggs are scrambled to your liking.
5. Remove baking pan from air fryer oven and fill rolls with scrambled egg mixture.
6. Place filled rolls in air fryer oven and air-fry at 390°F for 2 to 3 minutes or until rolls are lightly browned.

Cheddar Cheese Biscuits

Servings: 8
Cooking Time: 22 Minutes
Ingredients:

- 2⅓ cups self-rising flour
- 2 tablespoons sugar
- ½ cup butter (1 stick), frozen for 15 minutes
- ½ cup grated Cheddar cheese, plus more to melt on top
- 1⅓ cups buttermilk
- 1 cup all-purpose flour, for shaping
- 1 tablespoon butter, melted

Directions:

1. Line a buttered 7-inch metal cake pan with parchment paper or a silicone liner.
2. Combine the flour and sugar in a large mixing bowl. Grate the butter into the flour. Add the grated cheese and stir to coat the cheese and butter with flour. Then add the buttermilk and stir just until you can no longer see streaks of flour. The dough should be quite wet.
3. Spread the all-purpose (not self-rising) flour out on a small cookie sheet. With a spoon, scoop 8 evenly sized balls of dough into the flour, making sure they don't touch each other. With floured hands, coat each dough ball with flour and toss them gently from hand to hand to stir any excess flour. Place each floured dough ball into the prepared pan, right up next to the other. This will help the biscuits rise up, rather than spreading out.
4. Preheat the toaster oven to 380°F.
5. Transfer the cake pan to the air fryer oven, lowering it into the air fryer oven using a sling made of aluminum foil (fold a piece of aluminum foil into a strip about 2-inches wide by 24-inches long). Let the ends of the aluminum foil sling hang across the cake pan before returning to the air fryer oven.
6. Air-fry for 20 minutes. Check the biscuits a couple of times to make sure they are not getting too brown on top. If they are, re-arrange the aluminum foil strips to cover any brown parts. After 20 minutes, check the biscuits by inserting a toothpick into the center of the biscuits. It should come out clean. If it needs a little more time, continue to air-fry for a couple of extra minutes. Brush the tops of the biscuits with some melted butter and sprinkle a little more grated cheese on top if desired. Air-fry for another 2 minutes. Remove the cake pan from the air fryer oven using the aluminum sling. Let the biscuits cool for just a minute or two and then turn them out onto a plate and pull apart. Serve immediately.

Zucchini Walnut Bread

Servings: 6
Cooking Time: 30 Minutes
Ingredients:

- ¾ cup all-purpose flour
- ½ teaspoon baking soda
- 1 teaspoon ground cinnamon
- ⅛ teaspoon salt
- 1 large egg
- ⅓ cup packed brown sugar
- ¼ cup canola oil
- 1 teaspoon vanilla extract
- ⅓ cup milk
- 1 medium zucchini, shredded (about 1⅓ cups)
- ⅓ cup chopped walnuts

Directions:

1. Preheat the toaster oven to 320°F.
2. In a medium bowl, mix together the flour, baking soda, cinnamon, and salt.
3. In a large bowl, whisk together the egg, brown sugar, oil, vanilla, and milk. Stir in the zucchini.
4. Slowly fold the dry ingredients into the wet ingredients. Stir in the chopped walnuts. Then pour the batter into two 4-inch oven-safe loaf pans.
5. Bake for 30 minutes or until a toothpick inserted into the center comes out clean. Let cool before slicing.
6. Store tightly wrapped on the counter for up to 5 days, in the refrigerator for up to 10 days, or in the freezer for 3 months.

Apple Incredibles

Servings: 6
Cooking Time: 25 Minutes
Ingredients:

- Muffin mixture:
- 2 cups unbleached flour
- 1 teaspoon baking powder
- ¼ cup brown sugar
- ½ teaspoon salt
- ¼ cup margarine, at room temperature
- ½ cup skim milk
- 1 egg, beaten
- 2 tablespoons finely chopped raisins
- 2 tablespoons finely chopped pecans
- 1 apple, peeled, cored, and thinly sliced

Directions:

1. Preheat the toaster oven to 400° F.

2. Combine the muffin mixture ingredients in a large bowl, stirring just to blend. Fill the pans of an oiled or nonstick 6-muffin tin with the batter. Insert the apple slices vertically into the batter, standing and pushing them all the way down to the bottom of the pan.
3. BAKE for 25 minutes, or until the apples are tender and the muffins are lightly browned.

Rosemary Bread

Servings: 6
Cooking Time: 15 Minutes
Ingredients:

- Spread:
- 3 tablespoons olive oil
- 2 tablespoons margarine
- 1 teaspoon garlic
- 2 tablespoons grated Parmesan cheese
- 3 1 tablespoon finely chopped fresh rosemary leaves
- ½ teaspoon freshly ground black pepper
- Salt to taste
- 1 French baguette, sliced 2 inches thick

Directions:

1. Preheat the toaster oven to 350° F.
2. Combine the spread ingredients in a small bowl, blending well with a fork. Adjust the seasonings to taste.
3. Spread the mixture on both sides of the bread slices and wrap the loaf in aluminum foil.
4. BAKE for 10 minutes. Remove from the oven and peel back the foil, exposing the top of the bread loaf. Bake for another 5 minutes, or until the top is lightly browned.

Brunch Burritos

Servings: 4
Cooking Time: 14 Minutes
Ingredients:

- Egg mixture:
- 4 medium eggs, lightly beaten
- 3 tablespoons finely chopped bell pepper
- 2 tablespoons finely chopped onion
- 4 strips lean turkey bacon, uncooked and cut into small ¼ × ¼-inch pieces
- 1 tablespoon chopped fresh cilantro
- ½ teaspoon ground cumin
- ½ teaspoon chili powder
- Salt and red pepper flakes to taste
- 4 6-inch flour tortillas
- 4 tablespoons salsa
- 4 tablespoons shredded part-skim, low-moisture mozzarella

Directions:

1. Combine the egg mixture ingredients in an oiled or nonstick 8½ × 8½ × 2-inch square baking (cake) pan.
2. TOAST twice, or until the mixture is firm and cooked.
3. Spoon the egg mixture in equal portions onto the center of each tortilla. Add 1 tablespoon salsa and 1 tablespoon mozzarella cheese to each. Roll each tortilla around the filling and lay, seam side down, in an oiled or nonstick 8½ × 8½ × 2-inch square baking (cake) pan.
4. BROIL for 8 minutes, or until lightly browned.

Egg-loaded Potato Skins

Servings: 4
Cooking Time: 55 Minutes
Ingredients:

- 2 large russet potatoes
- ½ teaspoon olive oil
- ½ cup Gruyère cheese, shredded and divided
- 4 large eggs
- ¼ cup heavy (whipping) cream, divided
- 1 scallion, both white and green parts, finely chopped
- Sea salt, for seasoning
- Freshly ground black pepper, for seasoning

Directions:

1. Preheat the toaster oven to 400°F on BAKE.
2. Prick the potatoes all over with a fork and rub with the olive oil.
3. Place the potatoes directly on the rack and bake for 40 minutes. The potatoes should be soft and tender, and the skin lightly browned. If not done, set the timer for 5 minutes more.
4. Take the potatoes out and set aside until cool enough to handle, about 10 minutes.
5. Cut the potatoes in half lengthwise and scoop out the flesh so that you have about ½-inch flesh and the intact skin. Place the potato halves in the air-fryer basket (placed on the baking tray) and sprinkle 2 tablespoons of cheese in each skin. Crack an egg into each potato half and spoon 1 tablespoon of cream over each egg. Sprinkle with scallion and lightly season with salt and pepper.
6. In position 1, bake for 15 minutes until the egg whites are set, and the yolks are still runny. If the eggs need more time, set the timer for 3 to 5 minutes more. Serve.

Breakfast Pita

Servings: 2
Cooking Time: 3 Minutes
Ingredients:

- 1 5-inch whole wheat pita loaf
- 1 teaspoon olive oil
- 1 egg, well beaten
- 2 tablespoons shredded low-fat mozzarella cheese
- Garlic powder
- Salt and freshly ground black pepper

Directions:

1. Cut a circle out of the top layer of one pita bread loaf and remove the disk-shaped layer, leaving the bottom intact. Brush the pita loaf with the olive oil. Carefully pour the beaten egg into the cavity. Sprinkle with cheese and season with garlic powder and salt and pepper to taste.
2. TOAST once on the oven rack, or until the egg is cooked thoroughly and the cheese is lightly browned.

Corn Bread

Servings: 6
Cooking Time: 20 Minutes
Ingredients:

- 1 cup cornmeal
- ¾ cup unbleached flour
- 2 tablespoons sugar
- 4 teaspoons baking powder
- 1 egg, beaten
- 1 cup skim milk
- 2 tablespoons vegetable oil
- Salt to taste

Directions:

1. Preheat the toaster oven to 425° F.
2. Combine all the ingredients in a medium bowl and mix just to blend. The batter will be slightly lumpy. Pour into an oiled or nonstick regular-size 8½ × 4½ × 2¼-inch loaf pan.
3. BAKE for 20 minutes, or until a toothpick inserted in the center comes out clean.

Italian Strata

Servings: 6
Cooking Time: 55 Minutes
Ingredients:

- 1 cup boiling water
- 3 tablespoons chopped sun-dried tomatoes (dry-packed)
- 5 cups cubed French bread or country bread (cut into 1-inch cubes)
- Nonstick cooking spray
- 1 ½ ounces sliced turkey pepperoni, cut into fourths (about ¾ cup)
- 2 tablespoons chopped pepperoncini peppers
- 1 cup coarsely chopped fresh spinach
- 1 cup shredded Italian blend cheese or mozzarella cheese
- 4 large eggs
- 1 ½ cups whole milk
- 1 teaspoon Italian seasoning
- ¼ teaspoon kosher salt
- 2 tablespoons shredded Parmesan cheese

Directions:

1. Pour the boiling water the over sun-dried tomatoes in a small, deep bowl; set aside.
2. Preheat the toaster oven to 350 °F. Place the bread cubes on a 12 x 12-inch baking pan. Bake for 10 minutes, stirring once.
3. Spray an 8 x 8-inch square baking pan with nonstick cooking spray. Drain the sun-dried tomatoes and pat dry with paper towels. Arrange half the bread cubes evenly in the prepared pan. Top with half the pepperoni, half the pepperoncini, all the spinach, and all of the reconstituted tomatoes. Sprinkle with ½ cup of the Italian cheese. Repeat layers with the remaining bread, pepperoni, pepperoncini, and ½ cup cheese.
4. Whisk the eggs, milk, Italian seasoning, and salt in a large bowl. Pour the egg mixture over the bread layers. Press down lightly with the back of a large spoon. Sprinkle with the Parmesan cheese. Cover and chill for at least 2 hours or overnight.
5. Preheat the toaster oven to 350°F. Bake the strata, uncovered, for 35 to 45 minutes, or until a knife inserted into the center comes out clean. Let stand for 10 minutes before serving.

French Vegetable Tartines

Servings: 4
Cooking Time: 21 Minutes
Ingredients:

- ½ medium red bell pepper, cut into ½-inch slices
- ½ medium red onion, cut into ½-inch slices
- 2 tablespoons olive oil
- Kosher salt and freshly ground black pepper
- ¾ cup thick-sliced button or white mushrooms
- 8 asparagus spears, trimmed and halved crosswise
- 2 tablespoons unsalted butter, softened
- 1 small clove garlic, minced
- 1 tablespoon minced fresh rosemary leaves
- 4 thick slices French or artisan bread
- ⅓ cup shredded fontina, Gruyère, or Swiss cheese
- Minced fresh flat-leaf (Italian) parsley or thyme leaves

Directions:

1. Preheat the toaster oven to 375°F.
2. Place the red pepper and red onion in a medium bowl. Drizzle with 1 tablespoon of the olive oil and season with salt and pepper; toss to coat well. Arrange the red pepper and onion slices in an ungreased 12 x 12-inch baking pan. Bake, uncovered, for 10 minutes.
3. Place the mushrooms and asparagus pieces in that same bowl. Drizzle with the remaining tablespoon of olive oil and season with salt and pepper. Stir the roasted pepper and onion and add the asparagus and mushrooms to the pan. Bake for 7 to 9 minutes or until the vegetables are tender. Remove the baking pan from the toaster oven and set aside.
4. Meanwhile, stir the butter, garlic, and rosemary in a small bowl. Season with salt and pepper and set aside.
5. Toast the bread in the toaster oven. Spread one side of each slice of toast with the butter mixture. Place the toast, buttered side up, on a baking pan. Arrange the vegetables equally on the toast, then top with the cheese.
6. Preheat the toaster oven on 400°F. Broil the tartines for 1 to 2 minutes, or just until the cheese melts. Garnish with parsley. Serve warm.

Baked Curried Fruit

Servings: 4
Cooking Time: 25 Minutes
Ingredients:

- Curry mixture:
- 2 tablespoons dry white wine
- 1 teaspoon lemon juice
- ¼ teaspoon ground allspice
- ¼ teaspoon ground ginger
- ¼ teaspoon ground cardamom
- ¼ teaspoon turmeric
- ¼ teaspoon ground cumin

- ¼ teaspoon ground coriander
- Pinch of grated nutmeg
- Pinch of cayenne
- 2 tablespoons honey
- 1 teaspoon soy sauce
- 1 16-ounce can pear halves, drained
- 1 8-ounce can pineapple chunks, drained
- 1 16-ounce can peach halves

Directions:

1. Preheat the toaster oven to 350° F.
2. Combine the curry mixture ingredients in a 1-quart 8½ × 8½ × 4-inch ovenproof baking dish and add the fruit, mixing well.
3. BAKE, uncovered, for 25 minutes, or until bubbling and the sauce is thickened. Cool and serve on a sesame wafer with Creamy Yogurt Sauce.

Baked Macs

Servings: 2
Cooking Time: 30 Minutes

Ingredients:

- 2 tablespoons rolled oats
- 2 tablespoons applesauce
- 1 tablespoon honey
- 1 teaspoon ground cinnamon
- Pinch of ground allspice
- Pinch of salt
- 2 McIntosh apples, cored
- Maple Yogurt Sauce (recipe follows)

Directions:

1. Preheat the toaster oven to 375° F.
2. Mix together the oatmeal, applesauce, honey, and seasonings in a small bowl. Spoon the mixture into the cavities of the apples and place the apples in an oiled or nonstick 8½ × 8½ × 2-inch square baking (cake) pan.
3. BAKE the apples for 30 minutes, or until tender. Serve chilled or warm with Maple Yogurt Sauce.

Nutty Whole Wheat Muffins

Servings: 8
Cooking Time: 11 Minutes

Ingredients:

- ½ cup whole-wheat flour, plus 2 tablespoons
- ¼ cup oat bran
- 2 tablespoons flaxseed meal
- ¼ cup brown sugar
- ½ teaspoon baking soda
- ½ teaspoon baking powder
- ¼ teaspoon salt
- ½ teaspoon cinnamon
- ½ cup buttermilk
- 2 tablespoons melted butter
- 1 egg
- ½ teaspoon pure vanilla extract
- ½ cup grated carrots
- ¼ cup chopped pecans
- ¼ cup chopped walnuts
- 1 tablespoon pumpkin seeds
- 1 tablespoon sunflower seeds
- 16 foil muffin cups, paper liners removed
- cooking spray

Directions:

1. Preheat the toaster oven to 330°F.
2. In a large bowl, stir together the flour, bran, flaxseed meal, sugar, baking soda, baking powder, salt, and cinnamon.
3. In a medium bowl, beat together the buttermilk, butter, egg, and vanilla. Pour into flour mixture and stir just until dry ingredients moisten. Do not beat.
4. Gently stir in carrots, nuts, and seeds.
5. Double up the foil cups so you have 8 total and spray with cooking spray.
6. Place 4 foil cups in air fryer oven and divide half the batter among them.
7. Air-fry at 330°F for 11 minutes or until toothpick inserted in center comes out clean.
8. Repeat step 7 to cook remaining 4 muffins.

Crepes

Servings: 6
Cooking Time: 27 Minutes

Ingredients:

- ½ cup unbleached flour
- ¾ cup skim milk
- 1 egg
- 2 teaspoons vegetable oil
- Salt to taste

Directions:

1. Whisk together all the ingredients in a small bowl until smooth. Set aside.
2. Preheat an oiled or nonstick 9¾-inch round pie pan by placing it under the broiler for 2 minutes, or until the pan is heated but not smoking. Remove from the oven and spoon 2 tablespoons crepe batter into the pan, tilting the pan to spread the batter evenly into a circle. Return to the broiler.
3. BROIL for 4 minutes, or until the crepe is cooked but not browned. Remove the pan from the oven and invert onto paper towels to cool and drain. Repeat the procedure with the remaining batter.

Broiled Bananas

Servings: 2
Cooking Time: 10 Minutes

Ingredients:

- Sauce:
- 1 tablespoon margarine
- 2 tablespoons honey
- 2 tablespoons lemon juice
- Pinch of salt (optional)
- 2 bananas, peeled, halved and quartered
- Creamy Yogurt Sauce or fat-free half-and-half

Directions:

1. Place the sauce ingredients in an oiled or nonstick 8½ × 8½ × 2-inch square baking (cake) pan.
2. BROIL for 5 minutes, or until the mixture begins to bubble. Remove the pan carefully from the oven using oven

mitts and stir to blend. Add the bananas and spoon the sauce over them.

3. BROIL for 5 minutes, or until the bananas are tender and golden in color.

4. Place 4 banana quarters each in 2 dessert dishes and spoon equal portions of the sauce over them. Serve with Creamy Yogurt Sauce or drizzle with fat-free half-and-half.

Potato & Bacon Frittata

Servings: 4

Cooking Time: 15 Minutes

Ingredients:

- 2 slices bacon, chopped
- 1 tablespoon olive oil
- ½ onion, thinly sliced
- 1 large gold potato, diced into ½-inch cubes
- Salt & pepper, to taste 6 large eggs
- ½ cup grated Parmesan cheese

Directions:

1. Place the chopped bacon slices in a large nonstick skillet. Cook over medium high heat for 5 minutes or until the bacon is cooked and crispy. Move the bacon to a small plate.
2. Add olive oil to the skillet, then add the onion and potato. Season with salt and pepper. Sautee for 10-12 minutes, or until the potatoes are tender.
3. Remove from heat and place the bacon, potatoes, and onions into the greased baking dish.
4. Preheat the toaster Oven to 350°F.
5. Whisk together the eggs, Parmesan, and a pinch of salt and pepper in a bowl. Pour egg mixture over the bacon, potatoes, and onions.
6. Place the baking dish on the wire rack, then insert the rack at mid position in the preheated oven.
7. Select the Bake function, adjust time to 15 minutes, then press Start/Pause.
8. Remove when the frittata is set. Allow to cool for 10 minutes before slicing.

Flaky Granola

Servings: 3

Cooking Time: 20 Minutes

Ingredients:

- ¼ cup rolled oats
- ½ cup wheat flakes
- ½ cup bran flakes
- ¼ cup wheat germ
- 3 tablespoons sesame seeds
- 4 ¼ cup unsweetened shredded coconut
- ½ cup chopped almonds, walnuts, or pecans
- 2 tablespoons chopped pumpkin seeds
- ½ cup honey or molasses
- 2 tablespoons vegetable oil
- Salt to taste

Directions:

1. Preheat the toaster oven to 375° F.
2. Combine all the ingredients in a medium bowl, stirring to mix well.
3. Spread the mixture in an oiled or nonstick 6½ × 6½ × 2-inch square (cake) pan.
4. BAKE for 20 minutes, turning with tongs every 5 minutes to toast evenly. Cool and store in an airtight container in the refrigerator.

Berry Crisp

Servings: 4

Cooking Time: 25 Minutes

Ingredients:

- 2 16-ounce packages frozen berries or 4 cups fresh berries
- 2 tablespoons lemon juice
- ½ cup rolled oats
- 1 tablespoon margarine, at room temperature
- 3 tablespoons wheat germ
- 4 ¼ cup honey
- 5 1 teaspoon vanilla extract
- Salt to taste

Directions:

1. Preheat the toaster oven to 400° F.
2. Combine the berries or fruit and lemon juice in a 1-quart-size 8½ × 8½ × 4-inch ovenproof baking dish, tossing well to mix. Set aside.
3. Combine the rolled oats, margarine, wheat germ, honey, vanilla, and salt in a small bowl and stir with a fork until the mixture is crumbly. Sprinkle evenly on top of the berries.
4. BAKE, covered, for 20 minutes, or until the berries are bubbling. Remove from the oven and uncover.
5. BROIL for 5 minutes, or until the topping is lightly browned.

Not-so-english Muffins

Servings: 4

Cooking Time: 10 Minutes

Ingredients:

- 2 strips turkey bacon, cut in half crosswise
- 2 whole-grain English muffins, split
- 1 cup fresh baby spinach, long stems removed
- ¼ ripe pear, peeled and thinly sliced
- 4 slices Provolone cheese

Directions:

1. Place bacon strips in air fryer oven and air-fry for 2minutes. Check and separate strips if necessary so they cook evenly. Air-fry for 4 more minutes, until crispy. Remove and drain on paper towels.
2. Place split muffin halves in air fryer oven and air-fry at 390°F for 2minutes, just until lightly browned.
3. Open air fryer oven and top each muffin with a quarter of the baby spinach, several pear slices, a strip of bacon, and a slice of cheese.
4. Air-fry at 360°F for 2minutes, until cheese completely melts.

Carrot Orange Muffins

Servings: 12
Cooking Time: 12 Minutes
Ingredients:

- 1½ cups all-purpose flour
- ½ cup granulated sugar
- ½ teaspoon ground cinnamon
- 2 teaspoons baking powder
- ¼ teaspoon baking soda
- ½ teaspoon salt
- 2 large eggs
- ¼ cup vegetable oil
- ⅓ cup orange marmalade
- 2 cups grated carrots

Directions:

1. Preheat the toaster oven oven to 320°F.
2. In a large bowl, whisk together the flour, sugar, cinnamon, baking powder, baking soda, and salt; set aside.
3. In a separate bowl, whisk together the eggs, vegetable oil, orange marmalade, and grated carrots.
4. Make a well in the dry ingredients; then pour the wet ingredients into the well of the dry ingredients. Using a rubber spatula, mix the ingredients for 1 minute or until slightly lumpy.
5. Using silicone muffin liners, fill 6 muffin liners two-thirds full.
6. Carefully place the muffin liners in the air fryer oven and bake for 12 minutes (or until the tops are browned and a toothpick inserted in the center comes out clean). Carefully remove the muffins from the air fryer oven and repeat with remaining batter.
7. Serve warm.

Southern-style Biscuits

Servings: 10
Cooking Time: 12 Minutes
Ingredients:

- 2 cups all-purpose flour
- 1 tablespoon baking powder
- 1 teaspoon table salt
- 4 tablespoons cold, unsalted butter, cut into bits
- ¾ to 1 cup buttermilk

Directions:

1. Preheat the toaster oven to 450 °F.
2. Combine the flour, baking powder, and salt in a large bowl. Using a pastry cutter or two knives, cut the butter into the flour mixture until the mixture is crumbly throughout. Pour in the buttermilk and gently mix until just combined.
3. Turn the dough onto a lightly floured surface and knead lightly about 8 times. Roll the dough, using a rolling pin, until about ½ inch thick. Cut out rounds using a 2 ½ -inch cutter. Place on an ungreased 12 x 12-inch baking pan or 8-inch round pan.
4. Bake for 10 to 12 minutes or until golden brown. Let cool slightly before serving warm.

Mushroom Blue Cheese Crostini

Servings: 10
Cooking Time: 3 Minutes
Ingredients:

- 1 tablespoon olive oil
- 8 ounces mushrooms, wild or button, sliced
- 3 cloves garlic, minced
- 2 tablespoons fresh flat-leaf (Italian) parsley, minced
- 2 teaspoons chopped fresh thyme, rosemary, or sage leaves
- Kosher salt and freshly ground black pepper
- 10 to 12 country bread, artisan bread, or baguette slices
- 1 cup grated fontina cheese
- ½ cup blue cheese or Gorgonzola crumbles
- 1 tablespoon fresh lemon juice
- Whole flat-leaf (Italian) parsley, for garnish

Directions:

1. Heat the olive oil in a medium nonstick skillet over medium-high heat. Add the mushrooms and cook, stirring frequently, until the liquid has evaporated, 7 to 10 minutes. Add the garlic and cook for 1 minute. Remove from the heat. Stir in the parsley and thyme and season with salt and pepper. Allow the mixture to cool.
2. Toast the slices of bread in the toaster oven.
3. Stir the fontina and blue cheese into the mushroom mixture.
4. Preheat the toaster oven on 400°F. Arrange the toasted baguette slices on a 12 x 12-inch baking sheet. Distribute the mushroom cheese mixture evenly over the toasted bread slices. Broil until the cheese melts, 2 to 3 minutes. Drizzle with the lemon juice. Garnish each crostini with a parsley leaf. Serve immediately.

Honey Ham And Swiss Broiler

Servings: 2
Cooking Time: 5 Minutes
Ingredients:

- 4 slices pumpernickel bread
- 1 tablespoon olive oil
- 1 tablespoon spicy brown mustard
- 1 tablespoon horseradish
- 4 slices reduced-fat honey ham
- 4 slices reduced-fat Swiss cheese
- 2 tablespoons finely chopped fresh parsley

Directions:

1. Brush one side of the 4 bread slices with oil and lay, oil side down, in an oiled or nonstick 8½ × 8½ × 2-inch square baking (cake) pan.
2. Spread 2 slices with mustard and 2 slices with horseradish.
3. Layer each with 1 slice honey ham and 1 slice Swiss cheese.
4. BROIL for 5 minutes, or until the cheese is melted. Sprinkle with equal portions of parsley and serve.

Orange-glazed Pears

Servings: 4
Cooking Time: 19 Minutes

Ingredients:

- 2 ripe pears
- 1 tablespoon lemon juice
- 1 tablespoon margarine
- Pinch of salt
- Glaze:
- 2 tablespoons sugar
- 3 tablespoons orange juice

Directions:

1. Prepare the pears: peel, cut in half, remove the seeds and fibrous centers with a teaspoon, quarter and brush the pear pieces with the lemon juice, and set aside.
2. Combine the glaze ingredients in an oiled or nonstick 8½ × 8½ × 2-inch square baking (cake) pan.
3. BROIL for 4 minutes, or until the margarine is melted. Remove from the oven, stir to blend, add the pear quarters, and spoon the glaze mixture over the pears to coat well.
4. BROIL for 15 minutes, or until the glaze has thickened and the pears are tender and golden in color. Serve warm or chilled.

Nacho Chips

Servings: 12
Cooking Time: 20 Minutes

Ingredients:

- 3 jalapeño peppers
- 4 6-inch flour tortillas
- 1 cup shredded low-fat Cheddar cheese

Directions:

1. Seed and cut the jalapeño peppers into thin rings. Arrange one-fourth of the rings on the tortilla. It's a good idea to wear gloves, since the peppers can sometimes cause skin irritation.
2. Place the tortilla in an oiled or nonstick 8½ × 8½ × 2-inch square baking (cake) pan. Sprinkle evenly with ¼ cup cheese.
3. BROIL for 5 minutes, or until the cheese is melted. Repeat the process for the remaining tortillas. Cut each into 6 wedges with a sharp knife or scissors.

Sweet And Spicy Pumpkin Scones

Servings: 8
Cooking Time: 8 Minutes

Ingredients:

- 2 cups all-purpose flour
- 3 tablespoons packed brown sugar
- ½ teaspoon baking powder
- ¼ teaspoon baking soda
- ½ teaspoon kosher salt
- ½ teaspoon ground cinnamon
- ¼ teaspoon ground ginger
- ¼ teaspoon ground cardamom
- 4 tablespoons cold unsalted butter
- ½ cup plus 2 tablespoons pumpkin puree, divided
- 4 tablespoons milk, divided
- 1 large egg
- 1 cup powdered sugar

Directions:

1. In a large bowl, mix together the flour, brown sugar, baking powder, baking soda, salt, cinnamon, ginger, and cardamom. Using a pastry blender or two knives, cut in the butter until coarse crumbles appear.
2. In a small bowl, whisk together ½ cup of the pumpkin puree, 2 tablespoons of the milk, and the egg until combined. Pour the wet ingredients into the dry ingredients; stir to combine.
3. Form the dough into a ball and place onto a floured service. Press the dough out or use a rolling pin to roll out the dough until ½ inch thick and in a circle. Cut the dough into 8 wedges.
4. Bake at 360°F for 8 to 10 minutes or until completely cooked through. Cook in batches as needed.
5. In a medium bowl, whisk together the powdered sugar, the remaining 2 tablespoons of pumpkin puree, and the remaining 2 tablespoons of milk. When the pumpkin scones have cooled, drizzle the pumpkin glaze over the top before serving.

Almond Granola With Dried Fruit

Servings: 5
Cooking Time: 45 Minutes

Ingredients:

- 2½ tablespoons maple syrup
- 2½ tablespoons packed light brown sugar
- 2 teaspoons vanilla extract
- ¼ teaspoon table salt
- ¼ cup vegetable oil
- 2½ cups (7½ ounces) old-fashioned rolled oats
- 1 cup whole almonds, chopped
- 1 cup raisins, currants, dried cranberries, and/or chopped dried cherries

Directions:

1. Adjust toaster oven rack to middle position and preheat the toaster oven to 325 degrees. Line small rimmed baking sheet with parchment paper.
2. Whisk maple syrup, sugar, vanilla, and salt together in large bowl, then whisk in oil until fully combined. Fold in oats and almonds until thoroughly coated. Transfer oat mixture to prepared sheet and spread into even layer. Using stiff metal spatula, compress oat mixture until very compact. Bake until lightly browned, 35 to 45 minutes, rotating sheet halfway through baking.
3. Remove granola from oven and let cool on wire rack to room temperature, about 1 hour. Break cooled granola into pieces of desired size and transfer to large clean bowl. Add dried fruit and gently toss to combine. (Granola can be stored in airtight container for up to 2 weeks.)

Wild Blueberry Lemon Chia Bread

Servings: 6
Cooking Time: 27 Minutes
Ingredients:

- ¼ cup extra-virgin olive oil
- ⅓ cup plus 1 tablespoon cane sugar
- 1 large egg
- 3 tablespoons fresh lemon juice
- 1 tablespoon lemon zest
- ⅔ cup milk
- 1 cup all-purpose flour
- ¾ teaspoon baking powder
- ⅛ teaspoon salt
- 2 tablespoons chia seeds
- 1 cup frozen wild blueberries
- ⅓ cup powdered sugar
- 2 teaspoons milk

Directions:

1. Preheat the toaster oven to 310°F.
2. In a medium bowl, mix the olive oil with the sugar. Whisk in the egg, lemon juice, lemon zest, and milk; set aside.
3. In a small bowl, combine the all-purpose flour, baking powder, and salt.
4. Slowly mix the dry ingredients into the wet ingredients. Stir in the chia seeds and wild blueberries.
5. Liberally spray a 7-inch springform pan with olive-oil spray. Pour the batter into the pan and place the pan in the air fryer oven. Bake for 25 to 27 minutes, or until a toothpick inserted in the center comes out clean.
6. Remove and let cool on a wire rack for 10 minutes prior to removing from the pan.
7. Meanwhile, in a small bowl, mix the powdered sugar with the milk to create the glaze.
8. Slice and serve with a drizzle of the powdered sugar glaze.

Portable Omelet

Servings: 1
Cooking Time: 4 Minutes
Ingredients:

- 2 slices multigrain bread
- 2 eggs
- 1 tablespoon plain nonfat yogurt
- Salt and freshly ground black pepper
- 2 strips turkey bacon
- 2 tablespoons shredded low-moisture, part-skim mozzarella cheese

Directions:

1. TOAST the bread slices and set aside.
2. Whisk together the eggs and yogurt in a small bowl and season with salt and pepper to taste.
3. Layer bacon strips in a small 4 × 8 × 2¼-inch loaf pan. Pour the egg mixture on top and sprinkle with the cheese.
4. TOAST once, or until the egg is done to your preference. Cut the omelet into toast-size squares and place between the 2 slices of toast to make a sandwich. (TOAST takes 2 to 3 minutes.)

English Scones

Servings: 8
Cooking Time: 8 Minutes
Ingredients:

- 2 cups all-purpose flour
- 1 tablespoon baking powder
- ½ teaspoon salt
- 2 tablespoons sugar
- ¼ cup unsalted butter
- ⅔ cup plus 1 tablespoon whole milk, divided

Directions:

1. Preheat the toaster oven to 380°F.
2. In a large bowl, whisk together the flour, baking powder, salt, and sugar. Using a pastry blender or your fingers, cut in the butter until pea-size crumbles appear. Make a well in the center and pour in ⅔ cup of the milk. Quickly mix the batter until a ball forms. Knead the dough 3 times.
3. Place the dough onto a floured surface and, using your hands or a rolling pin, flatten the dough until it's ¾ inch thick. Using a biscuit cutter or drinking glass, cut out 10 circles, reforming the dough and flattening as needed to use up the batter.
4. Brush the tops lightly with the remaining 1 tablespoon of milk.
5. Place the scones into the air fryer oven. Air-fry for 8 minutes or until golden brown and cooked in the center.

Fancy Toasted Bagels

Servings: 2
Cooking Time: 2 Minutes
Ingredients:

- 2 bagels, cut in half
- 4 tablespoons grated Parmesan cheese
- Paprika
- Spread:
- 4 tablespoons low-fat cream cheese
- 2 tablespoons chopped pimientos
- 1 tablespoon chopped scallions
- 1 tablespoon chopped fresh parsley
- ¼ teaspoon Worcestershire sauce
- ½ teaspoon garlic powder
- Salt and freshly ground black pepper to taste

Directions:

1. Sprinkle each bagel slice with 2 tablespoons Parmesan cheese and paprika to taste.
2. TOAST once on the oven rack.
3. Combine the ingredients for the spread, mixing well. Adjust the seasonings to taste. Spread the mixture in equal portions on the toasted bagel slices and serve.

New York–style Crumb Cake

Servings: 8
Cooking Time: 90 Minutes
Ingredients:

- CRUMB TOPPING
- 8 tablespoons unsalted butter, melted
- ⅓ cup (2⅓ ounces) granulated sugar
- ⅓ cup packed (2⅓ ounces) dark brown sugar

- ¾ teaspoon ground cinnamon
- ⅛ teaspoon table salt
- 1¾ cups (7 ounces) cake flour
- CAKE
- 1¼ cups (5 ounces) cake flour
- ½ cup (3½ ounces) granulated sugar
- ¼ teaspoon baking soda
- ¼ teaspoon table salt
- 6 tablespoons unsalted butter, cut into 6 pieces and softened
- ⅓ cup buttermilk
- 1 large egg plus 1 large yolk
- 1 teaspoon vanilla extract
- Confectioners' sugar

Directions:

1. Adjust toaster oven rack to middle position and preheat the toaster oven to 325 degrees. Make foil sling for 8-inch square baking pan by folding 2 long sheets of aluminum foil so each is 8 inches wide. Lay sheets of foil in pan perpendicular to each other, with extra foil hanging over edges of pan. Push foil into corners and up sides of pan, smoothing foil flush to pan.
2. FOR THE CRUMB TOPPING: Whisk melted butter, granulated sugar, brown sugar, cinnamon, and salt in medium bowl until combined. Add flour and stir with rubber spatula or wooden spoon until mixture resembles thick, cohesive dough; set aside to cool to room temperature, 10 to 15 minutes.
3. FOR THE CAKE: Using stand mixer fitted with paddle, mix flour, sugar, baking soda, and salt on low speed to combine. With mixer running, add softened butter 1 piece at a time. Continue beating until mixture resembles moist crumbs with no visible butter pieces remaining, 1 to 2 minutes. Add buttermilk, egg and yolk, and vanilla and beat on medium-high speed until light and fluffy, about 1 minute, scraping down bowl as needed.
4. Transfer batter to prepared pan. Using rubber spatula, spread batter into even layer. Break apart crumb topping into large pea-size pieces and sprinkle in even layer over batter, beginning with edges and then working toward center. (Assembled cake can be wrapped tightly with plastic wrap and refrigerated for up to 24 hours; increase baking time to 40 to 45 minutes.)
5. Bake until crumbs are golden and toothpick inserted in center of cake comes out clean, 35 to 40 minutes, rotating pan halfway through baking. Let cool on wire rack for at least 30 minutes. Using foil overhang, lift cake out of pan. Dust with confectioners' sugar before serving.

Buttered Poppy Seed Bread

Servings: 6
Cooking Time: 25 Minutes

Ingredients:

- 3 tablespoons unsalted butter, melted
- 1 (1-pound) loaf frozen white bread dough
- 1 teaspoon poppy seeds
- ¼ teaspoon onion powder
- ¼ teaspoon garlic powder
- ¼ teaspoon freshly ground black pepper

Directions:

1. Pour about half of the melted butter into a 9 x 5-inch loaf pan. Brush the butter to cover the sides and bottom of the pan. Place the frozen bread loaf in the pan. Brush the top of the loaf with the remaining butter, covering completely. Stir the poppy seeds, onion powder, garlic powder, and pepper in a small bowl. Sprinkle the seasonings over the top of the bread. Cover with plastic wrap and refrigerate overnight.
2. Remove the bread from the refrigerator and loosen the plastic wrap so it is loosely covered. Let it rise at room temperature until the top of the bread is just over the top edge of the pan, about 2 to 4 hours.
3. Preheat the toaster oven to 350°F.
4. Bake for 20 to 25 minutes or until the bread is golden brown.
5. Let cool for 5 minutes, then remove the loaf from the pan and place on a wire rack to cool for a few minutes. Slice and serve warm.

Sun-dried Tomato Spread

Servings: 1
Cooking Time: 4 Minutes

Ingredients:

- ½ cup minced sun-dried tomatoes
- 3 tablespoons olive oil
- 2 tablespoons grated Parmesan cheese
- 1 teaspoon dried oregano or
- 1 tablespoon chopped fresh oregano
- 3 tablespoons chopped pecans or walnuts
- 2 garlic cloves, chopped
- Salt and freshly ground black pepper to taste

Directions:

1. Combine the sun-dried tomatoes and ⅔ cup water in an oiled or nonstick 8½ × 8½ × 2-inch baking (cake) pan.
2. BROIL for 4 minutes, or until the tomatoes are softened. Remove from the oven and transfer the tomatoes with the liquid to a bowl. Add all the other ingredients and mix well.
3. Process the mixture in a blender or food processor until smooth. Adjust the seasonings.

Strawberry Toast

Servings: 4
Cooking Time: 8 Minutes

Ingredients:

- 4 slices bread, ½-inch thick
- butter-flavored cooking spray
- 1 cup sliced strawberries
- 1 teaspoon sugar

Directions:

1. Spray one side of each bread slice with butter-flavored cooking spray. Lay slices sprayed side down.
2. Divide the strawberries among the bread slices.
3. Sprinkle evenly with the sugar and place in the air fryer oven in a single layer.
4. Air-fry at 390°F for 8 minutes. The bottom should look brown and crisp and the top should look glazed.

Orange Rolls

Servings: 8
Cooking Time: 10 Minutes
Ingredients:

- parchment paper
- 3 ounces low-fat cream cheese
- 1 tablespoon low-fat sour cream or plain yogurt (not Greek yogurt)
- 2 teaspoons sugar
- ¼ teaspoon pure vanilla extract
- ¼ teaspoon orange extract
- 1 can (8 count) organic crescent roll dough
- ¼ cup chopped walnuts
- ¼ cup dried cranberries
- ¼ cup shredded, sweetened coconut
- butter-flavored cooking spray
- Orange Glaze
- ½ cup powdered sugar
- 1 tablespoon orange juice
- ¼ teaspoon orange extract
- dash of salt

Directions:

1. Cut a circular piece of parchment paper slightly smaller than the bottom of your air fryer oven. Set aside.
2. In a small bowl, combine the cream cheese, sour cream or yogurt, sugar, and vanilla and orange extracts. Stir until smooth.
3. Preheat the toaster oven to 300°F.
4. Separate crescent roll dough into 8 triangles and divide cream cheese mixture among them. Starting at wide end, spread cheese mixture to within 1 inch of point.
5. Sprinkle nuts and cranberries evenly over cheese mixture.
6. Starting at wide end, roll up triangles, then sprinkle with coconut, pressing in lightly to make it stick. Spray tops of rolls with butter-flavored cooking spray.
7. Place parchment paper in air fryer oven, and place 4 rolls on top, spaced evenly.
8. Air-fry for 10minutes, until rolls are golden brown and cooked through.
9. Repeat steps 7 and 8 to cook remaining 4 rolls. You should be able to use the same piece of parchment paper twice.
10. In a small bowl, stir together ingredients for glaze and drizzle over warm rolls.

Zucchini Melt

Servings: 6
Cooking Time: 16 Minutes
Ingredients:

- Sandwich mixture:
- 1 small zucchini, chopped
- 1 plum tomato, chopped
- 2 tablespoons chopped scallions
- ¼ cup sliced mushrooms
- 1 bell pepper, seeded and chopped
- 1 tablespoon olive oil
- 2 tablespoons minced pimientos
- 1 teaspoon dried oregano
- ½ teaspoon dried basil
- 1 teaspoon minced garlic
- 6 slices multigrain or rye bread
- ½ cup shredded low-fat mozzarella cheese
- 2 tablespoons grated Parmesan cheese

Directions:

1. Combine the sandwich mixture ingredients in a medium bowl, mixing well.
2. Transfer to an oiled or nonstick 8½ × 8½ × 2-inch square baking (cake) pan.
3. BROIL for 10 minutes, or until the zucchini and scallions are tender.
4. Spoon the mixture onto each slice of bread in equal portions. Sprinkle each slice with equal portions of the cheeses. Place the bread slices on a broiling rack with a pan underneath.
5. BROIL for 6 minutes, or until the cheese is melted.

Breakfast Pizza

Servings: 2
Cooking Time: 60 Minutes
Ingredients:

- 3 tablespoons extra-virgin olive oil, divided, plus extra for drizzling
- 1 recipe Classic Pizza Dough (recipe follows), room temperature
- 4 ounces whole-milk mozzarella cheese, shredded (1 cup)
- ½ ounce Parmesan cheese, grated (¼ cup)
- 2 ounces (¼ cup) cottage cheese
- ⅛ teaspoon dried oregano
- 4 ounces breakfast sausage, casings removed
- 4 large eggs
- ⅛ teaspoon table salt
- ⅛ teaspoon pepper
- 2 tablespoons minced fresh chive

Directions:

1. Coat small rimmed baking sheet with 2 tablespoons oil. Press and roll dough into 11 by 8-inch rectangle on lightly floured counter. (If dough springs back during rolling, let rest for 10 minutes before rolling again.) Transfer dough to prepared sheet and re-stretch dough into 11 by 8-inch rectangle. Brush dough evenly with 1 teaspoon oil and cover with plastic wrap. Let sit in warm spot until slightly risen, about 20 minutes.
2. Adjust toaster oven rack to lowest position and preheat the toaster oven to 450 degrees. Remove plastic and, using your fingers, make indentations all over dough. Bake until dough has puffed slightly, 5 to 7 minutes.
3. Combine mozzarella and Parmesan in bowl. Combine cottage cheese, oregano, and remaining 2 teaspoons oil in separate bowl.
4. Remove sheet from oven and, using spatula, press down on any air bubbles. Spread cottage cheese mixture evenly over top, leaving ½-inch border around edges. Pinch sausage into dime-size pieces and arrange evenly over cottage cheese mixture. Sprinkle mozzarella mixture evenly over pizza, leaving ½-inch border. Using back of spoon, create 4 evenly

spaced indentations in cheese, each about 3 inches in diameter. Crack 1 egg into each well, then sprinkle with salt and pepper.

5. Bake until crust is golden brown on bottom and eggs are just set, 9 to 10 minutes for slightly runny yolks or 11 to 12 minutes for soft but set yolks. Remove pizza from pan and transfer to wire rack; let rest for 5 minutes. Sprinkle with chives and drizzle with extra oil. Cut into 8 equal pieces and serve.

Egg Muffins

Servings: 4
Cooking Time: 11 Minutes

Ingredients:

- 4 eggs
- salt and pepper
- olive oil
- 4 English muffins, split
- 1 cup shredded Colby Jack cheese
- 4 slices ham or Canadian bacon

Directions:

1. Preheat the toaster oven to 390°F.
2. Beat together eggs and add salt and pepper to taste. Spray air fryer oven baking pan lightly with oil and add eggs. Air-fry for 2 minutes, stir, and continue cooking for 4 minutes, stirring every minute, until eggs are scrambled to your preference. Remove pan from air fryer oven.
3. Place bottom halves of English muffins in air fryer oven. Take half of the shredded cheese and divide it among the muffins. Top each with a slice of ham and one-quarter of the eggs. Sprinkle remaining cheese on top of the eggs. Use a fork to press the cheese into the egg a little so it doesn't slip off before it melts.
4. Air-fry at 360°F for 1 minute. Add English muffin tops and air-fry for 4 minutes to heat through and toast the muffins.

Morning Glory Muffins

Servings: 6
Cooking Time: 25 Minutes

Ingredients:

- Oil spray (hand-pumped)
- ¼ cup raisins
- 1 cup whole-wheat flour
- ½ cup packed dark brown sugar
- 1 teaspoon baking soda
- 1¼ teaspoons pumpkin pie spice
- ¼ teaspoon sea salt
- 1 cup carrot, finely shredded
- 1 small apple, peeled, cored, and shredded
- ⅓ cup shredded, sweetened coconut
- 2 large eggs
- ¼ cup canola oil
- Juice and zest of ½ orange

Directions:

1. Place the rack on position 1 and preheat the toaster oven on BAKE to 350°F for 5 minutes. Lightly spray 6 muffin cups with the oil or line them with paper liners.
2. In a small bowl, cover the raisins with hot water and set aside.
3. In a large bowl, whisk the flour, brown sugar, baking soda, pumpkin pie spice, and salt. Add the carrot, apple, and coconut, and toss to mix.
4. In a small bowl, beat the eggs, oil, orange juice, and orange zest.
5. Drain the raisins, squeezing out as much water as possible.
6. Add the wet ingredients and raisins to the dry ingredients and mix until the batter is just combined.
7. Spoon the batter into the muffin cups.
8. Bake for 25 minutes or until a knife inserted in the center comes out clean.
9. Remove from the oven and let cool before serving.

Tarragon Beef Ragout

Servings: 6
Cooking Time: 53 Minutes
Ingredients:

- 1 pound lean round steak, cut across the grain of the meat into thin strips, approximately ¼ × 2 inches
- ½ cup dry red wine
- 1 small onion, chopped
- 2 carrots, peeled and thinly sliced
- 3 2 plum tomatoes, chopped
- 1 celery stalk, chopped
- 1 10-ounce package frozen peas
- 3 garlic gloves, minced
- 1 tablespoon Dijon mustard
- ½ teaspoon ground cumin
- ½ teaspoon dried tarragon
- Salt and freshly ground black pepper to taste

Directions:

1. Preheat the toaster oven to 375° F.
2. Combine all the ingredients with ½ cup water in an 8½ × 8½ × 4-inch ovenproof baking dish. Adjust the seasonings. Cover with aluminum foil.
3. BAKE, covered, for 45 minutes, or until the beef, onion, and celery are tender. Remove the cover.
4. BROIL 8 minutes to reduce the liquid and lightly brown the top.

Easy Oven Lasagne

Servings: 4
Cooking Time: 60 Minutes
Ingredients:

- 6 uncooked lasagna noodles, broken in half
- 1 15-ounce jar marinara sauce
- ½ pound ground turkey or chicken breast
- ½ cup part-skim ricotta cheese
- ½ cup shredded part-skim mozzarella cheese
- 2 tablespoons chopped fresh oregano leaves or 1 teaspoon dried oregano
- 2 tablespoons chopped fresh basil leaves or 1 teaspoon dried basil
- 1 tablespoon garlic cloves, minced
- ¼ cup grated Parmesan cheese
- Salt and freshly ground black pepper to taste

Directions:

1. Preheat the toaster oven to 375° F.
2. Layer in a 1-quart 8½ × 8½ × 4-inch ovenproof baking dish in this order: 6 lasagna noodle halves, ½ jar of the marinara sauce, ½ cup water, half of the ground meat, half of the ricotta and mozzarella cheeses, half of the oregano and basil leaves, and half of the minced garlic. Repeat the layer, starting with the noodles. Cover the dish with aluminum foil.
3. BAKE, covered, for 50 minutes, or until the noodles are tender. Uncover, sprinkle the top with Parmesan cheese and bake for another 10 minutes, or until the liquid is reduced and the top is browned.

Creamy Roasted Pepper Basil Soup

Servings: 4
Cooking Time: 35 Minutes
Ingredients:

- 1 5-ounce jar roasted peppers, drained ½ cup fresh basil leaves
- 1 cup fat-free half-and-half
- 1 cup skim milk
- 2 tablespoons reduced-fat cream cheese
- 1 teaspoon garlic powder
- 1 teaspoon paprika
- Salt and freshly ground black pepper to taste
- 2 tablespoons chopped fresh basil leaves (garnish for cold soup)
- 2 tablespoons grated Parmesan cheese (topping for hot soup)

Directions:

1. Preheat the toaster oven to 400° F.
2. Process all the ingredients in a blender or food processor until smooth. Transfer the mixture to a 1-quart 8½ × 8½ × 4-inch ovenproof baking dish.
3. BAKE, covered, for 35 minutes. Ladle into individual soup bowls and serve.

Middle Eastern Roasted Chicken

Servings: 4
Cooking Time: 25 Minutes
Ingredients:

- 3 tablespoons fresh lemon juice
- ¼ cup plus 1 tablespoon olive oil
- 4 cloves garlic, minced
- ½ teaspoon kosher salt
- 1 teaspoon freshly ground black pepper
- 1 teaspoon ground cumin
- 1 teaspoon paprika
- ½ teaspoon turmeric
- ⅛ teaspoon red pepper flakes
- 1 pound boneless, skinless chicken breasts
- 1 large onion, cut into thin wedges

Directions:

1. Whisk the lemon juice, ¼ cup olive oil, garlic, salt, pepper, cumin, paprika, turmeric, and red pepper flakes in a small bowl until blended.
2. Cut the chicken breast lengthwise into thin scaloppine slices. Place the chicken in a nonreactive dish and pour the marinade over the chicken. Turn the chicken to coat thoroughly and evenly. Cover, refrigerate, and marinate for at least 1 hour and up to 10 hours. (The longer the better, as the flavor melds with the chicken.)
3. Remove the chicken from the refrigerator and add the onion to the marinade.

4. Preheat the toaster oven to 425°F. Brush the remaining tablespoon of olive oil over the bottom of a 12 x 12-inch pan. Place the chicken pieces on one side of the baking sheet and the onion wedges on the other side in a single layer. Discard any remaining marinade.
5. Roast for 20 to 25 minutes or until the chicken is browned and a meat thermometer registers 165°F. Remove from the oven and let rest a few minutes, then slice the chicken into thin strips. Toss with the onion and serve.

Baked Picnic Pinto Beans

Servings: 4
Cooking Time: 40 Minutes
Ingredients:
- 1 tomato, peeled and finely chopped
- 2 15-ounce cans pinto beans, drained
- 6 lean turkey bacon strips, cooked, drained, and crumbled
- 1 cup good-quality dark beer or ale
- 3 tablespoons finely chopped onion
- 1 tablespoon ketchup
- 2 tablespoons molasses
- 1 teaspoon Dijon mustard
- 1 teaspoon Worcestershire sauce
- 1 teaspoon garlic powder
- Salt and butcher's pepper to taste

Directions:
1. Preheat the toaster oven to 375° F.
2. Peel the tomato by immersing it in boiling water for 1 minute. Remove with tongs and when cool enough to handle, pull the skin away with a sharp paring knife. Chop and place in a 1-quart 8½ × 8½ × 4-inch ovenproof baking dish. Add all the other ingredients, stirring to mix well. Adjust the seasonings to taste. Cover with aluminum foil.
3. BAKE, covered, for 40 minutes.

Oven-baked Barley

Servings: 2
Cooking Time: 60 Minutes
Ingredients:
- ⅓ cup barley, toasted
- Seasonings:
- 1 tablespoon sesame oil
- 1 tablespoon sesame seeds
- ¼ teaspoon ground cumin
- ¼ teaspoon turmeric
- ½ teaspoon garlic powder
- Salt and freshly ground black pepper to taste

Directions:
1. Combine the barley and 1½ cups water in a 1-quart 8½ × 8½ × 4-inch ovenproof baking dish. Cover with aluminum foil.
2. BAKE, covered, for 50 minutes, or until almost cooked, testing the grains after 30 minutes for softness.
3. Add the oil and seasonings and fluff with a fork to combine. Cover and let the barley sit for 10 minutes to finish cooking and absorb the flavors of the seasonings. Fluff once more before serving.

Salad Lentils

Servings: 4
Cooking Time: 35 Minutes
Ingredients:
- ¼ cup lentils
- 1 tablespoon olive oil
- Salad ingredients:
- 1 celery stalk, trimmed and Chopped
- 1 plum tomato, chopped
- 1 cucumber, peeled, seeded, and chopped
- 1½ cups spinach leaves, pulled into small pieces
- 1 tablespoon balsamic vinegar
- 1 tablespoon olive oil
- ½ teaspoon dried oregano
- 1 tablespoon chopped scallions
- 2 tablespoons sliced pitted black olives
- 1 teaspoon minced roasted garlic

Directions:
1. Preheat the toaster oven to 400° F.
2. Combine the lentils, ¼ cups water, and olive oil in a 1-quart 8½ × 8½ × 4-inch ovenproof baking dish. Cover with aluminum foil.
3. BAKE, covered, for 35 minutes, or until the lentils are tender. When cool, combine with all the salad ingredients in a serving bowl and toss well. Adjust the seasonings, chill, and serve.

French Bread Pizza

Servings: 6
Cooking Time: 8 Minutes
Ingredients:
- 2 tablespoons unsalted butter, melted
- 2 cloves garlic, minced
- ½ teaspoon Italian seasoning
- 1 tablespoon olive oil
- ½ cup chopped onion
- ½ cup chopped green pepper
- 1 cup sliced button or white mushrooms
- 1 (10- to 12-ounce) loaf French or Italian bread, about 12 inches long, split in half lengthwise
- ½ cup pizza sauce
- 6 to 8 slices Canadian bacon or ¼ cup pepperoni slices
- ¼ cup sliced ripe olives, drained
- 1 cup shredded mozzarella cheese
- 3 tablespoons shredded Parmesan cheese

Directions:
1. Preheat the toaster oven to 450°F.
2. Stir the melted butter, garlic, and Italian seasoning in a small bowl; set aside.
3. Heat the oil in a small skillet over medium-high heat. Add the onion and green pepper and sauté, stirring frequently, for 3 minutes. Add the mushrooms and cook, stirring frequently, for 7 to 10 minutes or until the liquid has evaporated. Remove from the heat; set aside.
4. Gently pull a little of the soft bread out of the center of the loaf, making a well. (Take care not to tear the crust.) Brush the garlic butter over the cut sides of the bread.

5. Place both halves of the bread, side by side, cut side up, on a 12 x 12-inch baking pan. Bake for 3 minutes or until heated through. Carefully remove the bread from the oven.
6. Spoon the pizza sauce evenly over the cut sides of the bread. Top evenly with the Canadian bacon, the onion-mushroom mixture, and the olives. Top with the mozzarella and Parmesan cheeses. Return to the oven and bake for 3 to 5 minutes or until the cheese is melted.
7. Cut the French bread pizza crosswise into slices.

Sage, Chicken + Mushroom Pasta Casserole

Servings: 6
Cooking Time: 35 Minutes
Ingredients:

- Nonstick cooking spray
- 8 ounces bow-tie pasta, uncooked
- 4 tablespoons unsalted butter
- 8 ounces button or white mushrooms, sliced
- 3 tablespoons all-purpose flour
- Kosher salt and freshly ground black pepper
- 2 cups whole milk
- ½ cup dry white wine
- 2 tablespoons minced fresh sage
- 1 ½ cups chopped cooked chicken
- 1 cup shredded fontina, Monterey Jack, or Swiss cheese
- ½ cup shredded Parmesan cheese

Directions:

1. Preheat the toaster oven to 350°F. Spray a 2-quart baking pan with nonstick cooking spray.
2. Cook the pasta according to the package directions; drain and set aside.
3. Melt the butter in a large skillet over medium-high heat. Add the mushrooms and cook, stirring frequently, until the liquid has evaporated, 7 to 10 minutes. Blend in the flour and cook, stirring constantly, for 1 minute. Season with salt and pepper. Gradually stir in the milk and wine. Cook, stirring constantly, until the mixture bubbles and begins to thicken. Remove from the heat. Stir in the sage, cooked pasta, chicken, and fontina. Season with salt and pepper.
4. Spoon into the prepared pan. Cover and bake for 25 to 30 minutes. Uncover, sprinkle with the Parmesan, and bake for an additional 5 minutes or until the cheese is melted.
5. Remove from the oven and let stand for 5 to 10 minutes before serving.

Chicken Tortilla Roll-ups

Servings: 4
Cooking Time: 10 Minutes
Ingredients:

- Nonstick cooking spray
- ¼ cup olive oil
- 2 cloves garlic, minced
- 1 ½ cups shredded cooked chicken
- 1 cup shredded Mexican blend or cheddar cheese
- ½ cup frozen corn, thawed
- ⅓ cup salsa verde
- 1 green onion, white and green portions, chopped
- 2 tablespoons minced fresh cilantro
- 1 tablespoon fresh lime juice
- ½ teaspoon ground cumin
- ¼ teaspoon Sriracha or hot sauce
- Kosher salt and freshly ground black pepper
- 8 flour tortillas, about 8 inches in diameter
- Optional toppings: minced cilantro, salsa, guacamole, sour cream

Directions:

1. Preheat the toaster oven to 375°F. Spray a 12 x 12-inch baking pan with nonstick cooking spray.
2. Stir the oil and garlic in a small bowl; set aside.
3. Stir the chicken, cheese, corn, salsa verde, green onion, cilantro, lime juice, cumin, and Sriracha in a large bowl. Season with salt and pepper.
4. Brush both sides of a tortilla very lightly with the garlic oil. Spoon about ⅓ cup chicken filling on the lower side of the tortilla. Roll the tortilla over the filling. Place the filled tortilla, seam side down, in the prepared baking pan. Repeat with the remaining tortillas and filling.
5. Brush the tops of each filled tortilla with the remaining garlic oil, coating them evenly and especially covering the edges of the tortillas.
6. Bake, uncovered, for 10 minutes or until the tortillas are crisp and the filling is hot. Serve with your choice of any of the various toppings.

Parmesan Artichoke Pizza

Servings: 6
Cooking Time: 15 Minutes
Ingredients:

- CRUST
- ¾ cup warm water (110°F)
- 1 ½ teaspoons active dry yeast
- ¼ teaspoon sugar
- 1 tablespoon olive oil
- 1 teaspoon table salt
- ⅓ cup whole wheat flour
- 1 ½ to 1 ⅔ cups bread flour
- TOPPINGS
- 2 tablespoons olive oil
- 1 teaspoon Italian seasoning
- 1 clove garlic, minced
- ½ cup whole milk ricotta cheese, at room temperature
- ⅔ cup drained, chopped marinated artichokes
- ¼ cup chopped red onion
- 3 tablespoons minced fresh basil
- ½ cup shredded Parmesan cheese
- ⅓ cup shredded mozzarella cheese

Directions:

1. Make the Crust: Place the warm water, yeast, and sugar in a large mixing bowl for a stand mixer. Stir, then let stand for 3 to 5 minutes or until bubbly.
2. Stir in the olive oil, salt, whole wheat flour, and 1 ½ cups bread flour. If the dough is too sticky, stir in an additional 1 to 2 tablespoons bread flour. Beat with the flat (paddle) beater at medium-speed for 5 minutes (or knead by hand for 5 to 7 minutes or until the dough is smooth and

elastic). Place in a greased large bowl, turn the dough over, cover with a clean towel, and let stand for 30 to 45 minutes, or until starting to rise.

3. Stir the olive oil, Italian seasoning, and garlic in a small bowl; set aside.

4. Preheat the toaster oven to 450°F. Place a 12-inch pizza pan in the toaster oven while it is preheating.

5. Turn the dough onto a lightly floured surface and pull or roll the dough to make a 12-inch circle. Carefully transfer the crust to the hot pan.

6. Brush the olive oil mixture over the crust. Spread the ricotta evenly over the crust. Top with the artichokes, red onions, fresh basil, Parmesan, and mozzarella. Bake for 13 to 15 minutes, or until the crust is golden brown and the cheese is melted. Let stand for 5 minutes before cutting.

Miso-glazed Salmon With Broccoli

Servings: 2
Cooking Time: 25 Minutes
Ingredients:

- Nonstick cooking spray
- 2 tablespoons miso, preferably yellow
- 2 tablespoons mirin
- 1 tablespoon packed dark brown sugar
- 2 teaspoons minced fresh ginger
- 1 ½ teaspoons sesame oil
- 8 ounces fresh broccoli, cut into spears
- 1 tablespoon canola or vegetable oil
- Kosher salt and freshly ground black pepper
- 2 salmon fillets (5 to 6 ounces each)

Directions:

1. Preheat the toaster oven to 425°F. Spray a 12 x 12-inch baking pan with nonstick cooking spray.
2. Stir the miso, mirin, brown sugar, ginger, and sesame oil in a small bowl; set aside.
3. Toss the broccoli spears with the canola oil and season with salt and pepper. Place the broccoli on the pan. Bake, uncovered, for 10 minutes. Stir the broccoli and move to one side of the pan.
4. Place the salmon, skin side down, on the other end of the pan. Brush lightly with olive oil and season with salt and pepper. Bake for 10 minutes.
5. Brush the fish generously with the miso sauce. Bake for an additional 3 to 5 minutes, or until the fish flakes easily with a fork and a meat thermometer registers 145°F.

Spanish Rice

Servings: 4
Cooking Time: 45 Minutes
Ingredients:

- ¾ cup rice
- 2 tablespoons dry white wine
- 3 tablespoons olive oil
- 1 15-ounce can whole tomatoes
- ¼ cup thinly sliced onions
- 3 tablespoons chopped fresh cilantro
- 4 ½ cup chopped bell pepper
- 5 2 bay leaves
- Salt and a pinch of red pepper flakes to taste

Directions:

1. Preheat the toaster oven to 375° F.
2. Combine all the ingredients with 1 cup water in a 1-quart 8½ × 8½ × 4-inch ovenproof baking dish and adjust the seasonings. Cover with aluminum foil.
3. BAKE, covered, for 45 minutes, or until the rice is cooked, removing the cover after 30 minutes.

Pesto Pizza

Servings: 1
Cooking Time: 20 Minutes
Ingredients:

- Topping:
- ½ cup chopped fresh basil
- 1 tablespoon pine nuts (pignoli)
- 1 tablespoon olive oil
- 2 tablespoons shredded Parmesan cheese
- 1 garlic clove, minced
- ½ teaspoon dried oregano or 1 tablespoon chopped fresh oregano
- 1 plum tomato, chopped
- Salt and pepper to taste
- 1 9-inch ready-made pizza crust
- 2 tablespoons shredded low-fat mozzarella

Directions:

1. Preheat the toaster oven to 375° F.
2. Combine the topping ingredients in a small bowl.
3. Process the mixture in a blender or food processor until smooth. Spread the mixture on the pizza crust, then sprinkle with the mozzarella cheese. Place the pizza crust on the toaster oven rack.
4. BAKE for 20 minutes, or until the cheese is melted and the crust is brown.

Honey Bourbon–glazed Pork Chops With Sweet Potatoes + Apples

Servings: 2
Cooking Time: 42 Minutes
Ingredients:

- Nonstick cooking spray
- 2 medium sweet potatoes, peeled and quartered
- 2 tablespoons bourbon
- 2 tablespoons honey
- 1 tablespoon canola or vegetable oil
- ½ teaspoon onion powder
- ½ teaspoon dry mustard
- ¼ teaspoon dried thyme leaves
- Kosher salt and freshly ground black pepper
- 2 bone-in pork chops, cut about ¾ inch thick
- 1 Granny Smith apple, not peeled, cored and cut into ½-inch wedges

Directions:

1. Preheat the toaster oven to 375°F. Spray a 12 x 12-inch baking pan with nonstick cooking spray.
2. Place the sweet potatoes on one side of the prepared pan. Spray with nonstick cooking spray. Bake, uncovered, for 20 minutes.

3. Meanwhile, stir the bourbon, honey, oil, onion powder, mustard, and thyme in a small bowl. Season with salt and pepper and set aside.
4. Turn the potatoes over. Place the pork chops on the other end of the pan in a single layer. Arrange the apple wedges around the potatoes and pork chops, stacking the apples as needed. Brush the bourbon mixture generously over all. Bake for 15 to 18 minutes or until the pork is done as desired and a meat thermometer registers a minimum of 145°F.
5. For additional browning, set the toaster oven to Broil and broil for 2 to 4 minutes, or until the edges are brown as desired.
6. Transfer to a serving platter. Spoon any drippings over the meat and vegetables. Let stand for 5 minutes before serving.

Narragansett Clam Chowder

Servings: 4
Cooking Time: 35 Minutes
Ingredients:
- 1 cup fat-free half-and-half
- 2 tablespoons unbleached flour
- 3 ½ cup chopped onion
- 1 cup peeled and diced potato
- 1 tablespoon vegetable oil
- 1 tablespoon chopped fresh parsley
- 1 6-ounce can clams, drained and chopped
- 1 15-ounce can fat-free low-sodium chicken broth
- Salt and freshly ground black pepper

Directions:
1. Whisk together the half-and-half and flour in a small bowl. Set aside.
2. Combine the onion, potato, and oil in an 8½ × 8½ × 2-inch square baking (cake) pan.
3. BROIL 15 minutes, turning every 5 minutes with tongs, or until the potato is tender and the onion is cooked. Transfer to a 1-quart baking dish. Add the parsley, clams, broth, and half-and-half/flour mixture. Stir well and season to taste with salt and pepper.
4. BAKE, uncovered, at 375° F. for 20 minutes, stirring after 10 minutes, or until the stock is reduced and thickened. Ladle into bowls and serve with Yogurt Bread.

Roasted Harissa Chicken + Vegetables

Servings: 4
Cooking Time: 30 Minutes
Ingredients:
- Nonstick cooking spray
- 1 medium zucchini, halved lengthwise and sliced crosswise ½ inch thick
- ½ large red onion, sliced ¼ inch thick
- 2 tablespoons olive oil
- Kosher salt and freshly ground black pepper
- 1 pound boneless, skinless chicken breasts, cut into 1-inch cubes
- ½ teaspoon ground cumin
- 1 clove garlic, minced
- 2 tablespoons harissa sauce or paste
- 1 tablespoon honey
- 2 tablespoons minced fresh cilantro
- 2 cups hot cooked rice
- Optional toppings: plain Greek yogurt or sour cream, sesame seeds (toasted or chopped), or dry-roasted peanuts

Directions:
1. Preheat the toaster oven to 400°F. Spray a 12 x 12-inch baking pan with nonstick cooking spray.
2. Place the zucchini and red onion in a medium bowl. Drizzle with 1 tablespoon olive oil and season with salt and pepper. Stir to coat the vegetables evenly. Arrange the vegetables in a single layer in the prepared baking pan. Roast, uncovered, for 10 minutes.
3. Place the chicken cubes in that same bowl. Drizzle with the remaining 1 tablespoon olive oil. Season with the cumin, garlic, salt, and pepper. Stir to coat the chicken evenly.
4. Stir the vegetables and move to one side of the pan. Arrange the chicken in a single layer on the other side of the pan. Roast for 10 minutes.
5. Blend the harissa and honey in a small bowl. Drizzle the sauce over the chicken and vegetables. Using a pastry brush, coat the chicken and vegetables evenly. Roast, uncovered, for an additional 8 to 10 minutes, or until the vegetables are tender and the chicken registers 165°F on a meat thermometer.
6. Spoon the chicken, vegetables, and any collected liquid onto a serving platter. Sprinkle with the cilantro. Serve the chicken and vegetables with the rice and, if desired, a dollop of plain Greek yogurt and a sprinkling of sesame seeds.

Moussaka

Servings: 6
Cooking Time: 50 Minutes
Ingredients:
- 2 cups eggplant, peeled and cut into 1-inch cubes
- Beef mixture:
- 1 pound very lean ground beef
- 2 tablespoons finely chopped onion
- 3 4 tablespoons tomato paste
- ¼ cup dry red wine
- 2 tablespoons finely chopped fresh parsley
- ¼ teaspoon ground cinnamon
- Salt and freshly ground black pepper to taste
- Cheese mixture:
- 2 eggs, beaten
- 1 tablespoon unbleached flour
- ½ cup fat-free half-and-half
- ¼ teaspoon grated nutmeg
- 1 cup low-fat ricotta cheese
- Bread crumb mixture:
- 1 cup multigrain bread crumbs
- 1 cup freshly grated Parmesan cheese
- Olive oil

Directions:
1. Preheat the toaster oven to 375° F.
2. Dissolve 1 tablespoon salt in 2 cups water. Add the eggplant cubes and let soak for 10 minutes. Rinse well, drain,

and pat with paper towel to remove any excess moisture. Set aside.
3. Combine the beef mixture ingredients in a medium bowl and set aside.
4. Whisk together the cheese mixture ingredients in a medium bowl and set aside.
5. Combine the bread crumb mixture in a medium bowl and set aside.
6. Layer half the eggplant cubes in a 1-quart 8½ × 8½ × 4-inch ovenproof baking dish that has been brushed with olive oil.
7. Sprinkle the eggplant with half the bread crumb mixture.
8. Add a layer of half the beef mixture. Repeat the layering process, using up the remaining eggplant, beef, and bread crumb mixtures.
9. Pour the cheese mixture over the top.
10. BAKE, uncovered, for 50 minutes, or until the eggplant is tender and the top is golden.

Glazed Pork Tenderloin With Carrots Sheet Pan Supper

Servings: 4-6
Cooking Time: 20 Minutes
Ingredients:

- 1 pound pork tenderloin
- 1 teaspoon steak seasoning blend
- 2 large carrots, sliced 1/2-inch thick
- 2 large parsnips, sliced 1/2-inch thick
- 1/2 small sweet onion, cut in thin wedges
- 1 tablespoon olive oil
- Salt and pepper to taste
- 1/2 cup apricot jam
- 1 tablespoon balsamic vinegar

Directions:
1. Place rack on bottom position of toaster oven. Heat the toaster oven to 425°F. Spray the toaster oven baking pan with nonstick cooking spray or line the pan with nonstick aluminum foil.
2. Place pork tenderloin diagonally in center of pan. Sprinkle pork with seasoning blend.
3. In a large bowl, combine carrots, parsnips and onion. Add olive oil, salt and black pepper and stir until vegetables are coated. Arrange vegetables evenly in pan around pork.
4. Bake 20 minutes. Stir vegetables.
5. Meanwhile, in a small bowl, combine apricot jam and balsamic vinegar. Spoon about half of mixture over pork.
6. Continue baking until pork reaches reaches 160°F when tested with a meat thermometer and vegetables are roasted, about 10 minutes. Slice pork and serve with remaining sauce, if desired.

Sheet Pan Loaded Nachos

Servings: 4
Cooking Time: 13 Minutes
Ingredients:

- 1 tablespoon canola or vegetable oil
- ½ pound lean ground beef
- ½ cup chopped onion
- 2 cloves garlic, minced
- 1 teaspoon chili powder
- ½ teaspoon ground cumin
- Kosher salt and freshly ground black pepper
- 6 ounces tortilla chips
- ½ cup canned black beans, rinsed and drained
- 1 ½ cups shredded sharp cheddar cheese or Mexican blend cheese
- ½ cup salsa
- Optional toppings: sliced jalapeño peppers, chopped bell peppers, sliced ripe olives, chopped tomatoes, minced fresh cilantro, sour cream, chopped avocado, guacamole, or chopped onion.

Directions:
1. Preheat the toaster oven to 400°F. Line a 12 x 12-inch baking pan with nonstick aluminum foil. (Or if lining the pan with regular foil, spray it with nonstick cooking spray.)
2. Heat the oil in a large skillet over medium-high heat. Add the ground beef and onion and cook, stirring frequently, until the beef is almost done. Add the garlic, chili powder, cumin, season with salt and pepper, and cook, stirring frequently, until the beef is fully cooked; drain.
3. Arrange the tortilla chips in an even layer in the prepared pan. Top with the beef-onion mixture, then top with the beans. Bake, uncovered, for 6 to 8 minutes. Top with the cheese and bake for 5 minutes more, or until the cheese is melted.
4. Drizzle with the salsa. Top as desired with any of the various toppings.

Light Beef Stroganoff

Servings: 4
Cooking Time: 40 Minutes
Ingredients:

- Sauce:
- 1 cup skim milk
- 1 cup fat-free half-and-half
- 2 tablespoons reduced-fat cream cheese, at room temperature
- 4 tablespoons unbleached flour
- 2 pounds lean round or sirloin steak, cut into strips 2 inches long and ½ inch thick
- Browning mixture:
- 1 tablespoon soy sauce
- 2 tablespoons spicy brown mustard
- 1 tablespoon olive oil
- 2 teaspoons garlic powder
- Salt and freshly ground black pepper to taste

Directions:
1. Whisk together the sauce ingredients in a medium bowl until smooth. Set aside.
2. Combine the beef strips and browning mixture ingredients in an oiled or nonstick 8½ × 8½ × 2-inch square baking (cake) pan.
3. BROIL for 8 minutes, or until the strips are browned, turning with tongs after 4 minutes. Transfer to a 1-quart 8½ × 8½ × 4-inch ovenproof baking dish. Add the sauce and mix well. Adjust the seasonings to taste. Cover with aluminum foil.

4. BAKE, covered, for 40 minutes, or until the meat is tender.

Fillets En Casserole

Servings: 4
Cooking Time: 20 Minutes
Ingredients:

- ½ cup multigrain bread crumbs
- 4 6-ounce fish fillets
- Sauce:
- 2 tablespoons white wine
- 1 teaspoon Worcestershire sauce
- 1 teaspoon lemon juice
- 1 tablespoon vegetable oil
- 1 teaspoon Dijon mustard
- Salt and freshly ground black pepper to taste
- 2 tablespoons capers

Directions:

1. Preheat the toaster oven to 400° F.
2. Layer the bottom of an oiled or nonstick 8½ × 8½ × 2-inch square baking (cake) pan with the bread crumbs and place the fillets on the crumbs.
3. Combine the sauce ingredients, mixing well, and spoon over the fillets. Sprinkle with the capers.
4. BAKE, covered, for 20 minutes, or until the fish flakes easily with a fork.

Favorite Baked Ziti

Servings: 4
Cooking Time: 30 Minutes
Ingredients:

- 2 tablespoons olive oil
- 1 small onion, diced
- 3 cloves garlic, minced
- ¼ teaspoon red pepper flakes
- 1 pound lean ground beef
- ½ teaspoon kosher salt
- ¼ cup dry red wine
- 1 (14.5-ounce) can crushed tomatoes
- 1 tablespoon tomato paste
- 16 ounces ziti, uncooked
- Nonstick cooking spray
- ⅓ cup grated Parmesan cheese
- 1 ½ cups shredded mozzarella cheese
- 2 ounces fresh mozzarella cheese, cut into cubes (about ½ cup)

Directions:

1. Heat the olive oil in a large skillet over medium-high heat. Add the onion and cook, stirring frequently, until tender, 3 to 4 minutes. Stir in the garlic and red pepper flakes. Add the ground beef and salt. Cook, breaking up the ground beef, until the meat is brown and cooked through. Drain well, if needed, and return to the skillet.
2. Add the wine and cook for 2 minutes. Add the tomatoes, tomato paste, and ¾ cup water. Reduce the heat and simmer, uncovered, for 20 to 25 minutes, stirring occasionally.
3. Cook the ziti according to the package directions, except reduce the cooking time to 7 minutes. The ziti will be harder than Al Dente, which is what you want. Drain and rinse under cold water. Transfer to a large bowl.
4. Preheat the toaster oven to 425 °F. Spray an 11 x 7 x 2 ½-inch baking dish with nonstick cooking spray. Spoon about 1 cup of the meat sauce into the prepared dish. Add half of the ziti in an even layer. Spoon about half of the remaining sauce over the ziti. Sprinkle with half the Parmesan and all the shredded mozzarella. Add the remaining half of ziti and cover with the remaining sauce. Sprinkle the remaining Parmesan on top.
5. Bake, covered, for 20 minutes. Remove from the oven and add the cubes of fresh mozzarella. Bake, uncovered, for an additional 10 minutes. If desired, turn to broil for a few minutes to make the top crispy and brown.
6. Remove from the oven and let stand for 10 minutes before serving.

Homemade Beef Enchiladas

Servings: 4
Cooking Time: 20 Minutes
Ingredients:

- 1 tablespoon canola or vegetable oil
- 1 tablespoon plus 1 teaspoon all-purpose flour
- 2 tablespoons chili powder
- ½ teaspoon ground cumin
- ½ teaspoon garlic powder
- ¼ teaspoon kosher salt
- 1 ¼ cups chicken or vegetable broth
- ¾ pound lean ground beef
- Nonstick cooking spray
- 8 flour or corn tortillas
- ¼ cup finely chopped onion
- 1 ½ cups shredded Mexican-blend or cheddar cheese

Directions:

1. Heat the oil in a small saucepan over medium-high heat. Add the flour and whisk for about a minute. Stir in the chili powder, cumin, garlic powder, and salt. Gradually stir in the broth, whisking until smooth. Reduce the heat to a simmer and cook the sauce for 10 to 12 minutes.
2. Cook the ground beef in a medium skillet over medium-high heat until browned and cooked through, stirring to crumble into a fine texture. Remove from the heat and drain.
3. Preheat the toaster oven to 350°F. Spray an 11 x 7 x 2 ½-inch baking dish with nonstick cooking spray. Place about ½ cup sauce over the bottom of the dish. Lay a tortilla on a large plate and spread about 2 tablespoons of sauce over the surface of the tortilla. Spoon 2 tablespoons of the ground beef down the center of the tortilla. Sprinkle with some onion and cheese (amount is up to you). Roll up and place in the baking dish. Repeat with the remaining tortillas. Pour the remaining sauce over the top. Sprinkle with remaining cheese. Bake, uncovered, for 20 minutes or until the tortillas are heated through and slightly crisp on the outside.

Broiled Chipotle Tilapia With Avocado Sauce

Servings: 2
Cooking Time: 10 Minutes
Ingredients:

- 1 small avocado, halved, pitted and peeled
- 3 tablespoons sour cream
- 1 teaspoon lime juice
- 2 1/2 teaspoons chipotle and roasted garlic seasoning, divided
- 1 tablespoon mayonnaise
- 1/2 pound tilapia fillets
- Chopped cilantro

Directions:

1. Using a chopper or small food processor, blend avocado, sour cream, lime juice and 1 1/2 teaspoons seasoning until smooth. Cover and refrigerate.
2. Spray toaster oven baking pan with nonstick cooking spray.
3. in small bowl, mix mayonnaise and remaining 1 teaspoon seasoning.
4. Brush mayonnaise mixture on both sides of tilapia fillets.
5. Place coated fish in pan.
6. Set toaster oven to BROIL. Broil fish for 10 minutes or until fish flakes with a fork.
7. Serve with avocado sauce and garnish with lime slices and cilantro, if desired.

Crab Chowder

Servings: 4
Cooking Time: 40 Minutes
Ingredients:

- 1 6-ounce can lump crabmeat, drained and chopped, or ½ pound fresh crabmeat, cleaned and chopped
- 1 cup skim milk or low-fat soy milk
- 1 cup fat-free half-and-half
- 2 tablespoons unbleached flour
- ¼ cup chopped onion
- ½ cup peeled and diced potato
- 1 carrot, peeled and chopped
- 1 celery stalk, chopped
- 2 garlic cloves, minced
- 2 tablespoons chopped fresh parsley
- ½ teaspoon ground cumin
- 1 teaspoon paprika
- Salt and butcher's pepper to taste

Directions:

1. Preheat the toaster oven to 400° F.
2. Whisk together the milk, half-and-half, and flour in a bowl. Transfer the mixture to a 1-quart 8½ × 8½ × 4-inch ovenproof baking dish. Add all the other ingredients, mixing well. Adjust the seasonings to taste.
3. BAKE, covered, for 40 minutes, or until the vegetables are tender.

Classic Beef Stew

Servings: 4
Cooking Time: 50 Minutes
Ingredients:

- 1½ cups dark beer
- 4 tablespoons unbleached flour
- 2 cups (approximately 1 pound) lean top round steak, cut into 1-inch cubes
- 1 cup peeled and coarsely chopped carrots
- 1 cup peeled and coarsely chopped potatoes
- ½ cup coarsely chopped onion
- 1 cup fresh or frozen peas
- 2 plum tomatoes, chopped
- 3 garlic cloves, minced
- 4 3 bay leaves
- ¼ teaspoon ground cumin
- Salt and butcher's pepper to taste

Directions:

1. Preheat the toaster oven to 400° F.
2. Whisk together the beer and flour in a 1-quart 8½ × 8½ × 4-inch ovenproof baking dish. Add all the other ingredients and seasonings and mix well, adjusting the seasonings to taste. Cover the dish with aluminum foil.
3. BAKE, covered, for 50 minutes, or until the meat is cooked and the vegetables are tender. Remove the bay leaves before serving.

Kashaburgers

Servings: 4
Cooking Time: 50 Minutes
Ingredients:

- 1 cup kasha
- 2 tablespoons minced onion or scallions
- 1 tablespoon minced garlic
- ½ cup multigrain bread crumbs
- 1 egg
- ¼ teaspoon paprika
- ½ teaspoon chili powder
- ¼ teaspoon sesame oil
- 1 tablespoon vegetable oil
- Salt and freshly ground black pepper to taste

Directions:

1. Preheat the toaster oven to 400° F.
2. Combine 2 cups water and the kasha in a 1-quart 8½ × 8½ × 4-inch ovenproof baking dish.
3. BAKE, uncovered, for 30 minutes, or until the grains are cooked. Remove from the oven and add all the other ingredients, stirring to mix well. When the mixture is cooled, shape into 4 to 6 patties and place on a rack with a broiling pan underneath.
4. BROIL for 20 minutes, turn with a spatula, then broil for another 10 minutes, or until browned.

Individual Chicken Pot Pies

Servings: 4
Cooking Time: 25 Minutes
Ingredients:

- 3 tablespoons unsalted butter
- ½ medium onion, chopped
- 1 carrot, chopped
- 1 stalk celery, chopped

- 1 ¼ cups sliced button or white mushrooms
- 2 tablespoons all-purpose flour
- 1 ¼ cups whole milk
- 1 tablespoon fresh lemon juice
- ½ teaspoon dried thyme leaves
- Kosher salt and freshly ground black pepper
- 1 ½ cups chopped cooked chicken
- ½ cup frozen peas
- Nonstick cooking spray
- 1 sheet frozen puff pastry, about 9 inches square, thawed (½ of a 17.3-ounce package)
- 1 large egg

Directions:

1. Melt the butter in a large skillet over medium-high heat. Add the onion, carrot, and celery and cook, stirring frequently, for 3 minutes. Add the mushrooms and cook, stirring frequently, for 7 to 10 minutes or until the liquid has evaporated. Blend in the flour and cook, stirring for 1 minute. (Be sure all of the flour is blended into the butter and vegetables.) Gradually stir in the milk. Cook, stirring constantly, until the mixture bubbles and thickens. Stir in the lemon juice and thyme and season with salt and pepper. Stir in the chicken and peas. Remove from the heat and set aside.
2. Preheat the toaster oven to 375°F. Spray 4 (8-ounce) oven-safe ramekins with nonstick cooking spray.
3. Roll the puff pastry out on a lightly floured board, to make an even 10-inch square. Cut the pastry into circles using a 4-inch cutter.
4. Spoon a heaping ¾ cup of filling into each prepared ramekin. Place a puff pastry circle on top of each and crimp the edges to seal to the ramekin. Using the tip of a paring knife, cut 3 slits in each crust to allow steam to escape. Whisk the egg with 1 tablespoon water in a small bowl. Brush the egg mixture over the top of the crust.
5. Bake for 20 to 25 minutes, or until the crust is golden brown. Remove from the oven and let stand for 5 minutes before serving.

Sun-dried Tomato Pizza

Servings: 4
Cooking Time: 25 Minutes

Ingredients:

- Tomato mixture:
- 1 cup chopped sun-dried tomatoes
- 2 tablespoons tomato paste
- 2 tablespoons olive oil
- 2 tablespoons chopped onion
- 2 garlic cloves, minced
- 1 teaspoon dried oregano
- 1 teaspoon dried basil
- Salt and red pepper flakes to taste
- 1 9-inch ready-made pizza crust
- 1 5-ounce can mushrooms
- ¼ cup pitted and sliced black olives
- ½ cup shredded low-fat mozzarella cheese

Directions:

1. Combine the tomato mixture ingredients with ½ cup water in an 8½ × 8½ × 2-inch square baking (cake) pan.
2. BROIL for 8 minutes, or until the tomatoes are softened. Remove from the oven and cool for 5 minutes.
3. Process the mixture in a blender or food processor until well blended. Spread on the pizza crust and layer with the mushrooms, olives, and cheese.
4. BAKE at 400° F. for 25 minutes, or until the cheese is melted.

Lentil And Carrot Soup

Servings: 4
Cooking Time: 40 Minutes

Ingredients:

- ½ cup lentils
- ½ cup dry white wine
- 1 small onion, chopped
- 3 carrots, peeled and finely chopped
- ½ cup fresh mushrooms, cleaned and sliced, or 1 5-ounce can mushroom pieces, well drained
- 3 garlic cloves, minced
- 1 tablespoon chopped fresh parsley
- 1 tablespoon Worcestershire sauce
- Salt and freshly ground black pepper to taste

Directions:

1. Preheat the toaster oven to 375° F.
2. Combine all the ingredients with 2 cups water in a 1-quart 8½ × 8½ × 4-inch ovenproof baking dish. Adjust the seasonings.
3. BAKE for 40 minutes, or until the lentils, carrots, and onions are tender. Ladle into individual soup bowls and serve.

Baked Parsleyed Cheese Grits

Servings: 4
Cooking Time: 30 Minutes

Ingredients:

- 4 strips lean uncooked turkey bacon, cut in half
- 1 cup grits
- 2 cups skim or low-fat soy milk
- 1 egg
- ½ cup shredded Parmesan cheese
- 1 tablespoon chopped fresh parsley
- ½ teaspoon garlic powder
- Salt and butcher's pepper to taste

Directions:

1. Preheat the toaster oven to 350° F.
2. Layer an 8½ × 8½ × 2-inch square baking (cake) pan with the bacon strips.
3. Combine the remaining ingredients in a medium bowl and pour the mixture over the strips.
4. BAKE, uncovered, for 30 minutes, or until the grits are cooked. Cut into squares with a spatula and serve.

Chicken Thighs With Roasted Rosemary Root Vegetables

Servings: 2
Cooking Time: 70 Minutes
Ingredients:

- 2 sprigs fresh rosemary
- 1 small turnip, peeled and cut into 1 1/2-inch cubes
- 1 parsnip, peeled and cut into 1/2-inch slices
- 1 small onion, quartered
- 1 large sweet potato, peeled and cut into 1-inch cubes
- 2 cloves garlic, peeled
- 2 tablespoons olive oil
- 1 teaspoon salt, divided
- 1/2 teaspoon coarse pepper, divided
- 1/2 teaspoon rotisserie chicken seasoning
- 4 chicken thighs with bone and skin

Directions:

1. Place rack on bottom position of toaster oven. Preheat the toaster oven to 425°F.
2. Spray the toaster oven baking pan with nonstick cooking spray. Place rosemary sprigs on pan.
3. In a large bowl, mix turnip. parsnip, onion, sweet potato, garlic, oil, 1/2 teaspoon salt and 1/4 teaspoon pepper until vegetables are coated with oil. Add to baking pan.
4. Bake 30 minutes. Stir vegetables.
5. Sprinkle remaining salt, pepper and rotisserie chicken seasoning over chicken pieces.
6. Place chicken on top of vegetables in pan. Continue baking for an additional 35 to 40 minutes or until chicken reaches 165°F when tested with a meat thermometer and vegetables are roasted.

Italian Baked Stuffed Tomatoes

Servings: 4
Cooking Time: 30 Minutes
Ingredients:

- 4 large tomatoes
- 1 cup shredded chicken
- 1 1/2 cup shredded mozzarella, divided
- 1 1/2 cup cooked rice
- 2 tablespoon minced onion
- 1/4 cup grated parmesan cheese
- 1 tablespoon dried Italian seasoning
- salt
- pepper
- Basil

Directions:

1. Preheat the toaster oven to 350°F. Spray toaster oven pan with nonstick cooking spray.
2. Cut the top off each tomato and scoop centers out. Place bottoms on prepared pan. Chop 3 tomatoes (about 1 1/2 cup, chopped) and add to large bowl.
3. Add shredded chicken, 1 cup shredded mozzarella cheese, rice, onion, Parmesan cheese, Italian seasoning, salt and pepper to large bowl and stir until blended. Divide between tomatoes, about 1 cup per tomato. Top with remaining mozzarella and tomato top.
4. Bake 25 to 30 minutes until cheese is melted and mixture is heated through.
5. Garnish with basil before serving.

Salad Couscous

Servings: 4
Cooking Time: 10 Minutes
Ingredients:

- 1 10-ounce package precooked couscous
- 2 tablespoons olive oil
- Salt and freshly ground black pepper
- ¼ cup chopped fresh tomatoes
- 2 tablespoons chopped fresh basil leaves
- 1 tablespoon sliced almonds
- ½ bell pepper, chopped
- 3 scallions, chopped
- 2 tablespoons lemon juice

Directions:

1. Preheat the toaster oven to 400° F.
2. Mix together the couscous, 2 cups water, and olive oil in a 1-quart 8½ × 8½ × 4-inch ovenproof baking dish. Add salt and pepper to taste. Cover with aluminum foil.
3. BAKE, covered, for 10 minutes, or until the couscous is cooked. Remove from the oven, fluff with a fork and, when cool, add the tomatoes, basil leaves, almonds, pepper, scallions, and lemon juice. Adjust the seasonings to taste. Chill before serving.

French Onion Soup

Servings: 4
Cooking Time: 46 Minutes
Ingredients:

- 1 cup finely chopped onions
- 1 teaspoon toasted sesame oil
- 1 tablespoon vegetable oil
- 2 ½ cup dry white wine
- 3 teaspoons soy sauce
- ½ teaspoon garlic powder
- Freshly ground black pepper to taste
- 4 French bread rounds, sliced 1 inch thick
- 4 tablespoons grated Parmesan cheese
- 1 tablespoon chopped fresh parsley

Directions:

1. Place the onions, sesame oil, and vegetable oil in an 8½ × 8½ × 2-inch square baking (cake) pan.
2. BROIL for 10 minutes, stirring every 3 minutes until the onions are tender. Remove from the oven and transfer to a 1-quart 8½ × 8½ × 4-inch ovenproof baking dish. Add 2 cups water, the wine, and the soy sauce. Add the garlic powder and pepper and adjust the seasonings.
3. BAKE, covered, at 400° F. for 30 minutes. Remove from the oven, uncover, and add the 4 bread rounds, letting them float on top of the soup. Sprinkle each with 1 tablespoon Parmesan cheese.
4. BROIL, uncovered, for 6 minutes, or until the cheese is lightly browned. With tongs, transfer the bread rounds to 4 individual soup bowls. Ladle the soup on top of the bread rounds. Garnish with the parsley and serve immediately.

Scalloped Corn Casserole

Servings: 4
Cooking Time: 38 Minutes
Ingredients:

- Casserole mixture:
- 2 15-ounce cans corn
- 1 red bell pepper, chopped
- ¼ cup chopped scallions
- ½ cup fat-free half-and-half
- 2 tablespoons unbleached flour
- 2 eggs
- ½ teaspoon chili powder
- 1 teaspoon ground cumin
- 1 teaspoon garlic powder
- Salt and freshly ground black pepper to taste
- ¼ cup multigrain seasoned bread Crumbs
- 1 tablespoon margarine

Directions:

1. Preheat the toaster oven to 400° F.
2. Combine all the casserole mixture ingredients in a 1-quart 8½ × 8½ × 4-inch ovenproof baking dish, mixing well. Adjust the seasonings to taste. Cover with aluminum foil.
3. BAKE, covered, for 30 minutes, or until the pepper and onions are tender. Remove from the oven and uncover. Sprinkle with the bread crumbs and dot with the margarine.
4. BROIL for 8 minutes, or until the bread crumb topping is lightly browned.

Parmesan Crusted Tilapia

Servings: 2
Cooking Time: 14 Minutes
Ingredients:

- 2 ounces Parmesan cheese
- 1/4 cup Italian seasoned Panko bread crumbs
- 1/2 teaspoon Italian seasoning
- 1/4 teaspoon ground black pepper
- 1 tablespoon mayonnaise
- 2 tilapia fillets or other white fish fillets (about 4 ounces each)

Directions:

1. Preheat the toaster oven to 425°F. Spray baking pan with nonstick cooking spray.
2. Using a spiralizer, grate Parmesan cheese and place in a large resealable plastic bag. Add Panko bread crumbs, Italian seasoning and black pepper. Seal and shake bag.
3. Spread mayonnaise on both sides of fish fillets. Add fish to bag and shake until coated with crumb mixture.
4. Press remaining crumbs from bag onto fish. Place on prepared baking pan.
5. Bake until fish flakes easily with a fork, 12 to 14 minutes.

Very Quick Pizza

Servings: 1
Cooking Time: 3 Minutes
Ingredients:

- 2 tablespoons salsa
- 1 6-inch whole wheat pita bread
- 2 tablespoons shredded part-skim, low-moisture mozzarella cheese

Directions:

1. Spread the salsa on the pita bread and sprinkle with the cheese.
2. TOAST once, or until the cheese is melted.

Nice + Easy Baked Macaroni + Cheese

Servings: 6
Cooking Time: 35 Minutes
Ingredients:

- Nonstick cooking spray
- 2 cups whole milk
- 3 ounces cream cheese
- ½ teaspoon kosher salt
- 1 clove garlic
- ¼ teaspoon freshly ground black pepper
- 8 ounces macaroni, uncooked
- 2 cups shredded cheddar cheese
- 2 tablespoons unsalted butter, melted
- ¼ cup grated Parmesan cheese
- 1 cup panko bread crumbs

Directions:

1. Preheat the toaster oven to 425°F. Spray an 11 x 7 x 2 ½-inch baking dish with nonstick cooking spray.
2. Place the milk, cream cheese, salt, garlic, and pepper into a blender. Blend until smooth.
3. Add macaroni to the prepared dish. Sprinkle with the cheddar cheese. Pour the milk mixture over all.
4. Combine the butter, Parmesan, and panko in a small bowl. Sprinkle the crumb mixture over the macaroni. Bake, uncovered, for 25 to 35 minutes or until the top is golden brown. Remove from the oven and let stand for at least 10 minutes.

Baked Tomato Casserole

Servings: 4
Cooking Time:45 Minutes
Ingredients:

- Casserole mixture:
- 1 medium onion, coarsely chopped
- 3 medium tomatoes, coarsely chopped
- 1 medium green pepper, coarsely chopped
- 2 garlic cloves, minced
- ½ teaspoon crushed oregano
- ½ teaspoon crushed basil
- 1 tablespoon extra virgin olive oil
- 2 tablespoons chopped fresh cilantro
- Salt and freshly ground black pepper
- 3 4 tablespoons grated Parmesan cheese
- ¼ cup multigrain bread crumbs

Directions:

1. Preheat the toaster oven to 400° F.
2. Combine the casserole mixture ingredients in a 1-quart 8½ × 8½ × 4-inch ovenproof baking dish. Adjust the seasonings to taste and cover with aluminum foil.

3. BAKE, covered, for 35 minutes, or until the tomatoes and pepper are tender. Remove from the oven, uncover, and sprinkle with the bread crumbs and Parmesan cheese.
4. BROIL for 10 minutes, or until the topping is lightly browned.

Cheesy Chicken–stuffed Shells

Servings: 4
Cooking Time: 40 Minutes
Ingredients:

- Nonstick cooking spray
- 16 jumbo pasta shells
- 1 cup finely diced cooked chicken
- 1 cup whole milk ricotta cheese
- 1 ¼ cups shredded mozzarella cheese
- 1 large egg, slightly beaten
- ⅓ cup grated Parmesan cheese
- 1 teaspoon Italian seasoning
- 2 cloves garlic, minced
- ¼ teaspoon kosher salt
- ¼ teaspoon freshly ground black pepper
- 1 ½ cups marinara sauce

Directions:

1. Preheat the toaster oven to 350 °F. Spray an 8 x 8-inch square baking pan with nonstick cooking spray.
2. Cook the shells according to the package directions, drain, and rinse with cool water.
3. Combine the chicken, ricotta, ¾ cup of the mozzarella, egg, Parmesan, Italian seasoning, garlic, salt, and pepper in a large bowl.
4. Spread about ¾ cup of the marinara sauce in the prepared pan. Fill each shell with a heaping tablespoon of the chicken-cheese mixture. Place the prepared shells, stuffed side up, in the pan. Pour the remaining marinara over the shells.
5. Cover and bake for 25 to 30 minutes. Sprinkle with the remaining ½ cup mozzarella and bake, uncovered, for an additional 5 to 10 minutes or until the cheese is melted. Remove from the oven and let stand for 5 to 10 minutes before serving.

Crunchy Baked Chicken Tenders

Servings: 3-4
Cooking Time: 18 Minutes
Ingredients:

- 2/3 cup seasoned panko breadcrumbs
- 2/3 cup cheese crackers, crushed
- 2 teaspoons melted butter
- 2 large eggs, beaten
- Salt and pepper
- 1 1/2 pounds chicken tenders
- Barbecue sauce

Directions:

1. Preheat the toaster oven to 450°F. Spray the toaster oven baking pan with nonstick cooking spray.
2. In medium bowl, combine breadcrumbs, cheese cracker crumbs and butter.
3. In another medium bowl, mix eggs, salt and pepper.
4. Dip chicken tenders in eggs and dredge in breadcrumb mixture.
5. Place on pan.
6. Bake for 15 to 18 minutes, turning once. Serve with barbecue sauce for dipping.

Yeast Dough For Two Pizzas

Servings: 8
Cooking Time: 20 Minutes
Ingredients:

- ¼ cup tepid water
- 1 cup tepid skim milk
- ½ teaspoon sugar
- 1 1¼-ounce envelope dry yeast
- 2 cups unbleached flour
- 1 tablespoon olive oil

Directions:

1. Preheat the toaster oven to 400° F.
2. Combine the water, milk, and sugar in a bowl. Add the yeast and set aside for 3 to 5 minutes, or until the yeast is dissolved.
3. Stir in the flour gradually, adding just enough to form a ball of the dough.
4. KNEAD on a floured surface until the dough is satiny, and then put the dough in a bowl in a warm place with a damp towel over the top. In 1 hour or when the dough has doubled in bulk, punch it down and divide it in half. Flatten the dough and spread it out to the desired thickness on an oiled or nonstick 9¾-inch-diameter pie pan. Spread with Homemade Pizza Sauce (recipe follows) and add any desired toppings.
5. BAKE for 20 minutes, or until the topping ingredients are cooked and the cheese is melted.

Fresh Herb Veggie Pizza

Servings: 4
Cooking Time: 25 Minutes
Ingredients:

- 1 9-inch ready-made pizza crust
- 1 tablespoon olive oil
- 1 4-ounce can tomato paste
- 2 tablespoons shredded part-skim mozzarella
- 2 tablespoons grated Parmesan cheese
- 2 tablespoons crumbled feta cheese
- ½ bell pepper, chopped
- 1 tablespoon chopped fresh parsley
- 1 tablespoon chopped fresh oregano
- 1 tablespoon chopped fresh basil
- ½ teaspoon red pepper flakes
- Salt and freshly ground black pepper to taste
- Pizza mixture:
- 2 garlic cloves, minced
- 1 plum tomato, chopped

Directions:

1. Preheat the toaster oven to 400° F.
2. Brush the pizza crust with olive oil and spread the tomato paste evenly to cover.

3. Combine the ingredients for the pizza mixture and spread evenly on top of the tomato paste layer. Sprinkle the cheeses over all and season to taste. Place the pizza on the toaster oven rack.
4. BAKE for 25 minutes, or until the vegetables are cooked and the cheese is melted.

Chicken Noodle Soup

Servings: 4
Cooking Time: 45 Minutes
Ingredients:

- 1 cup egg noodles, uncooked
- 1 skinless, boneless chicken breast filet, cut into 1-inch pieces
- 1 carrot, peeled and chopped
- 1 celery stalk, chopped
- 1 plum tomato, chopped
- 1 small onion, peeled and chopped
- 1 tablespoon chopped fresh parsley
- 1 teaspoon dried basil
- Salt and freshly ground black pepper to taste

Directions:

1. Preheat the toaster oven to 400° F.
2. Combine all the ingredients with 3 cups water in a 1-quart 8½ × 8½ × 4-inch ovenproof baking dish.
3. BAKE, covered, for 45 minutes, or until the vegetables and chicken are tender.

Pork And Brown Rice Casserole

Servings: 4
Cooking Time: 45 Minutes
Ingredients:

- 2 very lean 6-ounce boneless pork chops, cut into 1-inch cubes
- ½ cup brown rice
- 1 cup chunky tomato sauce
- ½ cup dry white wine
- 3 tablespoons finely chopped onion
- 2 small zucchini squashes, finely chopped
- 2 plum tomatoes, chopped
- ½ teaspoon ground cumin
- ½ teaspoon ground ginger
- 1 teaspoon garlic powder
- 2 bay leaves
- Salt and freshly ground black pepper

Directions:

1. Preheat the toaster oven to 400° F.
2. Combine all the ingredients in a 1-quart 8½ × 8½ × 4-inch ovenproof baking dish. Cover with aluminum foil.
3. BAKE, covered, for 45 minutes, or until the rice is cooked to your preference. Discard the bay leaves before serving.

Tomato Bisque

Servings: 4
Cooking Time: 25 Minutes
Ingredients:

- 1 8-ounce can tomato sauce
- 1 7-ounce jar diced pimientos, drained
- 1 tablespoon finely chopped onion
- 2 cups low-fat buttermilk
- 1 cup fat-free half-and-half
- 1 tablespoon low-fat cream cheese
- 1 teaspoon garlic powder
- ½ teaspoon paprika
- ½ teaspoon ground bay leaf
- 1 teaspoon hot sauce (optional)
- Salt and white pepper to taste
- 2 tablespoons minced fresh basil leaves

Directions:

1. Preheat the toaster oven to 350° F.
2. Process all the ingredients except the basil in a blender or food processor until smooth. Pour into a 1-quart 8½ × 8½ × 4-inch ovenproof baking dish. Adjust the seasonings to taste.
3. BAKE, covered, for 25 minutes. Ladle into small soup bowls and garnish each with fresh basil leaves before serving.

Kasha Loaf

Servings: 4
Cooking Time: 30 Minutes
Ingredients:

- 1 cup whole grain kasha
- 2 cups tomato sauce or 3 2 8-ounce cans tomato sauce (add a small amount of water to make 4 2 cups)
- 3 tablespoons minced onion or scallions
- 1 tablespoon minced garlic
- 1 cup multigrain bread crumbs
- 1 egg
- 1 teaspoon paprika
- 1 teaspoon chili powder
- 1 teaspoon sesame oil

Directions:

1. Preheat the toaster oven to 400° F.
2. Combine all the ingredients in a bowl and transfer to an oiled or nonstick regular-size 4½ × 8½ × 2/4-inch loaf pan.
3. BAKE, uncovered, for 30 minutes, or until lightly browned.

Classic Tuna Casserole

Servings: 4
Cooking Time: 65 Minutes
Ingredients:

- 1 cup elbow macaroni
- 2 6-ounce cans tuna packed in water, drained well and crumbled
- 1 cup frozen peas 1 6-ounce can button mushrooms, drained
- 1 tablespoon margarine
- Salt and freshly ground black pepper
- 1 cup fat-free half-and-half
- 4 tablespoons unbleached flour
- 1 teaspoon garlic powder
- 1 cup multigrain bread crumbs

Directions:

1. Preheat the toaster oven to 400° F.
2. Combine the macaroni and 3 cups water in a 1-quart 8½ × 8½ × 4-inch ovenproof baking dish, stirring to blend well. Cover with aluminum foil.
3. BAKE, covered, for 35 minutes, or until the macaroni is tender. Remove from the oven and drain well. Return to the baking dish and add the tuna, peas, and mushrooms. Add salt and pepper to taste.
4. Whisk together the half-and-half, flour, and garlic powder in a small bowl until smooth. Add to the macaroni mixture and stir to blend well.
5. BAKE, covered, for 25 minutes. Remove from the oven, sprinkle the top with the bread crumbs, and dot with the margarine. Bake, uncovered, for 10 minutes, or until the top is browned.

Pea Soup

Servings: 6
Cooking Time: 55 Minutes
Ingredients:

- 1 cup dried split peas, ground in a blender to a powderlike consistency
- 3 strips lean turkey bacon, uncooked and chopped
- ¼ cup grated carrots
- ¼ cup grated celery
- 2 tablespoons grated onion
- ½ teaspoon garlic powder
- Salt and freshly ground black pepper to taste
- Garnish:
- 2 tablespoons chopped fresh chives

Directions:
1. Preheat the toaster oven to 400° F.
2. Combine all the ingredients in a 1-quart 8½ × 8½ × 4-inch ovenproof baking dish, mixing well. Adjust the seasonings.
3. BAKE, covered, for 35 minutes. Remove from the oven and stir.
4. BAKE, covered, for another 20 minutes, or until the soup is thickened. Ladle the soup into individual soup bowls and garnish each with chopped fresh chives.

Light Quiche Lorraine

Servings: 4
Cooking Time: 35 Minutes
Ingredients:

- Crust:
- 1½ cups bread crumbs
- 1 tablespoon olive oil
- Filling:
- 4 eggs
- ½ cup plain nonfat yogurt
- 2 tablespoons finely chopped scallions
- ¼ cup shredded low-fat mozzarella
- 4 strips lean turkey bacon, broiled, blotted with paper towels, and chopped
- Salt and freshly ground black pepper to taste

Directions:
1. Preheat the toaster oven to 350° F.
2. Combine the bread crumbs, 1 tablespoon water, and the oil in a small bowl and transfer to a pie pan, pressing the mixture flat, starting at the center and working out to the sides. Chill for at least 5 minutes in the refrigerator.
3. Combine the filling ingredients and pour into the chilled bread crumb mixture in the pie pan.
4. BAKE for 40 minutes, or until the center is firm and springy to the touch.

Thai Chicken Pizza With Cauliflower Crust

Servings: 6
Cooking Time: 20 Minutes
Ingredients:

- Nonstick cooking spray
- ½ large head cauliflower (about 1 pound), cut into florets (3 ½ to 4 cups)
- 2 large eggs, lightly beaten
- ⅓ cup shredded mozzarella cheese
- 3 tablespoons shredded Parmesan cheese
- 2 teaspoons Italian seasoning
- ½ teaspoon garlic powder
- Kosher salt and freshly ground black pepper
- SAUCE
- ¼ cup creamy peanut butter
- 1 ½ tablespoons reduced-sodium soy sauce
- 1 ½ tablespoons fresh lime juice
- 1 tablespoon honey
- 1 tablespoon unseasoned rice vinegar
- ½ teaspoon chili garlic sauce
- TOPPINGS
- 1 cup chopped or shredded cooked chicken
- 1 carrot, shredded
- 2 green onions, white and green portions, thinly sliced
- 1 cup shredded Monterey Jack cheese

Directions:
1. Preheat the toaster oven to 425°F. Line a 12-inch pizza pan with parchment paper. Spray with nonstick cooking spray.
2. Place the cauliflower in the work bowl of a food processor. Pulse until finely chopped. (Work in batches, as necessary, so as not to overload the food processor.) Transfer the cauliflower rice to a large, microwave-safe bowl. Add 1 tablespoon water. Cover and microwave on High (100 percent) power for 3 minutes or until the cauliflower is tender. Uncover and let the cauliflower cool to room temperature.
3. Spoon the cauliflower into a clean kitchen towel and twist to drain the cauliflower well. Return the drained cauliflower to the bowl. Stir in the eggs, mozzarella, Parmesan, Italian seasoning, and garlic powder and season with salt and pepper. Stir well.
4. Spoon the cauliflower mixture onto the prepared pan. Gently spread or pat the mixture into an even circle, about 11 inches in diameter. Bake for 12 to 15 minutes or until the crust is set and beginning to brown.

5. Meanwhile, make the sauce: Stir the peanut butter, soy sauce, lime juice, honey, vinegar, and chili garlic sauce in a small bowl.
6. Remove the cauliflower crust from the toaster oven. Spread the peanut sauce over the crust. Top with the chicken, carrot, green onions, and Monterey Jack cheese. Bake for 5 minutes or until hot and the cheese is melted.

Oven-baked Rice

Servings: 2
Cooking Time: 40 Minutes
Ingredients:
- ¼ cup regular rice (not parboiled or precooked)
- Seasonings:
- 1 tablespoon olive oil
- 1 teaspoon dried parsley or
- 1 tablespoon chopped fresh parsley
- 1 teaspoon garlic powder or roasted garlic
- Salt and freshly ground black pepper to taste

Directions:
1. Preheat the toaster oven to 400° F.
2. Combine ¼ cups water and the rice in a 1-quart 8½ × 8½ × 4-inch ovenproof baking dish. Stir well to blend. Cover with aluminum foil.
3. BAKE, covered, for 30 minutes, or until the rice is almost cooked. Add the seasonings, fluff with a fork to combine the seasonings well, then let the rice sit, covered, for 10 minutes. Fluff once more before serving.

Meat Lovers Pan Pizza

Servings: 9
Cooking Time: 15 Minutes
Ingredients:
- Dough
- ¾ cup plus 1½ tablespoons warm water, 100°-110°F
- 1¾ teaspoons instant yeast
- 2 cups all-purpose flour, plus more for dusting
- 1 teaspoon kosher salt
- 1 tablespoon extra virgin olive oil, plus more for drizzling
- Toppings
- 6 tablespoons pizza sauce
- 8 ounces shredded low-moisture mozzarella
- Pepperoni slices
- 8 ounces cooked Italian sausage
- Crushed red pepper, for sprinkling
- Dried oregano, for sprinkling
- Black pepper, for sprinkling

Directions:
1. Pour water into a large mixing bowl, then whisk in the yeast. Allow to bloom for 10 minutes.
2. Add the flour and salt and mix with your hands until no dry flour remains.
3. Cover the dough tightly with plastic wrap and allow to rest at room temperature for 15 hours.
4. Add the olive oil and form into a ball.
5. Drizzle extra-virgin olive oil generously on the food tray and use your hands to coat evenly.
6. Place the dough on the food tray and spread it out slightly toward the corners of the pan.
7. Drizzle some more extra-virgin olive oil on top and use your hands to evenly coat the top of the dough.
8. Cover the dough and allow it to rest for 90 minutes.
9. Spread the dough out further so that it covers the bottom of the pan, then pop any bubbles that formed in the dough.
10. Spread pizza sauce on the dough, followed by cheese, then pepperoni and sausage.
11. Sprinkle the pizza with crushed red pepper, dried oregano, and black pepper.
12. Preheat the toaster Oven to 450°F.
13. Insert the pizza at low position in the preheated oven.
14. Select the Pizza function, adjust time to 15 minutes, and press Start/Pause.
15. Remove when done and allow to rest for 5 minutes before cutting.
16. Cut the pizza into squares and serve.

Connecticut Garden Chowder

Servings: 4
Cooking Time: 60 Minutes
Ingredients:
- Soup:
- ½ cup peeled and shredded potato
- ½ cup shredded carrot
- ½ cup shredded celery 2 plum tomatoes, chopped
- 1 small zucchini, shredded
- 2 bay leaves
- ¼ teaspoon sage
- 1 teaspoon garlic powder
- Salt and butcher's pepper to taste
- Chowder base:
- 2 tablespoons reduced-fat cream cheese, at room temperature
- ½ cup fat-free half-and-half
- 2 tablespoons unbleached flour
- 2 tablespoons chopped fresh parsley

Directions:
1. Preheat the toaster oven to 375° F.
2. Combine the soup ingredients in a 1-quart 8½ × 8½ × 4-inch ovenproof baking dish, mixing well. Adjust the seasonings to taste.
3. BAKE, covered, for 40 minutes, or until the vegetables are tender.
4. Whisk the chowder mixture ingredients together until smooth. Add the mixture to the cooked soup ingredients and stir well to blend.
5. BAKE, uncovered for 20 minutes, or until the stock is thickened. Ladle the soup into individual soup bowls and garnish with the parsley.

Oven-baked Couscous

Servings: 4
Cooking Time: 10 Minutes
Ingredients:
- 1 10-ounce package couscous
- 2 tablespoons olive oil
- 2 tablespoons canned chickpeas
- 2 tablespoons canned or frozen green peas
- 1 tablespoon chopped fresh parsley
- 3 scallions, chopped
- Salt and pepper to taste

Directions:
1. Preheat the toaster oven to 400° F.
2. Mix together all the ingredients with 2 cups water in a 1-quart 8½ × 8½ × 4-inch ovenproof baking dish. Adjust the seasonings to taste. Cover with aluminum foil.
3. BAKE, covered, for 10 minutes, or until the couscous and vegetables are tender. Adjust the seasonings to taste and fluff with a fork before serving.

Spanako Pizza

Servings: 2
Cooking Time: 30 Minutes
Ingredients:
- 8 sheets phyllo dough, thawed and folded in half
- 4 tablespoons olive oil
- 4 tablespoons grated Parmesan cheese
- Topping mixture:
- 1 10-ounce package frozen chopped spinach, thawed and well drained
- 1 plum tomato, finely chopped
- ¼ cup finely chopped onion
- ¼ cup shredded low-fat mozzarella cheese
- 3 tablespoons crumbled feta cheese or part-skim ricotta cheese
- 2 garlic cloves, minced
- Salt and freshly ground black pepper to taste

Directions:
1. Preheat the toaster oven to 375° F.
2. Layer the sheets of phyllo dough in an oiled or nonstick 9¾-inch-diameter baking pan, lightly brushing the top of each sheet with olive oil and folding in the corner edges to fit the pan.
3. Combine the topping mixture ingredients in a bowl and adjust the seasonings to taste. Spread the mixture on top of the phyllo pastry layers and sprinkle with the Parmesan cheese.
4. BAKE for 30 minutes, or until the cheese is melted and the topping is lightly browned. Remove carefully from the pan with a metal spatula.

Baked French Toast With Maple Bourbon Syrup

Servings: 6
Cooking Time: 40 Minutes
Ingredients:
- Nonstick cooking spray
- 4 tablespoons unsalted butter, melted
- ½ cup packed dark brown sugar
- ⅔ cup chopped pecans, toasted
- 6 (1-inch-thick) slices crusty artisan, brioche, or firm country bread
- 3 large eggs
- 1 cup milk
- 1 teaspoon pure vanilla extract
- ⅓ cup maple syrup
- 2 tablespoons bourbon

Directions:
1. Spray an 11 x 7 x 2 ½-inch baking dish with nonstick cooking spray. Pour the butter into the dish. Stir in the brown sugar and pecans. Arrange the bread at an angle in the dish, overlapping the bottom of the slices as necessary.
2. Whisk the eggs, milk, and vanilla in a medium bowl. Drizzle the milk mixture over the bread, taking care to pour slowly and moisten the edges of the bread. Cover and refrigerate overnight.
3. When ready to bake, preheat the toaster oven to 350°F. Bake, uncovered, for 30 to 35 minutes or until golden and set.
4. Mix the maple syrup and bourbon in a small bowl. Drizzle the syrup over the French toast. Bake for 3 to 5 minutes. Let stand for 2 to 3 minutes, then serve warm.

Zucchini Casserole

Servings: 4
Cooking Time: 37 Minutes
Ingredients:
- 4 small zucchini squashes, halved and quartered
- 2 plum tomatoes, quartered
- 1 8-ounce can tomato sauce
- 2 tablespoons chopped onion
- 2 garlic cloves, minced
- 1 tablespoon olive oil
- 1 tablespoon chopped fresh oregano
- 1 tablespoon chopped fresh basil
- 2 tablespoons pine nuts (pignoli)
- Salt and freshly ground black pepper to taste
- ½ cup shredded low-fat mozzarella cheese

Directions:
1. Preheat the toaster oven to 400° F.
2. Combine all the ingredients, except the mozzarella cheese, in a 1-quart 8½ × 8½ × 4-inch ovenproof baking dish. Cover with aluminum foil.
3. BAKE, covered, for 30 minutes, or until the zucchini is tender. Uncover and sprinkle the top with the cheese.
4. BROIL for 7 minutes, or until the cheese is melted and lightly browned.

Beef Pork And Lamb

Stuffed Pork Chops

Servings: 4
Cooking Time: 12 Minutes

Ingredients:

- 4 boneless pork chops
- ½ teaspoon salt
- ½ teaspoon black pepper
- ¼ teaspoon paprika
- 1 cup frozen spinach, defrosted and squeezed dry
- 2 cloves garlic, minced
- 2 ounces cream cheese
- ¼ cup grated Parmesan cheese
- 1 tablespoon extra-virgin olive oil

Directions:

1. Pat the pork chops with a paper towel. Make a slit in the side of each pork chop to create a pouch.
2. Season the pork chops with the salt, pepper, and paprika.
3. In a small bowl, mix together the spinach, garlic, cream cheese, and Parmesan cheese.
4. Divide the mixture into fourths and stuff the pork chop pouches. Secure the pouches with toothpicks.
5. Preheat the toaster oven to 400°F.
6. Place the stuffed pork chops in the air fryer oven and spray liberally with cooking spray. Air-fry for 6 minutes, flip and coat with more cooking spray, and cook another 6 minutes. Check to make sure the meat is cooked to an internal temperature of 145°F. Cook the pork chops in batches, as needed.

Barbeque Ribs

Servings: 4
Cooking Time: 35 Minutes

Ingredients:

- 2 pounds pork spareribs or baby back ribs, silver skin removed
- 2 tablespoons brown sugar
- 1 teaspoon chili powder
- 1 teaspoon dry mustard
- Sea salt, for seasoning
- Freshly ground black pepper, for seasoning
- Oil spray (hand-pumped)
- 1 cup barbeque sauce

Directions:

1. Preheat the toaster oven to 375°F on AIR FRY for 5 minutes.
2. Cut the ribs into 4 bone sections or to fit in the basket.
3. In a small bowl, combine the brown sugar, chili powder, and mustard, and rub it all over the ribs.
4. Season the ribs with salt and pepper.
5. Place the air-fryer basket in the baking tray and spray it generously with the oil.
6. Arrange the ribs in the basket. There can be overlap if necessary.
7. In position 2, air fry for 35 minutes, turning halfway through, until the ribs are tender, browned, and crisp.
8. Baste the ribs with the barbeque sauce and serve.

Pesto Pork Chops

Servings: 2
Cooking Time: 15 Minutes

Ingredients:

- 2 (6-ounce) boneless pork loin chops
- 2 tablespoons basil pesto

Directions:

1. Preheat the toaster oven to 375°F on AIR FRY for 5 minutes.
2. Rub the pork chops all over with the pesto and set aside for 15 minutes.
3. Place the air-fryer basket in the baking tray and arrange the pork in the basket with no overlap.
4. In position 2, air fry for 15 minutes, turning halfway through, until the chops are lightly browned and have an internal temperature of 145°F.
5. Let the meat rest for 10 minutes and serve.

Slow Cooked Carnitas

Servings: 6
Cooking Time: 360 Minutes

Ingredients:

- 1 pork shoulder (5 pounds), bone-in
- 2½ teaspoons kosher salt
- 1½ teaspoons black pepper
- 1½ teaspoons ground cumin
- 1 teaspoon dried oregano
- ¼ teaspoon ground coriander
- 2 bay leaves
- 6 garlic cloves
- 1 small onion, quartered
- 1 cinnamon stick
- 1 full orange peel (no white)
- 2 oranges, juiced
- 1 lime, juiced

Directions:

1. Season the pork shoulder with salt, pepper, cumin, oregano, and coriander.
2. Place the seasoned pork shoulder in a large pot along with any seasoning that did not stick to the pork.
3. Add in the bay leaves, garlic cloves, onion, cinnamon stick, and orange peel.
4. Squeeze in the juice of two oranges and one lime and cover with foil.
5. Insert the wire rack at low position in the Air Fryer Toaster Oven, then place the pot on the rack.
6. Select the Slow Cook function and press Start/Pause.
7. Remove carefully when done, uncover, and remove the bone.
8. Shred the carnitas and use them in tacos, burritos, or any other way you please.

Almond And Sun-dried Tomato Crusted Pork Chops

Servings: 4
Cooking Time: 10 Minutes
Ingredients:

- ½ cup oil-packed sun-dried tomatoes
- ½ cup toasted almonds
- ¼ cup grated Parmesan cheese
- ½ cup olive oil
- 2 tablespoons water
- ½ teaspoon salt
- freshly ground black pepper
- 4 center-cut boneless pork chops (about 1¼ pounds)

Directions:

1. Place the sun-dried tomatoes into a food processor and pulse them until they are coarsely chopped. Add the almonds, Parmesan cheese, olive oil, water, salt and pepper. Process all the ingredients into a smooth paste. Spread most of the paste (leave a little in reserve) onto both sides of the pork chops and then pierce the meat several times with a needle-style meat tenderizer or a fork. Let the pork chops sit and marinate for at least 1 hour (refrigerate if marinating for longer than 1 hour).
2. Preheat the toaster oven to 370°F.
3. Brush a little olive oil on the bottom of the air fryer oven. Transfer the pork chops into the air fryer oven, spooning a little more of the sun-dried tomato paste onto the pork chops if there are any gaps where the paste may have been rubbed off. Air-fry the pork chops at 370°F for 10 minutes, turning the chops over halfway through the cooking process.
4. When the pork chops have finished cooking, transfer them to a serving plate and serve with mashed potatoes and vegetables for a hearty meal.

Red Curry Flank Steak

Servings: 4
Cooking Time: 18 Minutes
Ingredients:

- 3 tablespoons red curry paste
- ¼ cup olive oil
- 2 teaspoons grated fresh ginger
- 2 tablespoons soy sauce
- 2 tablespoons rice wine vinegar
- 3 scallions, minced
- 1½ pounds flank steak
- fresh cilantro (or parsley) leaves

Directions:

1. Mix the red curry paste, olive oil, ginger, soy sauce, rice vinegar and scallions together in a bowl. Place the flank steak in a shallow glass dish and pour half the marinade over the steak. Pierce the steak several times with a fork or meat tenderizer to let the marinade penetrate the meat. Turn the steak over, pour the remaining marinade over the top and pierce the steak several times again. Cover and marinate the steak in the refrigerator for 6 to 8 hours.
2. When you are ready to cook, remove the steak from the refrigerator and let it sit at room temperature for 30 minutes.
3. Preheat the toaster oven to 400°F.
4. Cut the flank steak in half so that it fits more easily into the air fryer oven and transfer both pieces to the air fryer oven. Pour the marinade over the steak. Air-fry for 18 minutes, depending on your preferred degree of doneness of the steak (12 minutes = medium rare). Flip the steak over halfway through the cooking time.
5. When your desired degree of doneness has been reached, remove the steak to a cutting board and let it rest for 5 minutes before slicing. Thinly slice the flank steak against the grain of the meat. Transfer the slices to a serving platter, pour any juice from the bottom of the air fryer oven over the sliced flank steak and sprinkle the fresh cilantro on top.

Spicy Little Beef Birds

Servings: 2
Cooking Time: 12 Minutes
Ingredients:

- Spicy mixture:
- 1 tablespoon olive oil
- 1 tablespoon brown mustard
- 1 teaspoon chili powder
- 1 teaspoon garlic powder
- 1 teaspoon hot sauce
- 1 tablespoon barbecue sauce or salsa
- Salt and freshly ground black pepper to taste
- ½ to ¾ pound pepper steaks, cut into 3 × 4-inch strips

Directions:

1. Blend the spicy mixture ingredients in a small bowl and brush both sides of the beef strips.
2. Roll up the strips lengthwise and fasten with toothpicks near each end. Place the beef rolls in an oiled or nonstick 8½ × 8½ × 2-inch square baking (cake) pan.
3. BROIL for 6 minutes, remove from the oven, and turn with tongs. Brush with the spicy mixture and broil again for 6 minutes, or until done to your preference.

Albóndigas

Servings: 4
Cooking Time: 15 Minutes
Ingredients:

- 1 pound Lean ground pork
- 3 tablespoons Very finely chopped trimmed scallions
- 3 tablespoons Finely chopped fresh cilantro leaves
- 3 tablespoons Plain panko bread crumbs (gluten-free, if a concern)
- 3 tablespoons Dry white wine, dry sherry, or unsweetened apple juice
- 1½ teaspoons Minced garlic
- 1¼ teaspoons Mild smoked paprika
- ¾ teaspoon Dried oregano
- ¾ teaspoon Table salt
- ¼ teaspoon Ground black pepper
- Olive oil spray

Directions:

1. Preheat the toaster oven to 400°F.
2. Mix the ground pork, scallions, cilantro, bread crumbs, wine or its substitute, garlic, smoked paprika, oregano, salt,

and pepper in a bowl until the herbs and spices are evenly distributed in the mixture.

3. Lightly coat your clean hands with olive oil spray, then form the ground pork mixture into balls, using 2 tablespoons for each one. Spray your hands frequently so that the meat mixture doesn't stick.

4. Set the balls in the air fryer oven so that they're not touching, even if they're close together. Air-fry undisturbed for 15 minutes, or until well browned and an instant-read meat thermometer inserted into one or two balls registers 165°F.

5. Use a nonstick-safe spatula and kitchen tongs for balance to gently transfer the fragile balls to a wire rack to cool for 5 minutes before serving.

Spicy Flank Steak With Fresh Tomato-corn Salsa

Servings: 4

Cooking Time: 20 Minutes

Ingredients:

- 2 large tomatoes, chopped
- 1 cup fresh (or canned) corn
- ½ English cucumber, chopped
- ¼ red onion, chopped
- 1 tablespoon jalapeño pepper, chopped
- 1 tablespoon fresh cilantro, chopped
- Sea salt, for seasoning
- Freshly ground black pepper, for seasoning
- 1 pound extra-lean beef flank steak, trimmed of fat
- Olive oil, for brushing
- 1 teaspoon garlic powder
- 1 teaspoon chili powder

Directions:

1. Preheat the toaster oven to 450°F on BROIL for 5 minutes.
2. In a small bowl, stir the tomato, corn, cucumber, onion, jalapeño, and cilantro, and season with salt and pepper.
3. Rub the steak all over with the oil and then season with garlic powder, chili powder, salt, and pepper.
4. Place the air-fryer basket in the baking tray and arrange the steak in the basket.
5. In position 2, broil for 20 minutes, turning halfway through, until browned and with an internal temperature of 140°F, for medium-rare.
6. Let the steak rest for 10 minutes and then cut it very thinly against the grain.
7. Serve with the salsa.

Pork Taco Gorditas

Servings: 4

Cooking Time: 21 Minutes

Ingredients:

- 1 pound lean ground pork
- 2 tablespoons chili powder
- 2 tablespoons ground cumin
- 1 teaspoon dried oregano
- 2 teaspoons paprika
- 1 teaspoon garlic powder
- ½ cup water
- 1 (15-ounce) can pinto beans, drained and rinsed
- ½ cup taco sauce
- salt and freshly ground black pepper
- 2 cups grated Cheddar cheese
- 5 (12-inch) flour tortillas
- 4 (8-inch) crispy corn tortilla shells
- 4 cups shredded lettuce
- 1 tomato, diced
- ⅓ cup sliced black olives
- sour cream, for serving
- tomato salsa, for serving

Directions:

1. Preheat the toaster oven to 400°F.
2. Place the ground pork in the air fryer oven and air-fry at 400°F for 10 minutes, stirring a few times during the cooking process to gently break up the meat. Combine the chili powder, cumin, oregano, paprika, garlic powder and water in a small bowl. Stir the spice mixture into the browned pork. Stir in the beans and taco sauce and air-fry for an additional minute. Transfer the pork mixture to a bowl. Season to taste with salt and freshly ground black pepper.
3. Sprinkle ½ cup of the shredded cheese in the center of four of the flour tortillas, making sure to leave a 2-inch border around the edge free of cheese and filling. Divide the pork mixture among the four tortillas, placing it on top of the cheese. Place a crunchy corn tortilla on top of the pork and top with shredded lettuce, diced tomatoes, and black olives. Cut the remaining flour tortilla into 4 quarters. These quarters of tortilla will serve as the bottom of the gordita. Place one quarter tortilla on top of each gordita and fold the edges of the bottom flour tortilla up over the sides, enclosing the filling. While holding the seams down, brush the bottom of the gordita with olive oil and place the seam side down on the countertop while you finish the remaining three gorditas.
4. Preheat the toaster oven to 380°F.
5. Air-fry one gordita at a time. Transfer the gordita carefully to the air fryer oven, seam side down. Brush or spray the top tortilla with oil and air-fry for 5 minutes. Carefully turn the gordita over and air-fry for an additional 5 minutes, until both sides are browned. When finished air frying all four gorditas, layer them back into the air fryer oven for an additional minute to make sure they are all warm before serving with sour cream and salsa.

Lamb Burger With Feta And Olives

Servings: 3

Cooking Time: 16 Minutes

Ingredients:

- 2 teaspoons olive oil
- ⅓ onion, finely chopped
- 1 clove garlic, minced
- 1 pound ground lamb
- 2 tablespoons fresh parsley, finely chopped
- 1½ teaspoons fresh oregano, finely chopped
- ½ cup black olives, finely chopped
- ⅓ cup crumbled feta cheese
- ½ teaspoon salt

- freshly ground black pepper
- 4 thick pita breads
- toppings and condiments

Directions:

1. Preheat a medium skillet over medium-high heat on the stovetop. Add the olive oil and cook the onion until tender, but not browned – about 4 to 5 minutes. Add the garlic and air-fry for another minute. Transfer the onion and garlic to a mixing bowl and add the ground lamb, parsley, oregano, olives, feta cheese, salt and pepper. Gently mix the ingredients together.
2. Divide the mixture into 3 or 4 equal portions and then form the hamburgers, being careful not to over-handle the meat. One good way to do this is to throw the meat back and forth between your hands like a baseball, packing the meat each time you catch it. Flatten the balls into patties, making an indentation in the center of each patty. Flatten the sides of the patties as well to make it easier to fit them into the air fryer oven.
3. Preheat the toaster oven to 370°F.
4. If you don't have room for all four burgers, air-fry two or three burgers at a time for 8 minutes at 370°F. Flip the burgers over and air-fry for another 8 minutes. If you cooked your burgers in batches, return the first batch of burgers to the air fryer oven for the last two minutes of cooking to re-heat. This should give you a medium-well burger. If you'd prefer a medium-rare burger, shorten the cooking time to about 13 minutes. Remove the burgers to a resting plate and let the burgers rest for a few minutes before dressing and serving.
5. While the burgers are resting, toast the pita breads in the air fryer oven for 2 minutes. Tuck the burgers into the toasted pita breads, or wrap the pitas around the burgers and serve with a tzatziki sauce or some mayonnaise.

Lamb Koftas Meatballs

Servings: 3
Cooking Time: 8 Minutes

Ingredients:

- 1 pound ground lamb
- 1 teaspoon ground cumin
- 1 teaspoon ground coriander
- 2 tablespoons chopped fresh mint
- 1 egg, beaten
- ½ teaspoon salt
- freshly ground black pepper

Directions:

1. Combine all ingredients in a bowl and mix together well. Divide the mixture into 10 portions. Roll each portion into a ball and then by cupping the meatball in your hand, shape it into an oval.
2. Preheat the toaster oven to 400°F.
3. Air-fry the koftas for 8 minutes.
4. Serve warm with the cucumber-yogurt dip.

Air-fried Roast Beef With Rosemary Roasted Potatoes

Servings: 8
Cooking Time: 60 Minutes

Ingredients:

- 1 (5-pound) top sirloin roast
- salt and freshly ground black pepper
- 1 teaspoon dried thyme
- 2 pounds red potatoes, halved or quartered
- 2 teaspoons olive oil
- 1 teaspoon very finely chopped fresh rosemary, plus more for garnish

Directions:

1. Start by making sure your roast will fit into the air fryer oven without touching the top element. Trim it if you have to in order to get it to fit nicely in your air fryer oven. (You can always save the trimmings for another use, like a beef sandwich.)
2. Preheat the toaster oven to 360°F.
3. Season the beef all over with salt, pepper and thyme. Transfer the seasoned roast to the air fryer oven.
4. Air-fry at 360°F for 20 minutes. Turn the roast over and continue to air-fry at 360°F for another 20 minutes.
5. Toss the potatoes with the olive oil, salt, pepper and fresh rosemary. Turn the roast over again in the air fryer oven and toss the potatoes in around the sides of the roast. Air-fry the roast and potatoes at 360°F for another 20 minutes. Check the internal temperature of the roast with an instant-read thermometer, and continue to roast until the beef is 5° lower than your desired degree of doneness. (Rare – 130°F, Medium – 150°F, Well done – 170°F.) Let the roast rest for 5 to 10 minutes before slicing and serving. While the roast is resting, continue to air-fry the potatoes if desired for extra browning and crispiness.
6. Slice the roast and serve with the potatoes, adding a little more fresh rosemary if desired.

Kielbasa Sausage With Pierogies And Caramelized Onions

Servings: 3
Cooking Time: 30 Minutes

Ingredients:

- 1 Vidalia or sweet onion, sliced
- olive oil
- salt and freshly ground black pepper
- 2 tablespoons butter, cut into small cubes
- 1 teaspoon sugar
- 1 pound light Polish kielbasa sausage, cut into 2-inch chunks
- 1 (13-ounce) package frozen mini pierogies
- 2 teaspoons vegetable or olive oil
- chopped scallions

Directions:

1. Preheat the toaster oven to 400°F.
2. Toss the sliced onions with a little olive oil, salt and pepper and transfer them to the air fryer oven. Dot the onions with pieces of butter and air-fry at 400°F for 2 minutes. Then sprinkle the sugar over the onions and stir. Pour any melted butter from the bottom of the air fryer oven over the onions (do this over the sink – some of the butter will spill through the pan). Continue to air-fry for another 13 minutes, stirring the pan every few minutes to cook the onions evenly.

3. Add the kielbasa chunks to the onions and toss. Air-fry for another 5 minutes. Transfer the kielbasa and onions to a bowl and cover with aluminum foil to keep warm.
4. Toss the frozen pierogies with the vegetable or olive oil and transfer them to the air fryer oven. Air-fry at 400°F for 8 minutes.
5. When the pierogies have finished cooking, return the kielbasa and onions to the air fryer oven and gently toss with the pierogies. Air-fry for 2 more minutes and then transfer everything to a serving platter. Garnish with the chopped scallions and serve hot with the spicy sour cream sauce below.
6. Kielbasa Sausage with Pierogies and Caramelized Onions

Crispy Smoked Pork Chops

Servings: 3
Cooking Time: 8 Minutes
Ingredients:

- ⅔ cup All-purpose flour or tapioca flour
- 1 Large egg white(s)
- 2 tablespoons Water
- 1½ cups Corn flake crumbs (gluten-free, if a concern)
- 3 ½-pound, ½-inch-thick bone-in smoked pork chops

Directions:

1. Preheat the toaster oven to 375°F.
2. Set up and fill three shallow soup plates or small pie plates on your counter: one for the flour; one for the egg white(s), whisked with the water until foamy; and one for the corn flake crumbs.
3. Set a chop in the flour and turn it several times, coating both sides and the edges. Gently shake off any excess flour, then set it in the beaten egg white mixture. Turn to coat both sides as well as the edges. Let any excess egg white slip back into the rest, then set the chop in the corn flake crumbs. Turn it several times, pressing gently to coat the chop evenly on both sides and around the edge. Set the chop aside and continue coating the remaining chop(s) in the same way.
4. Set the chops in the air fryer oven with as much air space between them as possible. Air-fry undisturbed for 8 minutes, or until the coating is crunchy and the chops are heated through.
5. Use kitchen tongs to transfer the chops to a wire rack and cool for a couple of minutes before serving.

Herbed Lamb Burgers

Servings: 4
Cooking Time: 15 Minutes
Ingredients:

- 1 pound lean ground lamb
- 1 large egg
- 1 tablespoon fresh parsley, chopped
- 2 teaspoons fresh mint, chopped
- 1 teaspoon minced garlic
- ¼ teaspoon sea salt
- ⅛ teaspoon freshly ground black pepper
- Olive oil spray (hand-pumped)
- 4 whole-wheat buns
- ¼ cup store-bought tzatziki sauce
- 1 tomato, cut into slices
- 4 thin red onion slices
- ½ cup shredded lettuce

Directions:

1. Preheat the toaster oven to 350°F on CONVECTION BROIL for 5 minutes.
2. In a large bowl, mix the lamb, egg, parsley, mint, garlic, salt, and pepper. Form the mixture into 4 patties.
3. Place the air-fryer basket in the baking tray and place the burger patties in the basket. Lightly spray the patties with the oil on both sides.
4. In position 2, broil for 15 minutes, turning halfway through.
5. Serve on the buns topped with tzatziki sauce, tomato, onion, and lettuce.

Steak With Herbed Butter

Servings: 2
Cooking Time: 16 Minutes
Ingredients:

- 4 tablespoons unsalted butter, softened
- 1 tablespoon minced flat-leaf (Italian) parsley
- 1 tablespoon chopped fresh chives
- 2 cloves garlic, minced
- 1 teaspoon Worcestershire sauce
- 2 beef strip steaks, cut about 1 ½ inches thick
- 1 tablespoon olive oil
- Kosher salt and freshly ground black pepper

Directions:

1. Combine the butter, parsley, chives, garlic, and Worcestershire sauce in a small bowl until well blended; set aside.
2. Preheat the toaster oven to broil.
3. Brush the steaks with olive oil and season with salt and pepper. Place the steak on the broiler rack set over the broiler pan. Place the pan in the toaster oven, positioning the steaks about 3 to 4 inches below the heating element. (Depending on your oven and the thickness of the steak, you may need to set the rack to the middle position.) Broil for 6 minutes, turn the steaks over, and broil for an additional 7 minutes. If necessary to reach the desired doneness, turn the steaks over again and broil for an additional 3 minutes or until you reach your desired doneness.
4. Spread the herb butter generously over the steaks. Allow the steaks to stand for 5 to 10 minutes before slicing and serving.

Skirt Steak Fajitas

Servings: 4
Cooking Time: 30 Minutes
Ingredients:

- 2 tablespoons olive oil
- ¼ cup lime juice
- 1 clove garlic, minced
- ½ teaspoon ground cumin
- ½ teaspoon hot sauce
- ½ teaspoon salt
- 2 tablespoons chopped fresh cilantro
- 1 pound skirt steak

- 1 onion, sliced
- 1 teaspoon chili powder
- 1 red pepper, sliced
- 1 green pepper, sliced
- salt and freshly ground black pepper
- 8 flour tortillas
- shredded lettuce, crumbled Queso Fresco (or grated Cheddar cheese), sliced black olives, diced tomatoes, sour cream and guacamole for serving

Directions:

1. Combine the olive oil, lime juice, garlic, cumin, hot sauce, salt and cilantro in a shallow dish. Add the skirt steak and turn it over several times to coat all sides. Pierce the steak with a needle-style meat tenderizer or paring knife. Marinate the steak in the refrigerator for at least 3 hours, or overnight. When you are ready to cook, remove the steak from the refrigerator and let it sit at room temperature for 30 minutes.
2. Preheat the toaster oven to 400°F.
3. Toss the onion slices with the chili powder and a little olive oil and transfer them to the air fryer oven. Air-fry at 400°F for 5 minutes. Add the red and green peppers to the air fryer oven with the onions, season with salt and pepper and air-fry for 8 more minutes, until the onions and peppers are soft. Transfer the vegetables to a dish and cover with aluminum foil to keep warm.
4. Place the skirt steak in the air fryer oven and pour the marinade over the top. Air-fry at 400°F for 12 minutes. Flip the steak over and air-fry at 400°F for an additional 5 minutes. (The time needed for your steak will depend on the thickness of the skirt steak. 17 minutes should bring your steak to roughly medium.) Transfer the cooked steak to a cutting board and let the steak rest for a few minutes. If the peppers and onions need to be heated, return them to the air fryer oven for just 1 to 2 minutes.
5. Thinly slice the steak at an angle, cutting against the grain of the steak. Serve the steak with the onions and peppers, the warm tortillas and the fajita toppings on the side so that everyone can make their own fajita.

Cilantro-crusted Flank Steak

Servings: 2
Cooking Time: 16 Minutes
Ingredients:

- Coating:
- 2 tablespoons chopped onion
- 1 tablespoon olive oil
- 2 tablespoons plain nonfat yogurt
- 1 plum tomato
- ½ cup fresh cilantro leaves
- 2 tablespoons cooking sherry
- ¼ teaspoon hot sauce
- 1 teaspoon garlic powder
- ½ teaspoon chili powder
- Salt and freshly ground black pepper
- 2 8-ounce flank steaks

Directions:

1. Process the coating ingredients in a blender or food processor until smooth. Spread half of the coating mixture on top of the flank steaks. Place the steaks on a broiling rack with a pan underneath.
2. BROIL for 8 minutes. Turn with tongs, spread the remaining mixture on the steaks, and broil again for 8 minutes, or until done to your preference.

Beef, Onion, And Pepper Shish Kebab

Servings: 4
Cooking Time: 20 Minutes
Ingredients:

- Marinade:
- 2 tablespoons olive oil
- ½ cup dry red wine
- 1 tablespoon soy sauce
- 1 teaspoon chili powder
- 1 teaspoon Worcestershire sauce
- 1 teaspoon garlic powder
- 1 teaspoon spicy brown mustard
- 1 teaspoon brown sugar
- 8 onion quarters, approximately 2 × 2-inch pieces
- 8 bell pepper quarters, 2 × 2-inch pieces
- 1 pound lean boneless beef (sirloin, round steak, London broil), cut into 8 2-inch cubes
- 4 8-inch metal or wooden (bamboo) skewers

Directions:

1. Combine the marinade ingredients in a large bowl. Add the onion, peppers, and beef. Refrigerate, covered, for at least 1 hour or
2. Skewer alternating beef, pepper, and onion pieces. Brush with the marinade mixture and place the skewers on a broiling rack with the pan underneath.
3. BROIL for 5 minutes, remove the pan with the skewers from the oven, turn the skewers, brush again, then broil for another 5 minutes. Repeat turning and brushing every 5 minutes, until the peppers and onions are well cooked and browned to your preference.

Steak Pinwheels With Pepper Slaw And Minneapolis Potato Salad

Servings: 4
Cooking Time: 16 Minutes
Ingredients:

- Brushing mixture:
- ½ cup cold strong brewed coffee
- 2 tablespoons molasses
- 1 tablespoon tomato paste
- 2 garlic cloves, minced
- 1 tablespoon olive oil
- Garlic powder
- 1 teaspoon butcher's pepper
- 1 pound lean, boneless beefsteak, flattened to ⅛-inch thickness with a meat mallet or rolling pin (place steak between 2 sheets of heavy-duty plastic wrap)

Directions:

1. Combine the brushing mixture ingredients in a small bowl and set aside.
2. Cut the steak into 2 × 3-inch strips, brush with the mixture, and roll up, securing the edges with toothpicks.

Brush again with the mixture and place in an oiled or nonstick 8½ × 8½ × 2-inch square baking (cake) pan.
3. BROIL for 8 minutes, then turn with tongs, brush with the mixture again, and broil for another 8 minutes, or until browned.

Wasabi-coated Pork Loin Chops

Servings: 3
Cooking Time: 14 Minutes
Ingredients:

- 1½ cups Wasabi peas
- ¼ cup Plain panko bread crumbs
- 1 Large egg white(s)
- 2 tablespoons Water
- 3 5- to 6-ounce boneless center-cut pork loin chops (about ½ inch thick)

Directions:

1. Preheat the toaster oven to 375°F .
2. Put the wasabi peas in a food processor. Cover and process until finely ground, about like panko bread crumbs. Add the bread crumbs and pulse a few times to blend.
3. Set up and fill two shallow soup plates or small pie plates on your counter: one for the egg white(s), whisked with the water until uniform; and one for the wasabi pea mixture.
4. Dip a pork chop in the egg white mixture, coating the chop on both sides as well as around the edge. Allow any excess egg white mixture to slip back into the rest, then set the chop in the wasabi pea mixture. Press gently and turn it several times to coat evenly on both sides and around the edge. Set aside, then dip and coat the remaining chop(s).
5. Set the chops in the air fryer oven with as much air space between them as possible. Air-fry, turning once at the 6-minute mark, for 12 minutes, or until the chops are crisp and browned and an instant-read meat thermometer inserted into the center of a chop registers 145°F. If the machine is at 360°F, you may need to add 2 minutes to the cooking time.
6. Use kitchen tongs to transfer the chops to a wire rack. Cool for a couple of minutes before serving.

Beer-baked Pork Tenderloin

Servings: 4
Cooking Time: 40 Minutes
Ingredients:

- 1 pound lean pork tenderloin, fat trimmed off
- 3 garlic cloves, minced
- 1 cup good-quality dark ale or beer
- 2 bay leaves
- Salt and freshly cracked black pepper
- Spiced apple slices

Directions:

1. Preheat the toaster oven to 400° F.
2. Place the tenderloin in an 8½ × 8½ × 4-inch ovenproof baking dish. Sprinkle the minced garlic over the pork, pour over the beer, add the bay leaves, and season to taste with the salt and pepper. Cover with aluminum foil.
3. BAKE, covered, for 40 minutes, or until the meat is tender. Discard the bay leaves and serve sliced with the liquid. Garnish with the spiced apple slices.

Italian Sausage & Peppers

Servings: 6
Cooking Time: 25 Minutes
Ingredients:

- 1 6-ounce can tomato paste
- ⅔ cup water
- 1 8-ounce can tomato sauce
- 1 teaspoon dried parsley flakes
- ½ teaspoon garlic powder
- ⅛ teaspoon oregano
- ½ pound mild Italian bulk sausage
- 1 tablespoon extra virgin olive oil
- ½ large onion, cut in 1-inch chunks
- 4 ounces fresh mushrooms, sliced
- 1 large green bell pepper, cut in 1-inch chunks
- 8 ounces spaghetti, cooked
- Parmesan cheese for serving

Directions:

1. In a large saucepan or skillet, stir together the tomato paste, water, tomato sauce, parsley, garlic, and oregano. Heat on stovetop over very low heat while preparing meat and vegetables.
2. Break sausage into small chunks, about ½-inch pieces. Place in air fryer oven baking pan.
3. Air-fry at 390°F for 5 minutes. Stir. Cook 7 minutes longer or until sausage is well done. Remove from pan, drain on paper towels, and add to the sauce mixture.
4. If any sausage grease remains in baking pan, pour it off or use paper towels to soak it up. (Be careful handling that hot pan!)
5. Place olive oil, onions, and mushrooms in pan and stir. Air-fry for 5 minutes or just until tender. Using a slotted spoon, transfer onions and mushrooms from baking pan into the sauce and sausage mixture.
6. Place bell pepper chunks in air fryer oven baking pan and air-fry for 8 minutes or until tender. When done, stir into sauce with sausage and other vegetables.
7. Serve over cooked spaghetti with plenty of Parmesan cheese.

Tuscan Pork Tenderloin

Servings: 4
Cooking Time: 35 Minutes
Ingredients:

- Nonstick cooking spray.
- 1 pork tenderloin (1 ¼ to 1 ½ pounds)
- Kosher salt and freshly ground black pepper
- 8 to 10 fresh basil leaves
- 1 ½ teaspoons minced garlic (about 3 cloves garlic)
- 2 slices prosciutto
- 2 ounces mozzarella cheese, cut into thin strips, or ½ cup shredded
- 1 tablespoon olive oil
- 1 teaspoon Italian seasoning

Directions:

1. Preheat the toaster oven to 400°F. Spray a 12 x 12-inch baking pan with nonstick cooking spray.

2. Cut the pork tenderloin in half lengthwise, not quite cutting through one side, and gently open it (like a book) so it lays flat. Cover the meat with plastic wrap. Pound the meat with the flat side of a meat pounder until the meat is even and about ½ inch thick.
3. Season the cut side of the meat with salt and pepper. Arrange the basil leaves evenly over the meat, then sprinkle with 1 teaspoon of the minced garlic. Top with an even layer of prosciutto and cheese. Roll the meat from the longer side covering the cheese and other filling ingredients completely. Tie the meat shut with kitchen twine, taking care to keep the roll tight and the filling inside.
4. Rub the outside of the meat with the olive oil. Mix the Italian seasoning and the remaining ½ teaspoon garlic in a small bowl. Season with salt and pepper. Rub the seasoning mixture evenly over the meat.
5. Place the meat in the prepared pan. Roast, uncovered, for 25 to 35 minutes or until the tenderloin is brown and the pork is just slightly pink inside.
6. Let stand for 5 to 10 minutes. Slice crosswise into slices about 1 inch thick.

Chinese Pork And Vegetable Non-stir-fry

Servings: 4
Cooking Time: 30 Minutes
Ingredients:

- Seasoning sauce:
- 1 tablespoon soy sauce
- ¼ cup dry white wine
- 1 tablespoon sesame oil
- 1 tablespoon vegetable oil
- 1 teaspoon Chinese five-spice powder
- 2 6-ounce lean boneless pork chops cut into ¼ × 2-inch strips
- 1 1-pound package frozen vegetable mix or 2 cups sliced assorted fresh vegetables: broccoli, carrots, cauliflower, bell pepper, and the like
- 1 4-ounce can mushroom pieces, drained, or ½ cup cleaned and sliced fresh mushrooms
- 2 tablespoons sesame seeds
- 2 tablespoons minced fresh garlic

Directions:

1. Whisk together the seasoning sauce ingredients in a small bowl. Set aside.
2. Combine the pork, vegetables, mushrooms, sesame seeds, and garlic in an oiled or nonstick 8½ × 8½ × 2-inch square baking (cake) pan. Add the seasoning sauce ingredients and toss to coat the pork, vegetables, and mushrooms well.
3. BROIL for 30 minutes, turning with tongs every 8 minutes, until the vegetables and meat are well cooked and lightly browned.

Ribeye Steak With Blue Cheese Compound Butter

Servings: 2
Cooking Time: 12 Minutes
Ingredients:

- 5 tablespoons unsalted butter, softened
- ¼ cup crumbled blue cheese 2 teaspoons lemon juice
- 1 tablespoon freshly chopped chives
- Salt & freshly ground black pepper, to taste
- 2 (12 ounce) boneless ribeye steaks

Directions:

1. Mix together butter, blue cheese, lemon juice, and chives until smooth.
2. Season the butter to taste with salt and pepper.
3. Place the butter on plastic wrap and form into a 3-inch log, tying the ends of the plastic wrap together.
4. Place the butter in the fridge for 4 hours to harden.
5. Allow the steaks to sit at room temperature for 1 hour.
6. Pat the steaks dry with paper towels and season to taste with salt and pepper.
7. Insert the fry basket at top position in the Cosori Smart Air Fryer Toaster Oven.
8. Preheat the toaster Oven to 450°F.
9. Place the steaks in the fry basket in the preheated oven.
10. Select the Broil function, adjust time to 12 minutes, and press Start/Pause.
11. Remove when done and allow to rest for 5 minutes.
12. Remove the butter from the fridge, unwrap, and slice into ¾-inch pieces.
13. Serve the steak with one or two pieces of sliced compound butter.

Sweet Potato–crusted Pork Rib Chops

Servings: 2
Cooking Time: 14 Minutes
Ingredients:

- 2 Large egg white(s), well beaten
- 1½ cups (about 6 ounces) Crushed sweet potato chips (certified gluten-free, if a concern)
- 1 teaspoon Ground cinnamon
- 1 teaspoon Ground dried ginger
- 1 teaspoon Table salt (optional)
- 2 10-ounce, 1-inch-thick bone-in pork rib chop(s)

Directions:

1. Preheat the toaster oven to 375°F .
2. Set up and fill two shallow soup plates or small pie plates on your counter: one for the beaten egg white(s); and one for the crushed chips, mixed with the cinnamon, ginger, and salt (if using).
3. Dip a chop in the egg white(s), coating it on both sides as well as the edges. Let the excess egg white slip back into the rest, then set it in the crushed chip mixture. Turn it several times, pressing gently, until evenly coated on both sides and the edges. If necessary, set the chop aside and coat the remaining chop(s).
4. Set the chop(s) in the air fryer oven with as much air space between them as possible. Air-fry undisturbed for 12 minutes, or until crunchy and browned and an instant-read meat thermometer inserted into the center of a chop (without touching bone) registers 145°F. If the machine is at 360°F, you may need to add 2 minutes to the cooking time.
5. Use kitchen tongs to transfer the chop(s) to a wire rack. Cool for 2 or 3 minutes before serving.

Better-than-chinese-take-out Pork Ribs

Servings: 3
Cooking Time: 35 Minutes
Ingredients:

- 1½ tablespoons Hoisin sauce (gluten-free, if a concern)
- 1½ tablespoons Regular or low-sodium soy sauce or gluten-free tamari sauce
- 1½ tablespoons Shaoxing (Chinese cooking rice wine), dry sherry, or white grape juice
- 1½ teaspoons Minced garlic
- ¾ teaspoon Ground dried ginger
- ¾ teaspoon Ground white pepper
- 1½ pounds Pork baby back rib rack(s), cut into 2-bone pieces

Directions:

1. Mix the hoisin sauce, soy or tamari sauce, Shaoxing or its substitute, garlic, ginger, and white pepper in a large bowl. Add the rib sections and stir well to coat. Cover and refrigerate for at least 2 hours or up to 24 hours, stirring the rib sections in the marinade occasionally.
2. Preheat the toaster oven to 350°F . Set the ribs in their bowl on the counter as the machine heats.
3. When the machine is at temperature, set the rib pieces on their sides in a single layer in the air fryer oven with as much air space between them as possible. Air-fry for 35 minutes, turning and rearranging the pieces once, until deeply browned and sizzling.
4. Use kitchen tongs to transfer the rib pieces to a large serving bowl or platter. Wait a minute or two before serving them so the meat can reabsorb some of its own juices.

Pretzel-coated Pork Tenderloin

Servings: 4
Cooking Time: 10 Minutes
Ingredients:

- 1 Large egg white(s)
- 2 teaspoons Dijon mustard (gluten-free, if a concern)
- 1½ cups (about 6 ounces) Crushed pretzel crumbs
- 1 pound (4 sections) Pork tenderloin, cut into ¼-pound (4-ounce) sections
- Vegetable oil spray

Directions:

1. Preheat the toaster oven to 350°F .
2. Set up and fill two shallow soup plates or small pie plates on your counter: one for the egg white(s), whisked with the mustard until foamy; and one for the pretzel crumbs.
3. Dip a section of pork tenderloin in the egg white mixture and turn it to coat well, even on the ends. Let any excess egg white mixture slip back into the rest, then set the pork in the pretzel crumbs. Roll it several times, pressing gently, until the pork is evenly coated, even on the ends. Generously coat the pork section with vegetable oil spray, set it aside, and continue coating and spraying the remaining sections.
4. Set the pork sections in the air fryer oven with at least ¼ inch between them. Air-fry undisturbed for 10 minutes, or until an instant-read meat thermometer inserted into the center of one section registers 145°F.
5. Use kitchen tongs to transfer the pieces to a wire rack. Cool for 3 to 5 minutes before serving.

Pork Cutlets With Almond-lemon Crust

Servings: 3
Cooking Time: 14 Minutes
Ingredients:

- ¾ cup Almond flour
- ¾ cup Plain dried bread crumbs (gluten-free, if a concern)
- 1½ teaspoons Finely grated lemon zest
- 1¼ teaspoons Table salt
- ¾ teaspoon Garlic powder
- ¾ teaspoon Dried oregano
- 1 Large egg white(s)
- 2 tablespoons Water
- 3 6-ounce center-cut boneless pork loin chops (about ¾ inch thick)
- Olive oil spray

Directions:

1. Preheat the toaster oven to 375°F .
2. Mix the almond flour, bread crumbs, lemon zest, salt, garlic powder, and dried oregano in a large bowl until well combined.
3. Whisk the egg white(s) and water in a shallow soup plate or small pie plate until uniform.
4. Dip a chop in the egg white mixture, turning it to coat all sides, even the ends. Let any excess egg white mixture slip back into the rest, then set it in the almond flour mixture. Turn it several times, pressing gently to coat it evenly. Generously coat the chop with olive oil spray, then set aside to dip and coat the remaining chop(s).
5. Set the chops in the air fryer oven with as much air space between them as possible. Air-fry undisturbed for 12 minutes, or until browned and crunchy. You may need to add 2 minutes to the cooking time if the machine is at 360°F.
6. Use kitchen tongs to transfer the chops to a wire rack. Cool for a few minutes before serving.

Vietnamese Beef Lettuce Wraps

Servings: 4
Cooking Time: 12 Minutes
Ingredients:

- ⅓ cup low-sodium soy sauce
- 2 teaspoons fish sauce
- 2 teaspoons brown sugar
- 1 tablespoon chili paste
- juice of 1 lime
- 2 cloves garlic, minced
- 2 teaspoons fresh ginger, minced
- 1 pound beef sirloin
- Sauce
- ⅓ cup low-sodium soy sauce
- juice of 2 limes
- 1 tablespoon mirin wine
- 2 teaspoons chili paste
- Serving

- 1 head butter lettuce
- ½ cup julienned carrots
- ½ cup julienned cucumber
- ½ cup sliced radishes, sliced into half moons
- 2 cups cooked rice noodles
- ⅓ cup chopped peanuts

Directions:

1. Combine the soy sauce, fish sauce, brown sugar, chili paste, lime juice, garlic and ginger in a bowl. Slice the beef into thin slices, then cut those slices in half. Add the beef to the marinade and marinate for 1 to 3 hours in the refrigerator. When you are ready to cook, remove the steak from the refrigerator and let it sit at room temperature for 30 minutes.
2. Preheat the toaster oven to 400°F.
3. Transfer the beef and marinade to the air fryer oven. Air-fry at 400°F for 12 minutes.
4. While the beef is cooking, prepare a wrap-building station. Combine the soy sauce, lime juice, mirin wine and chili paste in a bowl and transfer to a little pouring vessel. Separate the lettuce leaves from the head of lettuce and put them in a serving bowl. Place the carrots, cucumber, radish, rice noodles and chopped peanuts all in separate serving bowls.
5. When the beef has finished cooking, transfer it to another serving bowl and invite your guests to build their wraps. To build the wraps, place some beef in a lettuce leaf and top with carrots, cucumbers, some rice noodles and chopped peanuts. Drizzle a little sauce over top, fold the lettuce around the ingredients and enjoy!

Beef And Spinach Braciole

Servings: 4
Cooking Time: 92 Minutes

Ingredients:

- 7-inch oven-safe baking pan or casserole
- ½ onion, finely chopped
- 1 teaspoon olive oil
- ⅓ cup red wine
- 2 cups crushed tomatoes
- 1 teaspoon Italian seasoning
- ½ teaspoon garlic powder
- ¼ teaspoon crushed red pepper flakes
- 2 tablespoons chopped fresh parsley
- 2 top round steaks (about 1½ pounds)
- salt and freshly ground black pepper
- 2 cups fresh spinach, chopped
- 1 clove minced garlic
- ½ cup roasted red peppers, julienned
- ½ cup grated pecorino cheese
- ¼ cup pine nuts, toasted and rough chopped
- 2 tablespoons olive oil

Directions:

1. Preheat the toaster oven to 400°F.
2. Toss the onions and olive oil together in a 7-inch metal baking pan or casserole dish. Air-fry at 400°F for 5 minutes, stirring a couple times during the cooking process. Add the red wine, crushed tomatoes, Italian seasoning, garlic powder, red pepper flakes and parsley and stir. Cover the pan tightly with aluminum foil, lower the air fryer oven temperature to 350°F and continue to air-fry for 15 minutes.
3. While the sauce is simmering, prepare the beef. Using a meat mallet, pound the beef until it is ¼-inch thick. Season both sides of the beef with salt and pepper. Combine the spinach, garlic, red peppers, pecorino cheese, pine nuts and olive oil in a medium bowl. Season with salt and freshly ground black pepper. Spread the mixture evenly over the steaks. Starting at one of the short ends, roll the beef around the filling, tucking in the sides as you roll to ensure the filling is completely enclosed. Secure the beef rolls with toothpicks.
4. Remove the baking pan with the sauce from the air fryer oven and set it aside. Preheat the toaster oven to 400°F.
5. Brush or spray the beef rolls with a little olive oil and air-fry at 400°F for 12 minutes, rotating the beef during the cooking process for even browning. When the beef is browned, submerge the rolls into the sauce in the baking pan, cover the pan with foil and return it to the air fryer oven. Air-fry at 250°F for 60 minutes.
6. Remove the beef rolls from the sauce. Cut each roll into slices and serve with pasta, ladling some of the sauce overtop.

Glazed Meatloaf

Servings: 4
Cooking Time: 60 Minutes

Ingredients:

- 2 pounds extra-lean ground beef
- ½ cup fine bread crumbs
- 1 large egg
- 1 medium carrot, shredded
- 2 teaspoons minced garlic
- ¼ cup milk
- 1 tablespoon Italian seasoning
- ½ teaspoon sea salt
- ⅛ teaspoon freshly ground black pepper
- ½ cup ketchup
- 1 tablespoon dark brown sugar
- 1 teaspoon apple cider vinegar

Directions:

1. Place the rack in position 1 and preheat the toaster oven to 375°F on BAKE for 5 minutes.
2. In a large bowl, mix the ground beef, bread crumbs, egg, carrot, garlic, milk, Italian seasoning, salt, and pepper until well combined.
3. Press the mixture into a 9-by-5-inch loaf pan.
4. In a small bowl, stir the ketchup, brown sugar, and vinegar. Set aside.
5. Bake for 40 minutes.
6. Take the meatloaf out and spread the glaze over the top. Bake an additional 20 minutes until cooked through, with an internal temperature of 165°F. Serve.

Lime-ginger Pork Tenderloin

Servings: 4
Cooking Time: 26 Minutes
Ingredients:

- ½ cup packed dark brown sugar
- Juice of ½ lime
- 2 teaspoons fresh ginger, peeled and grated
- 1 teaspoon minced garlic
- 2 (1-pound) extra-lean pork tenderloins, trimmed of fat
- Sea salt, for seasoning
- Freshly ground black pepper, for seasoning
- 1 tablespoon olive oil

Directions:

1. Preheat the toaster oven to 400°F on CONVECTION BAKE for 5 minutes.
2. In a small bowl, stir the sugar, lime juice, ginger, and garlic together.
3. Lightly season the pork tenderloins all over with salt and pepper.
4. Heat the oil in a large skillet over medium-high heat. Brown the pork on all sides, about 6 minutes in total.
5. Place the air-fryer basket in the baking tray and place the tenderloins in the basket.
6. Brush the pork all over with the ginger-lime mixture.
7. In position 2, bake for 20 minutes, basting the pork at 10 minutes, until it reaches an internal temperature of about 145°F.
8. Let the pork rest for 10 minutes and serve.

Seasoned Boneless Pork Sirloin Chops

Servings: 2
Cooking Time: 16 Minutes
Ingredients:

- Seasoning mixture:
- ½ teaspoon ground cumin
- ¼ teaspoon turmeric
- Pinch of ground cardamom
- Pinch of grated nutmeg
- 1 teaspoon vegetable oil
- 1 teaspoon Pickapeppa sauce
- 2½- to ¾-pound boneless lean pork sirloin chops

Directions:

1. Combine the seasoning mixture ingredients in a small bowl and brush on both sides of the chops. Place the chops on the broiling rack with a pan underneath.
2. BROIL 8 minutes, remove the chops, turn, and brush with the mixture. Broil again for 8 minutes, or until the chops are done to your preference.

Pork Loin

Servings: 8
Cooking Time: 50 Minutes
Ingredients:

- 1 tablespoon lime juice
- 1 tablespoon orange marmalade
- 1 teaspoon coarse brown mustard
- 1 teaspoon curry powder
- 1 teaspoon dried lemongrass
- 2-pound boneless pork loin roast
- salt and pepper
- cooking spray

Directions:

1. Mix together the lime juice, marmalade, mustard, curry powder, and lemongrass.
2. Rub mixture all over the surface of the pork loin. Season to taste with salt and pepper.
3. Spray air fryer oven with nonstick spray and place pork roast diagonally in the pan.
4. Air-fry at 360°F for approximately 50 minutes, until roast registers 130°F on a meat thermometer.
5. Wrap roast in foil and let rest for 10minutes before slicing.

Italian Meatballs

Servings: 4
Cooking Time: 12 Minutes
Ingredients:

- 12 ounces lean ground beef
- 4 ounces Italian sausage, casing removed
- ½ cup breadcrumbs
- 1 cup grated Parmesan cheese
- 1 egg
- 2 tablespoons milk
- 2 teaspoons Italian seasoning
- ½ teaspoon onion powder
- ½ teaspoon garlic powder
- Pinch of red pepper flakes

Directions:

1. In a large bowl, place all the ingredients and mix well. Roll out 24 meatballs.
2. Preheat the toaster oven to 360°F.
3. Place the meatballs in the air fryer oven and air-fry for 12 minutes, tossing every 4 minutes. Using a food thermometer, check to ensure the internal temperature of the meatballs is 165°F.

Classic Pepperoni Pizza

Servings: 4
Cooking Time: 11 Minutes
Ingredients:

- Oil spray (hand-pumped)
- 1 pound premade pizza dough, or your favorite recipe
- ½ cup store-bought pizza sauce
- ¼ cup grated Parmesan cheese
- ¾ cup shredded mozzarella
- 10 to 12 slices pepperoni
- 2 tablespoons chopped fresh basil
- Pinch red pepper flakes

Directions:

1. Preheat the toaster oven to 425°F on BAKE for 5 minutes.
2. Spray the baking tray with the oil and spread the pizza dough with your fingertips so that it covers the tray. Prick the dough with a fork.
3. In position 2, bake for 8 minutes until the crust is lightly golden.

4. Take the crust out and spread with the pizza sauce, leaving a ½-inch border around the edge. Sprinkle with Parmesan and mozzarella cheeses and arrange the pepperoni on the pizza.
5. Bake for 3 minutes until the cheese is melted and bubbly.
6. Top with the basil and red pepper flakes and serve.

Chipotle-glazed Meat Loaf

Servings: 4
Cooking Time: 65 Minutes
Ingredients:
- 1 ½ pounds lean ground beef
- ¼ cup finely chopped onion
- ½ cup crushed tortilla chips
- 1 teaspoon ground cumin
- ½ teaspoon chili powder
- ½ teaspoon garlic powder
- ½ teaspoon kosher salt
- ¼ teaspoon freshly ground black pepper
- 3 tablespoons chopped pickled jalapeños
- 3 tablespoons chunky salsa
- 1 large egg
- ⅓ cup ketchup
- 3 ½ teaspoons minced chipotle chilies in adobo sauce

Directions:
1. Preheat the toaster oven to 375 °F. Line a 12 x 12-inch baking pan with aluminum foil.
2. Combine the ground beef, onion, tortilla chips, cumin, chili powder, garlic powder, salt, pepper, pickled jalapeños, salsa, and egg in a large bowl, stirring until blended well. Shape the meat mixture into a 9 x 5-inch loaf and place on the prepared pan.
3. Bake, uncovered, for 30 minutes. Carefully remove the meat loaf from the oven and spoon off any collected grease from the pan.
4. Place the ketchup in a small bowl and stir in the chipotle chilies in adobo sauce. Spread the ketchup mixture on top of the meat loaf. Continue to bake for an additional 25 to 35 minutes or until a meat thermometer registers 160 °F. Let stand for 10 minutes before slicing.

Beef Vegetable Stew

Servings: 4
Cooking Time: 120 Minutes
Ingredients:
- 1 pound lean stewing beef, cut into 1-inch chunks
- 2 carrots, diced
- 2 celery stalks
- 1 large potato, diced
- ½ sweet onion, chopped
- 2 teaspoons minced garlic
- 1 (15-ounce) can diced tomatoes, with juices
- 1 teaspoon sea salt
- ½ teaspoon freshly ground black pepper
- 1 cup low-sodium beef broth
- 3 tablespoons all-purpose flour
- 1 cup frozen peas

Directions:
1. Place the rack in position 1 and preheat the toaster oven to 375°F on BAKE for 5 minutes.
2. In a 1½-quart casserole dish, combine the beef, carrots, celery, potato, onion, garlic, tomatoes, salt, and pepper.
3. In a small bowl, stir the broth and flour until well combined. Add the broth mixture to the beef mixture and stir to combine.
4. Cover with foil or a lid and bake for 2 hours, stirring each time you reset the timer, until the meat is very tender.
5. Stir in the peas and let stand for 10 minutes. Serve.

Smokehouse-style Beef Ribs

Servings: 3
Cooking Time: 25 Minutes
Ingredients:
- ¼ teaspoon Mild smoked paprika
- ¼ teaspoon Garlic powder
- ¼ teaspoon Onion powder
- ¼ teaspoon Table salt
- ¼ teaspoon Ground black pepper
- 3 10- to 12-ounce beef back ribs (not beef short ribs)

Directions:
1. Preheat the toaster oven to 350°F .
2. Mix the smoked paprika, garlic powder, onion powder, salt, and pepper in a small bowl until uniform. Massage and pat this mixture onto the ribs.
3. When the machine is at temperature, set the ribs in the air fryer oven in one layer, turning them on their sides if necessary, sort of like they're spooning but with at least ¼ inch air space between them. Air-fry for 25 minutes, turning once, until deep brown and sizzling.
4. Use kitchen tongs to transfer the ribs to a wire rack. Cool for 5 minutes before serving.

Barbecued Broiled Pork Chops

Servings: 2
Cooking Time: 16 Minutes
Ingredients:
- Barbecue sauce mixture:
- 1 tablespoon ketchup
- ¼ cup dry red wine
- 1 tablespoon vegetable oil
- ⅛ teaspoon smoked flavoring (liquid smoke)
- 1 teaspoon chili powder
- 1 teaspoon ground cumin
- 1 teaspoon brown sugar
- ¼ teaspoon butcher's pepper
- 2 large (6- to 8-ounce) lean pork chops, approximately ¾ to 1 inch thick

Directions:
1. Combine the barbecue sauce mixture ingredients in a small bowl. Brush the chops with the sauce and place on a broiling rack with a pan underneath.
2. BROIL 8 minutes, turn with tongs, and broil for another 8 minutes, or until the meat is cooked to your preference.

Traditional Pot Roast

Servings: 6
Cooking Time: 75 Minutes
Ingredients:

- 2 tablespoons olive oil
- 1 teaspoon garlic powder
- 1 teaspoon fresh thyme, chopped
- ¼ teaspoon sea salt
- ¼ teaspoon freshly ground black pepper
- 1 (3-pound) beef rump roast

Directions:

1. Preheat the toaster oven to 350°F on CONVECTION BAKE for 5 minutes.
2. In a small bowl, stir the oil, garlic, thyme, salt, and pepper. Spread the mixture all over the beef.
3. Place the air-fryer basket in the baking tray and place the beef in the basket.
4. In position 1, bake for 1 hour and 15 minutes until browned and the internal temperature reaches 145°F for medium.
5. Let the roast rest 10 minutes and serve.

Bourbon Broiled Steak

Servings: 2
Cooking Time: 14 Minutes
Ingredients:

- Brushing mixture:
- ¼ cup bourbon
- 1 teaspoon garlic powder
- 1 tablespoon olive oil
- 1 teaspoon soy sauce
- 2 6- to 8-ounce sirloin steaks, ¾ inch thick

Directions:

1. Combine the brushing mixture ingredients in a small bowl. Brush the steaks on both sides with the mixture and place on the broiling rack with a pan underneath.
2. BROIL 4 minutes, remove from the oven, turn with tongs, brush the top and sides, and broil again for 4 minutes, or until done to your preference. To use the brushing mixture as a sauce or gravy, pour the mixture into a baking pan.
3. BROIL the mixture for 6 minutes, or until it begins to bubble.

Indian Fry Bread Tacos

Servings: 4
Cooking Time: 20 Minutes
Ingredients:

- 1 cup all-purpose flour
- 1½ teaspoons salt, divided
- 1½ teaspoons baking powder
- ¼ cup milk
- ¼ cup warm water
- ½ pound lean ground beef
- One 14.5-ounce can pinto beans, drained and rinsed
- 1 tablespoon taco seasoning
- ½ cup shredded cheddar cheese
- 2 cups shredded lettuce
- ¼ cup black olives, chopped
- 1 Roma tomato, diced
- 1 avocado, diced
- 1 lime

Directions:

1. In a large bowl, whisk together the flour, 1 teaspoon of the salt, and baking powder. Make a well in the center and add in the milk and water. Form a ball and gently knead the dough four times. Cover the bowl with a damp towel, and set aside.
2. Preheat the toaster oven to 380°F.
3. In a medium bowl, mix together the ground beef, beans, and taco seasoning. Crumble the meat mixture into the air fryer oven and air-fry for 5 minutes; toss the meat and cook an additional 2 to 3 minutes, or until cooked fully. Place the cooked meat in a bowl for taco assembly; season with the remaining ½ teaspoon salt as desired.
4. On a floured surface, place the dough. Cut the dough into 4 equal parts. Using a rolling pin, roll out each piece of dough to 5 inches in diameter. Spray the dough with cooking spray and place in the air fryer oven, working in batches as needed. Air-fry for 3 minutes, flip over, spray with cooking spray, and air-fry for an additional 1 to 3 minutes, until golden and puffy.
5. To assemble, place the fry breads on a serving platter. Equally divide the meat and bean mixture on top of the fry bread. Divide the cheese, lettuce, olives, tomatoes, and avocado among the four tacos. Squeeze lime over the top prior to serving.

Calzones South Of The Border

Servings: 8
Cooking Time: 8 Minutes
Ingredients:

- Filling
- ¼ pound ground pork sausage
- ½ teaspoon chile powder
- ¼ teaspoon ground cumin
- ⅛ teaspoon garlic powder
- ⅛ teaspoon onion powder
- ⅛ teaspoon oregano
- ½ cup ricotta cheese
- 1 ounce sharp Cheddar cheese, shredded
- 2 ounces Pepper Jack cheese, shredded
- 1 4-ounce can chopped green chiles, drained
- oil for misting or cooking spray
- salsa, sour cream, or guacamole
- Crust
- 2 cups white wheat flour, plus more for kneading and rolling
- 1 package (¼ ounce) RapidRise yeast
- 1 teaspoon salt
- ½ teaspoon chile powder
- ½ teaspoon ground cumin
- 1 cup warm water (115°F to 125°F)
- 2 teaspoons olive oil

Directions:

1. Crumble sausage into air fryer oven baking pan and stir in the filling seasonings: chile powder, cumin, garlic powder, onion powder, and oregano. Air-fry at 390°F for 2 minutes. Stir, breaking apart, and air-fry for 3 to 4 minutes, until well done. Remove and set aside on paper towels to drain.
2. To make dough, combine flour, yeast, salt, chile powder, and cumin. Stir in warm water and oil until soft dough forms. Turn out onto lightly floured board and knead for 3 or 4 minutes. Let dough rest for 10 minutes.
3. Place the three cheeses in a medium bowl. Add cooked sausage and chiles and stir until well mixed.
4. Cut dough into 8 pieces.
5. Working with 4 pieces of the dough, press each into a circle about 5 inches in diameter. Top each dough circle with 2 heaping tablespoons of filling. Fold over into a half-moon shape and press edges together. Seal edges firmly to prevent leakage. Spray both sides with oil or cooking spray.
6. Place 4 calzones in air fryer oven and air-fry at 360°F for 5 minutes. Mist with oil or spray and air-fry for 3 minutes, until crust is done and nicely browned.
7. While the first batch is cooking, press out the remaining dough, fill, and shape into calzones.
8. Spray both sides with oil or cooking spray and air-fry for 5 minutes. If needed, mist with oil and continue cooking for 3 minutes longer. This second batch will cook a little faster than the first because your air fryer oven is already hot.
9. Serve plain or with salsa, sour cream, or guacamole.

Crunchy Fried Pork Loin Chops

Servings: 3
Cooking Time: 12 Minutes
Ingredients:

- 1 cup All-purpose flour or tapioca flour
- 1 Large egg(s), well beaten
- 1½ cups Seasoned Italian-style dried bread crumbs (gluten-free, if a concern)
- 3 4- to 5-ounce boneless center-cut pork loin chops
- Vegetable oil spray

Directions:

1. Preheat the toaster oven to 350°F .
2. Set up and fill three shallow soup plates or small pie plates on your counter: one for the flour, one for the beaten egg(s), and one for the bread crumbs.
3. Dredge a pork chop in the flour, coating both sides as well as around the edge. Gently shake off any excess, then dip the chop in the egg(s), again coating both sides and the edge. Let any excess egg slip back into the rest, then set the chop in the bread crumbs, turning it and pressing gently to coat well on both sides and the edge. Coat the pork chop all over with vegetable oil spray and set aside so you can dredge, coat, and spray the additional chop(s).
4. Set the chops in the air fryer oven with as much air space between them as possible. Air-fry undisturbed for 12 minutes, or until brown and crunchy and an instant-read meat thermometer inserted into the center of a chop registers 145°F.
5. Use kitchen tongs to transfer the chops to a wire rack. Cool for 5 minutes before serving.

Beef Bourguignon

Servings: 6
Cooking Time: 240 Minutes
Ingredients:

- 4 slices bacon, chopped into ½-inch pieces
- 3 pounds chuck roast, cut into 2-inch chunks
- 1 tablespoon kosher salt, plus more to taste
- 1½ tablespoons black pepper, plus more to taste
- 4 tablespoons all purpose flour, divided
- 2 tablespoons olive oil
- 2 large carrots, cut into ½-inch thick slices
- ½ large white onion, diced
- 4 cloves garlic, minced
- 2 tablespoons tomato paste
- 3 cups red wine (Merlot, Pinot Noir, or Chianti)
- 2 cups beef stock
- 1 beef bouillon cube, crushed
- ½ teaspoon dried thyme
- ¼ teaspoon dried parsley
- 2 bay leaves
- 10 ounces fresh small white or brown mushrooms, quartered
- 2 tablespoons cornstarch (optional)
- 2 tablespoons water (optional)

Directions:

1. Render the bacon in a large pot over medium heat for 5 minutes or until crispy.
2. Drain the bacon and set aside, leaving the bacon fat in the pot.
3. Mix together chuck roast chunks, kosher salt, black pepper, and 2 tablespoons of all purpose flour until well combined.
4. Dredge the beef of any extra flour and sear in the bacon grease for about 4 minutes on each side. It is important not to overcrowd the pot, so you may need to work in batches.
5. Remove the beef when done and set aside with the bacon.
6. Add the olive oil, sliced carrots, and diced onion to the pot. Cook for 5 minutes, then add the garlic and cook for another minute.
7. Add the tomato paste and cook for 1 minute, then mix in the remaining 2 tablespoons of flour and cook on medium low for 4 minutes.
8. Pour in the wine and beef stock, scraping the bottom of the pot to make sure there aren't any bits stuck to the bottom.
9. Add the bacon and seared meat back into the pot, along with the bouillon cube, dried thyme, dried parsley, bay leaves, and mushrooms. Mix well and bring to a light boil.
10. Insert the wire rack at low position in the Air Fryer Toaster Oven.
11. Cover the pot with foil and place on the rack in the oven. Make sure the foil is secure so it doesn't lift and contact the heating elements.
12. Select the Slow Cook function, adjust time to 4 hours, and press Start/Pause.
13. Remove the pot carefully from the oven when done and place back on the stove.

14. Discard the foil, mix the stew, and season to taste with salt and pepper.
15. Thicken the stew if desired by using a cornstarch slurry of 2 tablespoons cornstarch and 2 tablespoons water. Add half, mix, and bring to a boil, stirring occasionally. If the sauce is still too thin, add the other half of the slurry.

Stuffed Bell Peppers

Servings: 4
Cooking Time: 10 Minutes
Ingredients:

- ¼ pound lean ground pork
- ¾ pound lean ground beef
- ¼ cup onion, minced
- 1 15-ounce can Red Gold crushed tomatoes
- 1 teaspoon Worcestershire sauce
- 1 teaspoon barbeque seasoning
- 1 teaspoon honey
- ½ teaspoon dried basil
- ½ cup cooked brown rice
- ½ teaspoon garlic powder
- ½ teaspoon oregano
- ½ teaspoon salt
- 2 small bell peppers

Directions:
1. Place pork, beef, and onion in air fryer oven baking pan and air-fry at 360°F for 5 minutes.
2. Stir to break apart chunks and cook 3 more minutes. Continue cooking and stirring in 2-minute intervals until meat is well done. Remove from pan and drain.
3. In a small saucepan, combine the tomatoes, Worcestershire, barbeque seasoning, honey, and basil. Stir well to mix in honey and seasonings.
4. In a large bowl, combine the cooked meat mixture, rice, garlic powder, oregano, and salt. Add ¼ cup of the seasoned crushed tomatoes. Stir until well mixed.
5. Cut peppers in half and remove stems and seeds.
6. Stuff each pepper half with one fourth of the meat mixture.
7. Place the peppers in air fryer oven and air-fry for 10 minutes, until peppers are crisp tender.
8. Heat remaining tomato sauce. Serve peppers with warm sauce spooned over top.

Lime And Cumin Lamb Kebabs

Servings: 4
Cooking Time: 16 Minutes
Ingredients:

- 1 pound boneless lean lamb, trimmed and cut into 1 × 1-inch pieces
- 2 plum tomatoes, cut into 2 × 2-inch pieces
- 1 bell pepper, cut into 2 × 2-inch pieces
- 1 small onion, cut into 2 × 2-inch pieces
- Brushing mixture:
- ¼ cup lime juice
- ½ teaspoon soy sauce
- 1 tablespoon honey
- 1½ teaspoon ground cumin

Directions:
1. Skewer alternating pieces of lamb, tomato, pepper, and onion on four 9-inch skewers.
2. Combine the brushing mixture ingredients in a small bowl and brush on the kebabs. Place the skewers on a broiling rack with a pan underneath.
3. BROIL for 8 minutes. Turn the skewers, brush the kebabs with the mixture, and broil for 8 minutes, or until the meat and vegetables are cooked and browned.

Spanish Pork Skewers

Servings: 4
Cooking Time: 16 Minutes
Ingredients:

- 1 pound pork tenderloin, cut into ¾- to 1-inch cubes
- 2 tablespoons olive oil
- 1 teaspoon ground cumin
- ½ teaspoon smoked paprika
- ½ teaspoon dried thyme leaves
- ½ teaspoon kosher salt, plus more for seasoning
- ⅛ teaspoon red pepper flakes
- 2 cloves garlic, minced
- 1 red bell pepper, cut into ¾- to 1-inch squares
- 1 small red onion, cut into ¾- to 1-inch wedges
- Freshly ground black pepper
- Nonstick cooking spray
- 2 tablespoons unsalted butter
- 1 tablespoon sherry or balsamic vinegar
- 1 teaspoon packed dark brown sugar

Directions:
1. Place the pork cubes in a medium bowl. Drizzle 1 tablespoon of oil over the pork. Stir the cumin, paprika, thyme, ½ teaspoon salt, the pepper flakes, and garlic in a small bowl. Sprinkle the seasonings over the pork. Stir to coat the pork evenly. Cover and refrigerate for at least 4 hours or up to overnight.
2. Place the bell pepper and onion pieces in a medium bowl. Drizzle with the remaining tablespoon olive oil and season with salt and pepper. Toss to coat evenly.
3. Alternately thread the pork and vegetables onto skewers. Spray a 12 x 12-inch baking pan with nonstick cooking spray. Place the filled skewers on the prepared pan. Place the pan in the toaster oven, positioning the skewers about 3 to 4 inches below the heating element. (Depending on your oven, you may need to set the rack to the middle position.)
4. Set the toaster oven on broil. Broil for 10 minutes. Turn the skewers. Broil for an additional 5 minutes, or until the vegetables are tender and a meat thermometer registers 145°F. Do not overcook.
5. Meanwhile, combine the butter, vinegar, and brown sugar in a small, glass, microwave-safe bowl. Season with salt and pepper. Microwave on High (100 percent) power for 45 seconds or until the butter melts and the mixture begins to bubble. Stir to dissolve the sugar.
6. Lightly brush the vinegar mixture over the skewers. Broil for 1 minute or until the skewers are browned.

Beef-stuffed Bell Peppers

Servings: 4
Cooking Time: 30 Minutes
Ingredients:

- 4 medium red or yellow bell peppers
- 1 pound extra-lean ground beef
- ½ sweet onion, finely chopped
- 2 teaspoons minced garlic
- 1 cup marinara sauce
- 1 cup ready-made brown or wild rice
- 1 cup fresh kale, chopped
- 1 teaspoon dried basil
- Sea salt, for seasoning
- Freshly ground black pepper, for seasoning
- 1 cup Swiss cheese, shredded

Directions:

1. Preheat the toaster oven to 350°F on AIR FRY for 5 minutes.
2. Cut the top off the peppers and scoop the seeds and membranes out. Set the pepper tops aside.
3. Place a large skillet over medium-high heat and brown the beef, about 10 minutes.
4. Add the onion and garlic and sauté until softened, about 4 minutes.
5. Add the marinara sauce, rice, kale, and basil, stirring to combine. Remove from the heat and season with salt and pepper.
6. Place the air-fryer basket in the baking tray and place the peppers in the basket, hollow-side up.
7. Evenly divide the filling among the peppers. You can place the pepper tops cut-side up and place the pepper bottoms in the tops to balance them, so that they do not tip over.
8. In position 1, air fry for 15 minutes until the peppers are tender. Top with the cheese and air fry for 2 more minutes more to melt the cheese. Serve.

Beef Al Carbon (street Taco Meat)

Servings: 6
Cooking Time: 8 Minutes
Ingredients:

- 1½ pounds sirloin steak, cut into ½-inch cubes
- ¾ cup lime juice
- ½ cup extra-virgin olive oil
- 1 teaspoon ground cumin
- 2 teaspoons garlic powder
- 1 teaspoon salt

Directions:

1. In a large bowl, toss together the steak, lime juice, olive oil, cumin, garlic powder, and salt. Allow the meat to marinate for 30 minutes. Drain off all the marinade and pat the meat dry with paper towels.
2. Preheat the toaster oven to 400°F.
3. Place the meat in the air fryer oven and spray with cooking spray. Cook the meat for 5 minutes, toss the meat, and continue cooking another 3 minutes, until slightly crispy.

Lamb Curry

Servings: 4
Cooking Time: 40 Minutes
Ingredients:

- 1 pound lean lamb for stewing, trimmed and cut into 1 × 1-inch pieces
- 1 small onion, chopped
- 3 garlic cloves, minced
- 2 plum tomatoes, chopped
- ½ cup dry white wine
- 2 tablespoons curry powder
- Salt and cayenne to taste

Directions:

1. Preheat the toaster oven to 400° F.
2. Combine all the ingredients in an 8½ × 8½ × 4-inch ovenproof baking dish. Adjust the seasonings.
3. BAKE, covered, for 40 minutes, or until the meat is tender and the onion is cooked.

Barbecue-style London Broil

Servings: 5
Cooking Time: 17 Minutes
Ingredients:

- ¾ teaspoon Mild smoked paprika
- ¾ teaspoon Dried oregano
- ¾ teaspoon Table salt
- ¾ teaspoon Ground black pepper
- ¼ teaspoon Garlic powder
- ¼ teaspoon Onion powder
- 1½ pounds Beef London broil (in one piece)
- Olive oil spray

Directions:

1. Preheat the toaster oven to 400°F.
2. Mix the smoked paprika, oregano, salt, pepper, garlic powder, and onion powder in a small bowl until uniform.
3. Pat and rub this mixture across all surfaces of the beef. Lightly coat the beef on all sides with olive oil spray.
4. When the machine is at temperature, lay the London broil flat in the air fryer oven and air-fry undisturbed for 8 minutes for the small batch, 10 minutes for the medium batch, or 12 minutes for the large batch for medium-rare, until an instant-read meat thermometer inserted into the center of the meat registers 130°F (not USDA-approved). Add 1, 2, or 3 minutes, respectively (based on the size of the cut) for medium, until an instant-read meat thermometer registers 135°F (not USDA-approved). Or add 3, 4, or 5 minutes respectively for medium, until an instant-read meat thermometer registers 145°F (USDA-approved).
5. Use kitchen tongs to transfer the London broil to a cutting board. Let the meat rest for 10 minutes. It needs a long time for the juices to be reincorporated into the meat's fibers. Carve it against the grain into very thin (less than ¼-inch-thick) slices to serve.

Crispy Lamb Shoulder Chops

Servings: 3
Cooking Time: 28 Minutes
Ingredients:

- ¾ cup All-purpose flour or gluten-free all-purpose flour
- 2 teaspoons Mild paprika
- 2 teaspoons Table salt
- 1½ teaspoons Garlic powder
- 1½ teaspoons Dried sage leaves
- 3 6-ounce bone-in lamb shoulder chops, any excess fat trimmed
- Olive oil spray

Directions:

1. Whisk the flour, paprika, salt, garlic powder, and sage in a large bowl until the mixture is of a uniform color. Add the chops and toss well to coat. Transfer them to a cutting board.
2. Preheat the toaster oven to 375°F .
3. When the machine is at temperature, again dredge the chops one by one in the flour mixture. Lightly coat both sides of each chop with olive oil spray before putting it in the air fryer oven. Continue on with the remaining chop(s), leaving air space between them in the air fryer oven.
4. Air-fry, turning once, for 25 minutes, or until the chops are well browned and tender when pierced with the point of a paring knife. If the machine is at 360°F, you may need to add up to 3 minutes to the cooking time.
5. Use kitchen tongs to transfer the chops to a wire rack. Cool for 5 minutes before serving.

Extra Crispy Country-style Pork Riblets

Servings: 3
Cooking Time: 30 Minutes
Ingredients:

- ⅓ cup Tapioca flour
- 2½ tablespoons Chile powder
- ¾ teaspoon Table salt (optional)
- 1¼ pounds Boneless country-style pork ribs, cut into 1½-inch chunks
- Vegetable oil spray

Directions:

1. Preheat the toaster oven to 375°F .
2. Mix the tapioca flour, chile powder, and salt (if using) in a large bowl until well combined. Add the country-style rib chunks and toss well to coat thoroughly.
3. When the machine is at temperature, gently shake off any excess tapioca coating from the chunks. Generously coat them on all sides with vegetable oil spray. Arrange the chunks in the air fryer oven in one (admittedly fairly tight) layer. The pieces may touch. Air-fry for 30 minutes, rearranging the pieces at the 10- and 20-minute marks to expose any touching bits, until very crisp and well browned.
4. Gently pour the contents of the pan onto a wire rack. Cool for 5 minutes before serving.

Perfect Strip Steaks

Servings: 2
Cooking Time: 17 Minutes
Ingredients:

- 1½ tablespoons Olive oil
- 1½ tablespoons Minced garlic
- 2 teaspoons Ground black pepper
- 1 teaspoon Table salt
- 2 ¾-pound boneless beef strip steak(s)

Directions:

1. Preheat the toaster oven to 375°F (or 380°F or 390°F, if one of these is the closest setting).
2. Mix the oil, garlic, pepper, and salt in a small bowl, then smear this mixture over both sides of the steak(s).
3. When the machine is at temperature, put the steak(s) in the air fryer oven with as much air space as possible between them for the larger batch. They should not overlap or even touch. That said, even just a ¼-inch between them will work. Air-fry for 12 minutes, turning once, until an instant-read meat thermometer inserted into the thickest part of a steak registers 127°F for rare (not USDA-approved). Or air-fry for 15 minutes, turning once, until an instant-read meat thermometer registers 145°F for medium (USDA-approved). If the machine is at 390°F, the steaks may cook 2 minutes more quickly than the stated timing.
4. Use kitchen tongs to transfer the steak(s) to a wire rack. Cool for 5 minutes before serving.

California Burritos

Servings: 4
Cooking Time: 17 Minutes
Ingredients:

- 1 pound sirloin steak, sliced thin
- 1 teaspoon dried oregano
- 1 teaspoon ground cumin
- ½ teaspoon garlic powder
- 16 tater tots
- ⅓ cup sour cream
- ½ lime, juiced
- 2 tablespoons hot sauce
- 1 large avocado, pitted
- 1 teaspoon salt, divided
- 4 large (8- to 10-inch) flour tortillas
- ½ cup shredded cheddar cheese or Monterey jack
- 2 tablespoons avocado oil

Directions:

1. Preheat the toaster oven to 380°F.
2. Season the steak with oregano, cumin, and garlic powder. Place the steak on one side of the air fryer oven and the tater tots on the other side. (It's okay for them to touch, because the flavors will all come together in the burrito.) Air-fry for 8 minutes, toss, and cook an additional 4 to 6 minutes.
3. Meanwhile, in a small bowl, stir together the sour cream, lime juice, and hot sauce.
4. In another small bowl, mash together the avocado and season with ½ teaspoon of the salt, to taste.
5. To assemble the burrito, lay out the tortillas, equally divide the meat amongst the tortillas. Season the steak equally with the remaining ½ teaspoon salt. Then layer the mashed avocado and sour cream mixture on top. Top each tortilla with 4 tater tots and finish each with 2 tablespoons cheese. Roll up the sides and, while holding in the sides, roll up the burrito. Place the burritos in the air fryer oven and brush with avocado oil (working in batches as needed); air-fry for 3 minutes or until lightly golden on the outside.

Pesto-crusted Chicken

Servings: 2
Cooking Time: 31 Minutes
Ingredients:

- Pesto:
- 1 cup fresh cilantro, parsley, and basil leaves
- 3 tablespoons nonfat plain yogurt
- ¼ cup pine nuts, walnut, or pecans
- 3 tablespoons grated Parmesan cheese
- 2 peeled garlic cloves
- 1 tablespoon lemon juice
- 3 tablespoons olive oil
- Salt and freshly ground black pepper to taste
- 2 skinless, boneless chicken breast halves

Directions:

1. Preheat the toaster oven to 450° F.
2. Blend the pesto ingredients in a blender or food processor until smooth. Set aside.
3. Place the chicken breast halves in an oiled or nonstick 8½ × 8½ × 2-inch square (cake) pan. With a butter knife or spatula, spread the mixture liberally on both sides of each chicken breast. Cover the dish with aluminum foil.
4. BAKE, covered, for 25 minutes, or until the chicken is tender. Remove from the oven and uncover.
5. BROIL for 6 minutes, or until the pesto coating is lightly browned.

I Forgot To Thaw—garlic Capered Chicken Thighs

Servings: 4
Cooking Time: 50 Minutes
Ingredients:

- 6 frozen skinless, boneless chicken thighs
- Garlic mixture:
- 3 garlic cloves, minced
- ¾ cup dry white wine
- 2 tablespoons capers
- ½ teaspoon paprika
- ¼ teaspoon ground cumin
- Salt and freshly ground black pepper to taste

Directions:

1. Preheat the toaster oven to 400° F.
2. Thaw the chicken as directed. Separate the pieces and add the garlic mixture, which has been combined in a small bowl, stirring well to coat. Cover the dish with aluminum foil.
3. BAKE for 30 minutes, or until the chicken is tender. Remove the cover and turn the chicken pieces, spooning the sauce over them.
4. BROIL for 8 minutes, or until the chicken is lightly browned.

Tender Chicken Meatballs

Servings: 4
Cooking Time: 30 Minutes
Ingredients:

- 1 pound lean ground chicken
- ½ cup bread crumbs
- 1 large egg
- 1 scallion, both white and green parts, finely chopped
- ¼ cup whole milk
- ¼ cup shredded, unsweetened coconut
- 1 tablespoon low-sodium soy sauce
- 1 teaspoon minced garlic
- 1 teaspoon fresh ginger, peeled and grated
- Pinch cayenne powder
- Oil spray (hand-pumped)

Directions:

1. Preheat the toaster oven to 375°F on BAKE for 5 minutes.
2. Line the baking tray with parchment and set aside.
3. In a large bowl, mix the chicken, bread crumbs, egg, scallion, milk, coconut, soy sauce, garlic, ginger, and cayenne until very well combined.
4. Shape the chicken mixture into 1½-inch balls and place them in a single layer on the baking tray. Do not overcrowd them.
5. In position 2, bake for 20 minutes, turning halfway through, until they are cooked through and evenly browned. Serve.

Honey Lemon Thyme Glazed Cornish Hen

Servings: 2
Cooking Time: 20 Minutes
Ingredients:

- 1 (2-pound) Cornish game hen, split in half
- olive oil
- salt and freshly ground black pepper
- ¼ teaspoon dried thyme
- ¼ cup honey
- 1 tablespoon lemon zest
- juice of 1 lemon
- 1½ teaspoons chopped fresh thyme leaves
- ½ teaspoon soy sauce
- freshly ground black pepper

Directions:

1. Split the game hen in half by cutting down each side of the backbone and then cutting through the breast. Brush or spray both halves of the game hen with the olive oil and then season with the salt, pepper and dried thyme.
2. Preheat the toaster oven to 390°F.
3. Place the game hen, skin side down, into the air fryer oven and air-fry for 5 minutes. Turn the hen halves over and air-fry for 10 minutes.
4. While the hen is cooking, combine the honey, lemon zest and juice, fresh thyme, soy sauce and pepper in a small bowl.

5. When the air fryer oven timer rings, brush the honey glaze onto the game hen and continue to air-fry for another 3 to 5 minutes, just until the hen is nicely glazed, browned and has an internal temperature of 165°F.
6. Let the hen rest for 5 minutes and serve warm.

Chicken Chunks

Servings: 4
Cooking Time: 10 Minutes
Ingredients:

- 1 pound chicken tenders cut in large chunks, about 1½ inches
- salt and pepper
- ½ cup cornstarch
- 2 eggs, beaten
- 1 cup panko breadcrumbs
- oil for misting or cooking spray

Directions:

1. Season chicken chunks to your liking with salt and pepper.
2. Dip chicken chunks in cornstarch. Then dip in egg and shake off excess. Then roll in panko crumbs to coat well.
3. Spray all sides of chicken chunks with oil or cooking spray.
4. Place chicken in air fryer oven in single layer and air-fry at 390°F for 5 minutes. Spray with oil, turn chunks over, and spray other side.
5. Air-fry for an additional 5 minutes or until chicken juices run clear and outside is golden brown.
6. Repeat steps 4 and 5 to cook remaining chicken.

Chicken Hand Pies

Servings: 8
Cooking Time: 10 Minutes
Ingredients:

- ¾ cup chicken broth
- ¾ cup frozen mixed peas and carrots
- 1 cup cooked chicken, chopped
- 1 tablespoon cornstarch
- 1 tablespoon milk
- salt and pepper
- 1 8-count can organic flaky biscuits
- oil for misting or cooking spray

Directions:

1. In a medium saucepan, bring chicken broth to a boil. Stir in the frozen peas and carrots and air-fry for 5 minutes over medium heat. Stir in chicken.
2. Mix the cornstarch into the milk until it dissolves. Stir it into the simmering chicken broth mixture and cook just until thickened.
3. Remove from heat, add salt and pepper to taste, and let cool slightly.
4. Lay biscuits out on wax paper. Peel each biscuit apart in the middle to make 2 rounds so you have 16 rounds total. Using your hands or a rolling pin, flatten each biscuit round slightly to make it larger and thinner.
5. Divide chicken filling among 8 of the biscuit rounds. Place remaining biscuit rounds on top and press edges all around. Use the tines of a fork to crimp biscuit edges and make sure they are sealed well.
6. Spray both sides lightly with oil or cooking spray.
7. Cook in a single layer, 4 at a time, at 330°F for 10 minutes or until biscuit dough is cooked through and golden brown.

Crispy Duck With Cherry Sauce

Servings: 2
Cooking Time: 33 Minutes
Ingredients:

- 1 whole duck (up to 5 pounds), split in half, back and rib bones removed
- 1 teaspoon olive oil
- salt and freshly ground black pepper
- Cherry Sauce:
- 1 tablespoon butter
- 1 shallot, minced
- ½ cup sherry
- ¾ cup cherry preserves 1 cup chicken stock
- 1 teaspoon white wine vinegar
- 1 teaspoon fresh thyme leaves
- salt and freshly ground black pepper

Directions:

1. Preheat the toaster oven to 400°F.
2. Trim some of the fat from the duck. Rub olive oil on the duck and season with salt and pepper. Place the duck halves in the air fryer oven, breast side up and facing the center of the air fryer oven.
3. Air-fry the duck for 20 minutes. Turn the duck over and air-fry for another 6 minutes.
4. While duck is air-frying, make the cherry sauce. Melt the butter in a large sauté pan. Add the shallot and sauté until it is just starting to brown – about 2 to 3 minutes. Add the sherry and deglaze the pan by scraping up any brown bits from the bottom of the pan. Simmer the liquid for a few minutes, until it has reduced by half. Add the cherry preserves, chicken stock and white wine vinegar. Whisk well to combine all the ingredients. Simmer the sauce until it thickens and coats the back of a spoon – about 5 to 7 minutes. Season with salt and pepper and stir in the fresh thyme leaves.
5. When the air fryer oven timer goes off, spoon some cherry sauce over the duck and continue to air-fry at 400°F for 4 more minutes. Then, turn the duck halves back over so that the breast side is facing up. Spoon more cherry sauce over the top of the duck, covering the skin completely. Air-fry for 3 more minutes and then remove the duck to a plate to rest for a few minutes.
6. Serve the duck in halves, or cut each piece in half again for a smaller serving. Spoon any additional sauce over the duck or serve it on the side.

Southwest Gluten-free Turkey Meatloaf

Servings: 8
Cooking Time: 35 Minutes

Ingredients:

- 1 pound lean ground turkey
- ¼ cup corn grits
- ¼ cup diced onion
- 1 teaspoon minced garlic
- ½ teaspoon black pepper
- ½ teaspoon salt
- 1 large egg
- ½ cup ketchup
- 4 teaspoons chipotle hot sauce
- ⅓ cup shredded cheddar cheese

Directions:

1. Preheat the toaster oven to 350°F.
2. In a large bowl, mix together the ground turkey, corn grits, onion, garlic, black pepper, and salt.
3. In a small bowl, whisk the egg. Add the egg to the turkey mixture and combine.
4. In a small bowl, mix the ketchup and hot sauce. Set aside.
5. Liberally spray a 9-x-4-inch loaf pan with olive oil spray. Depending on the size of your air fryer oven, you may need to use 2 or 3 mini loaf pans.
6. Spoon the ground turkey mixture into the loaf pan and evenly top with half of the ketchup mixture. Cover with foil and place the meatloaf into the air fryer oven. Air-fry for 30 minutes; remove the foil and discard. Check the internal temperature (it should be nearing 165°F).
7. Coat the top of the meatloaf with the remaining ketchup mixture, and sprinkle the cheese over the top. Place the meatloaf back in the air fryer oven for the remaining 5 minutes (or until the internal temperature reaches 165°F).
8. Remove from the oven and let cool 5 minutes before serving. Serve warm with desired sides.

Turkey Sausage Cassoulet

Servings: 4
Cooking Time: 52 Minutes

Ingredients:

- 3 turkey sausages
- 1 teaspoon olive oil
- ½ sweet onion
- 2 celery stalks, chopped
- 1 teaspoon minced garlic
- 2 (15-ounce) cans great northern beans, drained and rinsed
- 1(15-ounce) can fire-roasted tomatoes
- 1 small sweet potato, diced
- 1 teaspoon dried thyme
- 2 cups kale, chopped
- Sea salt, for seasoning
- Freshly ground black pepper, for seasoning

Directions:

1. Preheat the toaster oven to 375°F on AIR FRY for 5 minutes.
2. Place the air-fryer basket in the baking tray and place the sausages in the basket. Prick them all over with a fork.
3. In position 2, air fry for 12 minutes until cooked through. Set the sausages aside to cool until you can handle them. Then cut into ¼-inch slices.
4. Change the oven to BAKE at 375°F and place the rack in position 1.
5. Heat the oil in a small skillet over medium-high heat and sauté the onion, celery, and garlic until softened.
6. Transfer the cooked vegetables to a 1½-quart casserole dish and stir in the sausage, beans, tomatoes, sweet potato, and thyme. Cover with foil or a lid.
7. Bake for 35 to 40 minutes until tender and any liquid is absorbed. Take the casserole out and stir in the kale. Let it sit for 10 minutes to wilt.
8. Season with salt and pepper, and serve.

Nacho Chicken Fries

Servings: 4
Cooking Time: 7 Minutes

Ingredients:

- 1 pound chicken tenders
- salt
- ¼ cup flour
- 2 eggs
- ¾ cup panko breadcrumbs
- ¾ cup crushed organic nacho cheese tortilla chips
- oil for misting or cooking spray
- Seasoning Mix
- 1 tablespoon chili powder
- 1 teaspoon ground cumin
- ½ teaspoon garlic powder
- ½ teaspoon onion powder

Directions:

1. Stir together all seasonings in a small cup and set aside.
2. Cut chicken tenders in half crosswise, then cut into strips no wider than about ½ inch.
3. Preheat the toaster oven to 390°F.
4. Salt chicken to taste. Place strips in large bowl and sprinkle with 1 tablespoon of the seasoning mix. Stir well to distribute seasonings.
5. Add flour to chicken and stir well to coat all sides.
6. Beat eggs together in a shallow dish.
7. In a second shallow dish, combine the panko, crushed chips, and the remaining 2 teaspoons of seasoning mix.
8. Dip chicken strips in eggs, then roll in crumbs. Mist with oil or cooking spray.
9. Chicken strips will cook best if done in two batches. They can be crowded and overlapping a little but not stacked in double or triple layers.
10. Air-fry for 4 minutes. Mist with oil, and cook 3 more minutes, until chicken juices run clear and outside is crispy.
11. Repeat step 10 to cook remaining chicken fries.

Italian Roasted Chicken Thighs

Servings: 6
Cooking Time: 14 Minutes
Ingredients:

- 6 boneless chicken thighs
- ½ teaspoon dried oregano
- ½ teaspoon garlic powder
- ½ teaspoon sea salt
- ½ teaspoon black pepper
- ¼ teaspoon crushed red pepper flakes

Directions:

1. Pat the chicken thighs with paper towel.
2. In a small bowl, mix the oregano, garlic powder, salt, pepper, and crushed red pepper flakes. Rub the spice mixture onto the chicken thighs.
3. Preheat the toaster oven to 400°F.
4. Place the chicken thighs in the air fryer oven and spray with cooking spray. Air-fry for 10 minutes, turn over, and cook another 4 minutes. When cooking completes, the internal temperature should read 165°F.

Lemon Chicken

Servings: 4
Cooking Time: 36 Minutes
Ingredients:

- Marinade:
- Juice of 1 lemon, plus pulp (no seeds)
- ¼ cup dry white wine
- 2 tablespoons olive oil
- 1 tablespoon minced garlic
- 2 bay leaves
- 1 teaspoon dried thyme
- 1 teaspoon freshly ground black pepper
- Salt to taste
- 8 skinless, boneless chicken thighs
- Juice of 1 lemon
- 2 tablespoons olive oil

Directions:

1. Preheat the toaster oven to 400° F.
2. Blend the marinade ingredients in a bowl (reserving 3 tablespoons for basting), add the chicken thighs, cover, and chill for at least 1 hour. Transfer the chicken thighs to a 1-quart 8½ × 8½ × 4-inch ovenproof baking dish. Adjust the seasonings. Cover the dish with aluminum foil.
3. BAKE for 30 minutes, or until the chicken is tender. Uncover and spoon the reserved marinade over the chicken.
4. BROIL for 8 minutes, or until lightly browned. Remove the bay leaves before serving.

Poblano Bake

Servings: 4
Cooking Time: 11 Minutes
Ingredients:

- 2 large poblano peppers (approx. 5½ inches long excluding stem)
- ¾ pound ground turkey, raw
- ¾ cup cooked brown rice
- 1 teaspoon chile powder
- ½ teaspoon ground cumin
- ½ teaspoon garlic powder
- 4 ounces sharp Cheddar cheese, grated
- 1 8-ounce jar salsa, warmed

Directions:

1. Slice each pepper in half lengthwise so that you have four wide, flat pepper halves.
2. Remove seeds and membrane and discard. Rinse inside and out.
3. In a large bowl, combine turkey, rice, chile powder, cumin, and garlic powder. Mix well.
4. Divide turkey filling into 4 portions and stuff one into each of the 4 pepper halves. Press lightly to pack down.
5. Place 2 pepper halves in air fryer oven and air-fry at 390°F for 10 minutes or until turkey is well done.
6. Top each pepper half with ¼ of the grated cheese. Cook 1 more minute or just until cheese melts.
7. Repeat steps 5 and 6 to cook remaining pepper halves.
8. To serve, place each pepper half on a plate and top with ¼ cup warm salsa.

Pecan Turkey Cutlets

Servings: 4
Cooking Time: 12 Minutes
Ingredients:

- ¾ cup panko breadcrumbs
- ¼ teaspoon salt
- ¼ teaspoon pepper
- ¼ teaspoon dry mustard
- ¼ teaspoon poultry seasoning
- ½ cup pecans
- ¼ cup cornstarch
- 1 egg, beaten
- 1 pound turkey cutlets, ½-inch thick
- salt and pepper
- oil for misting or cooking spray

Directions:

1. Place the panko crumbs, ¼ teaspoon salt, ¼ teaspoon pepper, mustard, and poultry seasoning in food processor. Process until crumbs are finely crushed. Add pecans and process in short pulses just until nuts are finely chopped. Go easy so you don't overdo it!
2. Preheat the toaster oven to 360°F.
3. Place cornstarch in one shallow dish and beaten egg in another. Transfer coating mixture from food processor into a third shallow dish.
4. Sprinkle turkey cutlets with salt and pepper to taste.
5. Dip cutlets in cornstarch and shake off excess. Then dip in beaten egg and roll in crumbs, pressing to coat well. Spray both sides with oil or cooking spray.
6. Place 2 cutlets in air fryer oven in a single layer and air-fry for 12 minutes or until juices run clear.
7. Repeat step 6 to cook remaining cutlets.

East Indian Chicken

Servings: 4
Cooking Time: 45 Minutes
Ingredients:

- Sauce mixture:
- ¼ cup white wine
- ¼ cup red wine
- ½ cup low-sodium vegetable broth
- ½ cup finely chopped onion
- ½ cup finely chopped bell pepper
- ½ cup finely chopped fresh tomato
- 3 garlic cloves, minced
- 1 tablespoon peeled and minced fresh ginger
- 2 teaspoons curry powder
- ¼ teaspoon ground cinnamon
- ¼ teaspoon ground cumin
- 4 small dried chilies
- Salt and freshly ground black pepper to taste
- 6 skinless, boneless chicken thighs

Directions:

1. Preheat the toaster oven to 400° F.
2. Combine the sauce mixture ingredients in a 1-quart 8½ × 8½ × 4-inch ovenproof baking dish and mix well. Add the chicken and toss together to coat well. Cover the dish with aluminum foil.
3. BAKE for 45 minutes, or until the chicken is tender. Uncover and spoon the sauce over the chicken. Remove the chilies before serving.

Coconut Chicken With Apricot-ginger Sauce

Servings: 4
Cooking Time: 8 Minutes
Ingredients:

- 1½ pounds boneless, skinless chicken tenders, cut in large chunks (about 1¼ inches)
- salt and pepper
- ½ cup cornstarch
- 2 eggs
- 1 tablespoon milk
- 3 cups shredded coconut (see below)
- oil for misting or cooking spray
- Apricot-Ginger Sauce
- ½ cup apricot preserves
- 2 tablespoons white vinegar
- ¼ teaspoon ground ginger
- ¼ teaspoon low-sodium soy sauce
- 2 teaspoons white or yellow onion, grated or finely minced

Directions:

1. Mix all ingredients for the Apricot-Ginger Sauce well and let sit for flavors to blend while you cook the chicken.
2. Season chicken chunks with salt and pepper to taste.
3. Place cornstarch in a shallow dish.
4. In another shallow dish, beat together eggs and milk.
5. Place coconut in a third shallow dish. (If also using panko breadcrumbs, as suggested below, stir them to mix well.)
6. Spray air fryer oven with oil or cooking spray.
7. Dip each chicken chunk into cornstarch, shake off excess, and dip in egg mixture.
8. Shake off excess egg mixture and roll lightly in coconut or coconut mixture. Spray with oil.
9. Place coated chicken chunks in air fryer oven in a single layer, close together but without sides touching.
10. Air-fry at 360°F for 4 minutes, stop, and turn chunks over.
11. Cook an additional 4 minutes or until chicken is done inside and coating is crispy brown.
12. Repeat steps 9 through 11 to cook remaining chicken chunks.

Roasted Game Hens With Vegetable Stuffing

Servings: 2
Cooking Time: 50 Minutes
Ingredients:

- Stuffing:
- 1 cup multigrain bread crumbs
- 2 tablespoons chopped onion
- 1 carrot, shredded
- 1 celery stalk, shredded
- 1 garlic clove, minced
- 2 tablespoons chopped fresh parsley
- Salt and freshly ground black pepper to taste
- 2 whole game hens (thawed or fresh), giblets removed, rinsed, and patted dry with paper towels

Directions:

1. Preheat the toaster oven to 350° F.
2. Combine the stuffing ingredients in a medium bowl. Stuff the cavities of the game hens and place them in a baking dish.
3. BAKE, covered, for 45 minutes, or until the meat is tender and the juices run clear when the breast is pierced with a fork.
4. BROIL, uncovered, for 8 minutes, or until lightly browned.

Chicken Parmesan

Servings: 4
Cooking Time: 11 Minutes
Ingredients:

- 4 chicken tenders
- Italian seasoning
- salt
- ¼ cup cornstarch
- ½ cup Italian salad dressing
- ¼ cup panko breadcrumbs
- ¼ cup grated Parmesan cheese, plus more for serving
- oil for misting or cooking spray
- 8 ounces spaghetti, cooked
- 1 24-ounce jar marinara sauce

Directions:

1. Pound chicken tenders with meat mallet or rolling pin until about ¼-inch thick.
2. Sprinkle both sides with Italian seasoning and salt to taste.
3. Place cornstarch and salad dressing in 2 separate shallow dishes.
4. In a third shallow dish, mix together the panko crumbs and Parmesan cheese.
5. Dip flattened chicken in cornstarch, then salad dressing. Dip in the panko mixture, pressing into the chicken so the coating sticks well.
6. Spray both sides with oil or cooking spray. Place in air fryer oven in single layer.
7. Air-fry at 390°F for 5 minutes. Spray with oil again, turning chicken to coat both sides. See tip about turning.
8. Air-fry for an additional 6 minutes or until chicken juices run clear and outside is browned.
9. While chicken is cooking, heat marinara sauce and stir into cooked spaghetti.
10. To serve, divide spaghetti with sauce among 4 dinner plates, and top each with a fried chicken tender. Pass additional Parmesan at the table for those who want extra cheese.

Buffalo Egg Rolls

Servings: 8
Cooking Time: 9 Minutes
Ingredients:
- 1 teaspoon water
- 1 tablespoon cornstarch
- 1 egg
- 2½ cups cooked chicken, diced or shredded (see opposite page)
- ⅓ cup chopped green onion
- ⅓ cup diced celery
- ⅓ cup buffalo wing sauce
- 8 egg roll wraps
- oil for misting or cooking spray
- Blue Cheese Dip
- 3 ounces cream cheese, softened
- ⅓ cup blue cheese, crumbled
- 1 teaspoon Worcestershire sauce
- ¼ teaspoon garlic powder
- ¼ cup buttermilk (or sour cream)

Directions:
1. Mix water and cornstarch in a small bowl until dissolved. Add egg, beat well, and set aside.
2. In a medium size bowl, mix together chicken, green onion, celery, and buffalo wing sauce.
3. Divide chicken mixture evenly among 8 egg roll wraps, spooning ½ inch from one edge.
4. Moisten all edges of each wrap with beaten egg wash.
5. Fold the short ends over filling, then roll up tightly and press to seal edges.
6. Brush outside of wraps with egg wash, then spritz with oil or cooking spray.
7. Place 4 egg rolls in air fryer oven.
8. Air-fry at 390°F for 9 minutes or until outside is brown and crispy.
9. While the rolls are cooking, prepare the Blue Cheese Dip. With a fork, mash together cream cheese and blue cheese.
10. Stir in remaining ingredients.
11. Dip should be just thick enough to slightly cling to egg rolls. If too thick, stir in buttermilk or milk 1 tablespoon at a time until you reach the desired consistency.
12. Cook remaining 4 egg rolls as in steps 7 and 8.
13. Serve while hot with Blue Cheese Dip, more buffalo wing sauce, or both.

Light And Lovely Loaf

Servings: 4
Cooking Time: 30 Minutes
Ingredients:
- 2 cups ground chicken or turkey breast
- 1 egg
- ½ cup grated carrot
- ½ cup grated celery
- 1 tablespoon finely chopped onion
- ½ teaspoon garlic powder
- Salt and freshly ground black pepper to taste

Directions:
1. Preheat the toaster oven to 400° F.
2. Blend all ingredients in a bowl, mixing well, and transfer to an oiled or nonstick regular-size 4½ × 8½ × 2¼-inch loaf pan
3. BAKE, uncovered, for 30 minutes, until lightly browned.

Crispy Chicken Tenders

Servings: 4
Cooking Time: 22 Minutes
Ingredients:
- 1 pound boneless, skinless chicken breasts
- ½ cup all-purpose flour
- ½ teaspoon kosher salt
- ¼ teaspoon freshly ground black ground pepper
- 1 large egg, beaten
- 3 tablespoons whole milk
- 1 cup cornflake crumbs
- ½ cup grated Parmesan cheese
- Nonstick cooking spray

Directions:
1. Preheat the toaster oven to 375°F. Line a 12 x 12-inch baking pan with nonstick aluminum foil. (Or if lining the pan with regular foil, spray it with nonstick cooking spray.)
2. Cover the chicken with plastic wrap. Pound the chicken with the flat side of a meat pounder until it is even and about ½ inch thick. Cut the chicken into strips about 1 by 3 inches.
3. Combine the flour, salt, and pepper in a small shallow dish. Place the egg and milk in another small shallow dish and use a fork to combine. Place the cornflake crumbs and Parmesan in a third small shallow dish and combine.
4. Dredge each chicken piece in the flour, then dip in the egg mixture, and then coat with the cornflake crumb mixture. Place the chicken strips in a single layer in the prepared baking pan. Spray the chicken strips generously with nonstick cooking spray.

5. Bake for 10 minutes. Turn the chicken and spray with nonstick cooking spray. Bake for an additional 10 to 12 minutes, or until crisp and a meat thermometer registers 165 °F.

Chicken Breast With Chermoula Sauce

Servings: 4
Cooking Time: 15 Minutes
Ingredients:

- Chicken Ingredients
- 2 boneless skinless chicken breasts 1 tablespoon olive oil
- 1 teaspoon salt
- 1 teaspoon pepper
- Chermoula Ingredients
- 1 cup fresh cilantro
- 1 cup fresh parsley
- ¼ cup fresh mint
- ½ teaspoon red chili flakes
- ½ teaspoon cumin seeds
- ½ teaspoon coriander seeds
- 3 garlic cloves, peeled
- ½ cup extra virgin olive oil
- 1 lemon, zested and juiced
- ¾ teaspoons smoked paprika
- ¾ teaspoons salt

Directions:

1. Combine all the chermoula sauce ingredients in a blender or food processor. Pulse until smooth. Taste and add salt if needed. Place into a bowl and set aside.
2. Slice the chicken breast in half lengthwise and lightly pound with a meat tenderizer until both halves are about
3. ½-inch thick.
4. Preheat the toaster oven to 430°F.
5. Line the food tray with foil, then place the chicken breasts on the tray. Drizzle chicken with olive oil and season with salt and pepper.
6. Insert the food tray at top position in the preheated oven.
7. Select the Air Fry function, adjust time to 15 minutes, and press Start/Pause.
8. Remove when the chicken breast reaches an internal temperature of 160°F. Allow the chicken to rest for 5 minutes.
9. Brush the chermoula sauce over the chicken, or serve chicken with chermoula sauce on the side.

Quick Chicken For Filling

Servings: 2
Cooking Time: 8 Minutes
Ingredients:

- 1 pound chicken tenders, skinless and boneless
- ½ teaspoon ground cumin
- ½ teaspoon garlic powder
- cooking spray

Directions:

1. Sprinkle raw chicken tenders with seasonings.
2. Spray air fryer oven lightly with cooking spray to prevent sticking.
3. Place chicken in air fryer oven in single layer.
4. Air-fry at 390°F for 4 minutes, turn chicken strips over, and air-fry for an additional 4 minutes.
5. Test for doneness. Thick tenders may require an additional minute or two.

Gluten-free Nutty Chicken Fingers

Servings: 4
Cooking Time: 10 Minutes
Ingredients:

- ½ cup gluten-free flour
- ½ teaspoon garlic powder
- ¼ teaspoon onion powder
- ¼ teaspoon black pepper
- ¼ teaspoon salt
- 1 cup walnuts, pulsed into coarse flour
- ½ cup gluten-free breadcrumbs
- 2 large eggs
- 1 pound boneless, skinless chicken tenders

Directions:

1. Preheat the toaster oven to 400°F.
2. In a medium bowl, mix the flour, garlic, onion, pepper, and salt. Set aside.
3. In a separate bowl, mix the walnut flour and breadcrumbs.
4. In a third bowl, whisk the eggs.
5. Liberally spray the air fryer oven with olive oil spray.
6. Pat the chicken tenders dry with a paper towel. Dredge the tenders one at a time in the flour, then dip them in the egg, and toss them in the breadcrumb coating. Repeat until all tenders are coated.
7. Set each tender in the air fryer oven, leaving room on each side of the tender to allow for flipping.
8. When the air fryer oven is full, cook 5 minutes, flip, and cook another 5 minutes. Check the internal temperature after cooking completes; it should read 165°F. If it does not, cook another 2 to 4 minutes.
9. Remove the tenders and let cool 5 minutes before serving. Repeat until all the tenders are cooked.

Chicken Adobo

Servings: 6
Cooking Time: 12 Minutes
Ingredients:

- 6 boneless chicken thighs
- ¼ cup soy sauce or tamari
- ½ cup rice wine vinegar
- 4 cloves garlic, minced
- ⅛ teaspoon crushed red pepper flakes
- ½ teaspoon black pepper

Directions:

1. Place the chicken thighs into a resealable plastic bag with the soy sauce or tamari, the rice wine vinegar, the garlic, and the crushed red pepper flakes. Seal the bag and let the chicken marinate at least 1 hour in the refrigerator.
2. Preheat the toaster oven to 400°F.
3. Drain the chicken and pat dry with a paper towel. Season the chicken with black pepper and liberally spray with cooking spray.

4. Place the chicken in the air fryer oven and air-fry for 9 minutes, turn over at 9 minutes and check for an internal temperature of 165°F, and cook another 3 minutes.

Fried Chicken

Servings: 4
Cooking Time: 40 Minutes
Ingredients:

- 12 skin-on chicken drumsticks
- 1 cup buttermilk
- 1½ cups all-purpose flour
- 1 tablespoon smoked paprika
- ¾ teaspoon celery salt
- ¾ teaspoon dried mustard
- ½ teaspoon garlic powder
- ½ teaspoon freshly ground black pepper
- ½ teaspoon sea salt
- ½ teaspoon dried thyme
- ¼ teaspoon dried oregano
- 4 large eggs
- Oil spray (hand-pumped)

Directions:
1. Place the chicken and buttermilk in a medium bowl, cover, and refrigerate for at least 1 hour, up to overnight.
2. Preheat the toaster oven to 375°F on AIR FRY for 5 minutes.
3. In a large bowl, stir the flour, paprika, celery salt, mustard, garlic powder, pepper, salt, thyme, and oregano until well mixed.
4. Beat the eggs until frothy in a medium bowl and set them beside the flour.
5. Place the air-fryer basket in the baking tray and generously spray it with the oil.
6. Dredge a chicken drumstick in the flour, then the eggs, and then in the flour again, thickly coating it, and place the drumstick in the basket. Repeat with 5 more drumsticks and spray them all lightly with the oil on all sides.
7. In position 2, air fry for 20 minutes, turning halfway through, until golden brown and crispy with an internal temperature of 165°F.
8. Repeat with the remaining chicken, covering the cooked chicken loosely with foil to keep it warm. Serve.

Marinated Green Pepper And Pineapple Chicken

Servings: 4
Cooking Time: 20 Minutes
Ingredients:

- Marinade:
- 1 teaspoon finely chopped fresh ginger
- 2 garlic cloves, finely chopped
- 1 teaspoon toasted sesame oil
- 1 tablespoon brown sugar
- 2 tablespoons soy sauce
- ¾ cup dry white wine
- 2 skinless, boneless chicken breasts, cut into 1 × 3-inch strips
- 2 tablespoons chopped onion
- 1 bell pepper, chopped
- 1 5-ounce can pineapple chunks, drained
- 2 tablespoons grated unsweetened coconut

Directions:
1. Combine the marinade ingredients in a medium bowl and blend well. Add the chicken strips and spoon the mixture over them. Marinate in the refrigerator for at least 1 hour. Remove the strips from the marinade and place in an oiled or nonstick 8½ × 8½ × 2-inch square (cake) pan. Add the onion and pepper and mix well.
2. BROIL for 8 minutes. Then remove from the oven and, using tongs, turn the chicken, pepper, and onion pieces. (Spoon the reserved marinade over the pieces, if desired.)
3. BROIL again for 8 minutes, or until the chicken, pepper, and onion are cooked through and tender. Add the pineapple chunks and coconut and toss to mix well.
4. BROIL for another 4 minutes, or until the coconut is lightly browned.

Golden Seasoned Chicken Wings

Servings: 2
Cooking Time: 40 Minutes
Ingredients:

- Oil spray (hand-pumped)
- ¾ cup all-purpose flour
- 1 teaspoon garlic powder
- 1 teaspoon smoked paprika
- ½ teaspoon sea salt
- ¼ teaspoon freshly ground black pepper
- ¼ teaspoon onion powder
- 2 pounds chicken wing drumettes and flats

Directions:
1. Preheat the toaster oven to 400°F on AIR FRY for 5 minutes.
2. Place the air-fryer basket in the baking tray and spray it generously with the oil.
3. In a medium bowl, stir the flour, garlic powder, paprika, sea salt, pepper, and onion powder until well mixed.
4. Add half the chicken wings to the bowl and toss to coat with the flour.
5. Arrange the wings in the basket and spray both sides lightly with the oil.
6. In position 2, air fry for 20 minutes, turning halfway through, until golden brown and crispy.
7. Repeat with the remaining wings, covering the cooked wings loosely with foil to keep them warm. Serve.

Guiltless Bacon

Servings: 4
Cooking Time: 10 Minutes
Ingredients:

- 6 slices lean turkey bacon, placed on a broiling pan

Directions:
1. BROIL 5 minutes, turn the pieces, and broil again for 5 more minutes, or until done to your preference. Press the slices between paper towels and serve immediately.

Chicken Souvlaki Gyros

Servings: 4
Cooking Time: 18 Minutes
Ingredients:

- ¼ cup extra-virgin olive oil
- 1 clove garlic, crushed
- 1 tablespoon Italian seasoning
- ½ teaspoon paprika
- ½ lemon, sliced
- ¼ teaspoon salt
- 1 pound boneless, skinless chicken breasts
- 4 whole-grain pita breads
- 1 cup shredded lettuce
- ½ cup chopped tomatoes
- ¼ cup chopped red onion
- ¼ cup cucumber yogurt sauce

Directions:

1. In a large resealable plastic bag, combine the olive oil, garlic, Italian seasoning, paprika, lemon, and salt. Add the chicken to the bag and secure shut. Vigorously shake until all the ingredients are combined. Set in the fridge for 2 hours to marinate.
2. When ready to cook, preheat the toaster oven to 360°F.
3. Liberally spray the air fryer oven with olive oil mist. Remove the chicken from the bag and discard the leftover marinade. Place the chicken into the air fryer oven, allowing enough room between the chicken breasts to flip.
4. Air-fry for 10 minutes, flip, and cook another 8 minutes.
5. Remove the chicken from the air fryer oven when it has cooked (or the internal temperature of the chicken reaches 165°F). Let rest 5 minutes. Then thinly slice the chicken into strips.
6. Assemble the gyros by placing the pita bread on a flat surface and topping with chicken, lettuce, tomatoes, onion, and a drizzle of yogurt sauce.
7. Serve warm.

Turkey-hummus Wraps

Servings: 4
Cooking Time: 7 Minutes
Ingredients:

- 4 large whole wheat wraps
- ½ cup hummus
- 16 thin slices deli turkey
- 8 slices provolone cheese
- 1 cup fresh baby spinach (or more to taste)

Directions:

1. To assemble, place 2 tablespoons of hummus on each wrap and spread to within about a half inch from edges. Top with 4 slices of turkey and 2 slices of provolone. Finish with ¼ cup of baby spinach—or pile on as much as you like.
2. Roll up each wrap. You don't need to fold or seal the ends.
3. Place 2 wraps in air fryer oven, seam side down.
4. Air-fry at 360°F for 4 minutes to warm filling and melt cheese. If you like, you can continue cooking for 3 more minutes, until the wrap is slightly crispy.
5. Repeat step 4 to cook remaining wraps.

Crispy Fried Onion Chicken Breasts

Servings: 2
Cooking Time: 13 Minutes
Ingredients:

- ¼ cup all-purpose flour
- salt and freshly ground black pepper
- 1 egg
- 2 tablespoons Dijon mustard
- 1½ cups crispy fried onions (like French's®)
- ½ teaspoon paprika
- 2 (5-ounce) boneless, skinless chicken breasts
- vegetable or olive oil, in a spray bottle

Directions:

1. Preheat the toaster oven to 380°F.
2. Set up a dredging station with three shallow dishes. Place the flour in the first shallow dish and season well with salt and freshly ground black pepper. Combine the egg and Dijon mustard in a second shallow dish and whisk until smooth. Place the fried onions in a sealed bag and using a rolling pin, crush them into coarse crumbs. Combine these crumbs with the paprika in the third shallow dish.
3. Dredge the chicken breasts in the flour. Shake off any excess flour and dip them into the egg mixture. Let any excess egg drip off. Then coat both sides of the chicken breasts with the crispy onions. Press the crumbs onto the chicken breasts with your hands to make sure they are well adhered.
4. Spray or brush the bottom of the air fryer oven with oil. Transfer the chicken breasts to the air fryer oven and air-fry at 380°F for 13 minutes, turning the chicken over halfway through the cooking time.
5. Serve immediately.

Crispy "fried" Chicken

Servings: 4
Cooking Time: 14 Minutes
Ingredients:

- ¾ cup all-purpose flour
- ½ teaspoon paprika
- ¼ teaspoon black pepper
- ¼ teaspoon salt
- 2 large eggs
- 1½ cups panko breadcrumbs
- 1 pound boneless, skinless chicken tenders

Directions:

1. Preheat the toaster oven to 400°F.
2. In a shallow bowl, mix the flour with the paprika, pepper, and salt.
3. In a separate bowl, whisk the eggs; set aside.
4. In a third bowl, place the breadcrumbs.
5. Liberally spray the air fryer oven with olive oil spray.
6. Pat the chicken tenders dry with a paper towel. Dredge the tenders one at a time in the flour, then dip them in the egg, and toss them in the breadcrumb coating. Repeat until all tenders are coated.
7. Set each tender in the air fryer oven, leaving room on each side of the tender to allow for flipping.

8. When the air fryer oven is full, cook 4 to 7 minutes, flip, and cook another 4 to 7 minutes.
9. Remove the tenders and let cool 5 minutes before serving. Repeat until all tenders are cooked.

Chicken-fried Steak With Gravy

Servings: 2
Cooking Time: 16 Minutes
Ingredients:

- FOR THE STEAK
- Oil spray (hand-pumped)
- 1 cup all-purpose flour
- 1 teaspoon garlic powder
- 1 teaspoon onion powder
- 1 teaspoon smoked paprika
- 2 large eggs
- 2 (½-pound) cube steaks
- Sea salt, for seasoning
- Freshly ground black pepper, for seasoning
- FOR THE GRAVY
- 2 tablespoons salted butter
- 2 tablespoons all-purpose flour
- 1½ cups whole milk
- ¼ cup heavy (whipping) cream
- Sea salt, for seasoning
- Freshly ground black pepper, for seasoning

Directions:

1. To make the steak
2. Preheat the toaster oven to 400°F on AIR FRY for 5 minutes.
3. Place the air-fryer basket in the baking tray and spray it generously with the oil.
4. In a medium bowl, stir the flour, garlic powder, onion powder, and paprika until well blended.
5. In a medium bowl, beat the eggs and place them next to the flour.
6. Season the steaks all over with salt and pepper.
7. Dredge a steak in the egg and then in the flour mixture, making sure it is well coated. Shake off any excess flour.
8. Place the steak in the basket and repeat the process with the other steak.
9. Spray the tops of the steaks with the oil.
10. In position 2, air fry for 9 minutes until golden brown and crispy. Turn the steaks over, spray the second side with the oil, and air fry for an additional 7 minutes.
11. Set the steaks aside to rest for 5 minutes.
12. To make the gravy
13. While the steak is air frying, melt the butter in a medium saucepan over medium-high heat.
14. Whisk in the flour and cook for 2 minutes until lightly browned.
15. Whisk in the milk until the gravy is creamy and thick, about 5 minutes. Whisk in the cream and season with salt and pepper.
16. Serve the steak topped with the gravy.

Air-fried Turkey Breast With Cherry Glaze

Servings: 6
Cooking Time: 54 Minutes
Ingredients:

- 1 (5-pound) turkey breast
- 2 teaspoons olive oil
- 1 teaspoon dried thyme
- ½ teaspoon dried sage
- 1 teaspoon salt
- ½ teaspoon freshly ground black pepper
- ½ cup cherry preserves
- 1 tablespoon chopped fresh thyme leaves
- 1 teaspoon soy sauce
- freshly ground black pepper

Directions:

1. All turkeys are built differently, so depending on the turkey breast and how your butcher has prepared it, you may need to trim the bottom of the ribs in order to get the turkey to sit upright in the air fryer oven without touching the heating element. The key to this recipe is getting the right size turkey breast. Once you've managed that, the rest is easy, so make sure your turkey breast fits into the air fryer oven before you Preheat the toaster oven oven.
2. Preheat the toaster oven to 350°F.
3. Brush the turkey breast all over with the olive oil. Combine the thyme, sage, salt and pepper and rub the outside of the turkey breast with the spice mixture.
4. Transfer the seasoned turkey breast to the air fryer oven, breast side up, and air-fry at 350°F for 25 minutes. Turn the turkey breast on its side and air-fry for another 12 minutes. Turn the turkey breast on the opposite side and air-fry for 12 more minutes. The internal temperature of the turkey breast should reach 165°F when fully cooked.
5. While the turkey is air-frying, make the glaze by combining the cherry preserves, fresh thyme, soy sauce and pepper in a small bowl. When the cooking time is up, return the turkey breast to an upright position and brush the glaze all over the turkey. Air-fry for a final 5 minutes, until the skin is nicely browned and crispy. Let the turkey rest, loosely tented with foil, for at least 5 minutes before slicing and serving.

Hot Thighs

Servings: 4
Cooking Time: 40 Minutes
Ingredients:

- 6 skinless, boneless chicken thighs
- ¼ cup fresh lemon juice
- Seasonings:
- 1 teaspoon garlic powder
- ¼ teaspoon cayenne
- ½ teaspoon chili powder
- 1 teaspoon onion powder
- Salt and freshly ground black pepper to taste

Directions:

1. Preheat the toaster oven to 450° F.

2. Brush the chicken thighs liberally with the lemon juice. Set aside.
3. Combine the seasonings in a small bowl and transfer to a paper or plastic bag. Add the thighs and shake well to coat. Remove from the bag and place in an oiled or nonstick 8½ × 8½ × 2-inch square (cake) pan. Cover the pan with aluminum foil.
4. BAKE, covered, for 20 minutes. Turn the pieces with tongs and bake again for another 20 minutes, or until the meat is tender and lightly browned.

Sticky Soy Chicken Thighs

Servings: 2
Cooking Time: 20 Minutes
Ingredients:

- 2 tablespoons less-sodium soy sauce
- 1 tablespoon olive oil
- 1 tablespoon honey
- 1 tablespoon balsamic vinegar
- 1 tablespoon chili sauce
- Juice of 1 lime
- 1 teaspoon minced garlic
- 1 teaspoon ginger, peeled and grated
- 2 bone-in, skin-on chicken thighs
- Oil spray (hand-pumped)
- 1 scallion, both white and green parts, thinly sliced, for garnish
- 2 teaspoons sesame seeds, for garnish

Directions:

1. Preheat the toaster oven to 400°F on AIR FRY for 5 minutes.
2. In a large bowl, combine the soy sauce, olive oil, honey, balsamic vinegar, chili sauce, lime juice, garlic, and ginger. Add the chicken thighs to the bowl and toss to coat. Cover the bowl and refrigerate for 30 minutes.
3. Place the air-fryer basket in the baking tray and generously spray with oil.
4. Place the thighs in the basket, and in position 2, air fry for 20 minutes until cooked through and the thighs are browned and lightly caramelized, with an internal temperature of 165°F.
5. Garnish the chicken with the scallion and sesame seeds and serve.

Orange-glazed Roast Chicken

Servings: 6
Cooking Time: 100 Minutes
Ingredients:

- 1 3-pound whole chicken, rinsed and patted dry with paper towels
- Brushing mixture:
- 2 tablespoons orange juice concentrate
- 1 tablespoon soy sauce
- 1 tablespoon toasted sesame oil
- 1 teaspoon ground ginger
- Salt and freshly ground black pepper to taste

Directions:

1. Preheat the toaster oven to 400° F.
2. Place the chicken, breast side up, in an oiled or nonstick 8½ × 8½ × 2-inch square (cake) pan and brush with the mixture, which has been combined in a small bowl, reserving the remaining mixture. Cover with aluminum foil.
3. BAKE for 1 hour and 20 minutes. Uncover and brush the chicken with remaining mixture.
4. BAKE, uncovered, for 20 minutes, or until the breast is tender when pierced with a fork and golden brown.

Oven-crisped Chicken

Servings: 4
Cooking Time: 35 Minutes
Ingredients:

- Coating mixture:
- 1 cup cornmeal
- ¼ cup wheat germ
- 1 teaspoon paprika
- 1 teaspoon garlic powder
- Salt and butcher's pepper to taste
- 3 tablespoons olive oil
- 1 tablespoon spicy brown mustard
- 6 skinless, boneless chicken thighs

Directions:

1. Preheat the toaster oven to 375° F.
2. Combine the coating mixture ingredients in a small bowl and transfer to a plate, spreading the mixture evenly over the plate's surface. Set aside.
3. Whisk together the oil and mustard in a bowl. Add the chicken pieces and toss to coat thoroughly. Press both sides of each piece into the coating mixture to coat well. Chill in the refrigerator for 10 minutes. Transfer the chicken pieces to a broiling rack with a pan underneath.
4. BAKE, uncovered, for 35 minutes, or until the meat is tender and the coating is crisp and golden brown or browned to your preference.

Teriyaki Chicken Drumsticks

Servings: 2
Cooking Time: 17 Minutes
Ingredients:

- 2 tablespoons soy sauce
- ¼ cup dry sherry
- 1 tablespoon brown sugar
- 2 tablespoons water
- 1 tablespoon rice wine vinegar
- 1 clove garlic, crushed
- 1-inch fresh ginger, peeled and sliced
- pinch crushed red pepper flakes
- 4 to 6 bone-in, skin-on chicken drumsticks
- 1 tablespoon cornstarch
- fresh cilantro leaves

Directions:

1. Make the marinade by combining the soy sauce, dry sherry, brown sugar, water, rice vinegar, garlic, ginger and crushed red pepper flakes. Pour the marinade over the chicken legs, cover and let the chicken marinate for 1 to 4 hours in the refrigerator.
2. Preheat the toaster oven to 380°F.

3. Transfer the chicken from the marinade to the air fryer oven, transferring any extra marinade to a small saucepan. Air-fry at 380°F for 8 minutes. Flip the chicken over and continue to air-fry for another 6 minutes, watching to make sure it doesn't brown too much.
4. While the chicken is cooking, bring the reserved marinade to a simmer on the stovetop. Dissolve the cornstarch in 2 tablespoons of water and stir this into the saucepan. Bring to a boil to thicken the sauce. Remove the garlic clove and slices of ginger from the sauce and set aside.
5. When the time is up on the air fryer oven, brush the thickened sauce on the chicken and air-fry for 3 more minutes. Remove the chicken from the air fryer oven and brush with the remaining sauce.
6. Serve over rice and sprinkle the cilantro leaves on top.

Foiled Rosemary Chicken Breasts

Servings: 2
Cooking Time: 30 Minutes
Ingredients:
- 2 skinless, boneless chicken breast halves
- Sauce:
- 3 tablespoons dry white wine
- 1 tablespoon Dijon mustard
- 2 tablespoons nonfat plain yogurt
- Salt and freshly ground black pepper to taste
- 2 rosemary sprigs

Directions:
1. Preheat the toaster oven to 400° F.
2. Place each breast on a 12 × 12-inch square of heavy-duty aluminum foil (or regular foil doubled) and turn up the edges of the foil.
3. Mix together the sauce ingredients and spoon over the chicken breasts. Lay a rosemary sprig on each breast. Bring up the edges of the foil and fold to form a sealed packet.
4. BAKE for 25 minutes or until juices run clear when the meat is pierced with a fork. Remove the rosemary sprigs.
5. BROIL for 5 minutes, or until lightly browned. Replace the sprigs and serve.

Chicken Schnitzel Dogs

Servings: 4
Cooking Time: 10 Minutes
Ingredients:
- ½ cup flour
- ½ teaspoon salt
- 1 teaspoon marjoram
- 1 teaspoon dried parsley flakes
- ½ teaspoon thyme
- 1 egg
- 1 teaspoon lemon juice
- 1 teaspoon water
- 1 cup breadcrumbs
- 4 chicken tenders, pounded thin
- oil for misting or cooking spray
- 4 whole-grain hotdog buns
- 4 slices Gouda cheese
- 1 small Granny Smith apple, thinly sliced
- ½ cup shredded Napa cabbage
- coleslaw dressing

Directions:
1. In a shallow dish, mix together the flour, salt, marjoram, parsley, and thyme.
2. In another shallow dish, beat together egg, lemon juice, and water.
3. Place breadcrumbs in a third shallow dish.
4. Cut each of the flattened chicken tenders in half lengthwise.
5. Dip flattened chicken strips in flour mixture, then egg wash. Let excess egg drip off and roll in breadcrumbs. Spray both sides with oil or cooking spray.
6. Air-fry at 390°F for 5 minutes. Spray with oil, turn over, and spray other side.
7. Air-fry for 3 to 5 minutes more, until well done and crispy brown.
8. To serve, place 2 schnitzel strips on bottom of each hot dog bun. Top with cheese, sliced apple, and cabbage. Drizzle with coleslaw dressing and top with other half of bun.

Roast Chicken

Servings: 6
Cooking Time: 90 Minutes
Ingredients:
- Nonstick cooking spray
- 1 whole (3 ½ -pound) chicken
- Grated zest and juice of 1 lemon
- 1 tablespoon olive oil
- 1 ½ teaspoons kosher salt
- 1 teaspoon garlic powder
- ½ teaspoon dried thyme leaves
- ½ teaspoon freshly ground black pepper

Directions:
1. Preheat the toaster oven to 350°F. Spray a 12 x 12-inch baking pan with nonstick cooking spray.
2. Drizzle the chicken cavity with about half of the lemon juice. Place half of the juiced lemon into the chicken cavity. Truss the chicken using kitchen twine.
3. Rub the chicken evenly with the olive oil.
4. Stir the salt, garlic powder, lemon zest, thyme, and pepper in a small bowl. Using your fingertips, rub the seasonings evenly over the chicken. Place the chicken, breast side up, in the prepared pan. Drizzle with the remaining lemon juice.
5. Roast, uncovered, for 1 ¼ hours to 1 ½ hours, or until a meat thermometer registers 165°F. Let stand for 10 minutes before carving.

Chicken Nuggets

Servings: 20
Cooking Time: 14 Minutes
Ingredients:
- 1 pound boneless, skinless chicken thighs, cut into 1-inch chunks
- ¾ teaspoon salt
- ½ teaspoon black pepper
- ½ teaspoon garlic powder

- ½ teaspoon onion powder
- ½ cup flour
- 2 eggs, beaten
- ½ cup panko breadcrumbs
- 3 tablespoons plain breadcrumbs
- oil for misting or cooking spray

Directions:

1. In the bowl of a food processor, combine chicken, ½ teaspoon salt, pepper, garlic powder, and onion powder. Process in short pulses until chicken is very finely chopped and well blended.
2. Place flour in one shallow dish and beaten eggs in another. In a third dish or plastic bag, mix together the panko crumbs, plain breadcrumbs, and ¼ teaspoon salt.
3. Shape chicken mixture into small nuggets. Dip nuggets in flour, then eggs, then panko crumb mixture.
4. Spray nuggets on both sides with oil or cooking spray and place in air fryer oven in a single layer, close but not overlapping.
5. Air-fry at 360°F for 10 minutes. Spray with oil and cook 4 minutes, until chicken is done and coating is golden brown.
6. Repeat step 5 to cook remaining nuggets.

Chicken Cordon Bleu

Servings: 4
Cooking Time: 25 Minutes
Ingredients:

- Oil spray (hand-pumped)
- 4 (4-ounce) chicken breasts
- 4 teaspoons Dijon mustard
- 4 slices Gruyère cheese
- 4 slices lean ham
- 1 cup all-purpose flour
- 2 large eggs
- 1 cup bread crumbs
- ½ cup Parmesan cheese

Directions:

1. Preheat the toaster oven to 350°F on AIR FRY for 5 minutes.
2. Place the air-fryer basket in the baking tray and generously spray it with the oil.
3. Place a chicken breast flat on a clean work surface and cut along the length of the breast, almost in half, holding the knife parallel to the counter. Open the breast up like a book and place it between two pieces of plastic wrap. Pound the chicken breast to about ¼-inch thick with a rolling pin or mallet. Repeat with the remaining breasts.
4. Spread the mustard on each breast, place a piece of cheese and ham in the center, and fold the sides of the breast over the cheese and ham. Roll the breast up from the unfolded sides to form a sealed packet. Secure with a toothpick.
5. Repeat with the remaining breasts.
6. Sprinkle the flour on a plate and set it on your work surface.
7. In a small bowl, whisk the eggs until well beaten and place next to the flour.
8. In a medium bowl, stir the bread crumbs and Parmesan and place next to the eggs.
9. Dredge the chicken rolls in the flour, then egg, then the bread crumb mixture, making sure they are completely breaded.
10. Arrange the chicken in the basket and spray lightly all over with the oil.
11. In position 2, air fry for 25 minutes, turning halfway through, until golden brown. Serve.

Mediterranean Stuffed Chicken Breasts

Servings: 4
Cooking Time: 24 Minutes
Ingredients:

- 4 boneless, skinless chicken breasts
- ½ teaspoon salt
- ½ teaspoon black pepper
- ½ teaspoon garlic powder
- ½ teaspoon paprika
- ½ cup canned artichoke hearts, chopped
- 4 ounces cream cheese
- ¼ cup grated Parmesan cheese

Directions:

1. Pat the chicken breasts with a paper towel. Using a sharp knife, cut a pouch in the side of each chicken breast for filling.
2. In a small bowl, mix the salt, pepper, garlic powder, and paprika. Season the chicken breasts with this mixture.
3. In a medium bowl, mix together the artichokes, cream cheese, and grated Parmesan cheese. Divide the filling between the 4 breasts, stuffing it inside the pouches. Use toothpicks to close the pouches and secure the filling.
4. Preheat the toaster oven to 360°F.
5. Spray the air fryer oven liberally with cooking spray, add the stuffed chicken breasts to the air fryer oven, and spray liberally with cooking spray again. Air-fry for 14 minutes, carefully turn over the chicken breasts, and cook another 10 minutes. Check the temperature at 20 minutes cooking. Chicken breasts are fully cooked when the center measures 165°F. Cook in batches, if needed.

Italian Baked Chicken

Servings: 4
Cooking Time: 28 Minutes
Ingredients:

- 1 pound boneless, skinless chicken breasts
- ½ cup dry white wine
- 3 tablespoons olive oil
- 2 tablespoons white wine vinegar
- 2 tablespoons fresh lemon juice
- 2 teaspoons Italian seasoning
- 3 cloves garlic, minced
- ½ teaspoon kosher salt
- ¼ teaspoon freshly ground black pepper
- 4 slices salami, cut in half
- 3 tablespoons shredded Parmesan cheese

Directions:

1. If the chicken breasts are large and thick, slice each breast in half lengthwise. Place the chicken in a shallow baking dish.

2. Combine the white wine, olive oil, vinegar, lemon juice, Italian seasoning, garlic, salt, and pepper in a small bowl. Pour over the chicken breasts. Cover and refrigerate for 2 to 8 hours, turning the chicken occasionally to coat.
3. Preheat the toaster oven to 375 °F.
4. Drain the chicken, discarding the marinade, and place the chicken in an ungreased 12 x 12-inch baking pan. Bake, uncovered, for 20 to 25 minutes or until the chicken is done and a meat thermometer registers 165 °F. Place one slice salami (two pieces) on top of each piece of the chicken. Sprinkle the Parmesan evenly over the chicken breasts and broil for 2 to 3 minutes, or until the cheese is melted and starting to brown.

Chicken Wellington

Servings: 4
Cooking Time: 30 Minutes
Ingredients:
- 2 small (5- to 6-ounce) boneless, skinless chicken breast halves
- Kosher salt and freshly ground black pepper
- 2 teaspoons Italian seasoning
- 2 tablespoons olive oil
- 3 tablespoons unsalted butter, softened
- 3 ounces cream cheese, softened (about ⅓ cup)
- ¾ cup shredded Monterey Jack cheese
- ¼ cup grated Parmesan cheese
- 1 cup frozen (loose-pack) chopped spinach, thawed and squeezed dry
- ¾ cup chopped canned artichoke hearts, drained
- ½ teaspoon garlic powder
- 1 sheet frozen puff pastry, about 9 inches square, thawed (½ of a 17.3-ounce package)
- 1 large egg, lightly beaten

Directions:
1. Preheat the toaster oven to 425° F. Line a 12 x 12-inch baking pan with parchment paper.
2. Cut the chicken breasts in half lengthwise. Season each piece with the salt, pepper, and Italian seasoning. Fold the thinner end under the larger piece to make the chicken breasts into a rounded shape. Secure with toothpicks.
3. Heat a large skillet over medium-high heat. Add the olive oil and heat. Add the chicken breasts and brown well, turning to brown evenly. Remove from the skillet and set aside to cool. Remove the toothpicks.
4. Stir the butter, cream cheese, Monterey Jack, and Parmesan in a large bowl. Stir in the spinach, artichoke hearts, and garlic powder. Season with salt and pepper.
5. Roll out the puff pastry sheet on a lightly floured board until it makes a 12-inch square. Cut into four equal pieces. Spread one-fourth of the spinach-artichoke mixture on the surface of each pastry square to within ½ inch of all four edges. Place the chicken in the center of each. Gently fold the puff pastry up over the chicken and pinch the edges to seal tightly.
6. Place each chicken bundle, seam side down, on the prepared pan. Brush the top of each bundle lightly with the beaten egg. Bake for 25 to 30 minutes, or until the pastry is golden brown and crisp and a meat thermometer inserted into the chicken reaches 165°F.

Lemon Sage Roast Chicken

Servings: 4
Cooking Time: 60 Minutes
Ingredients:
- 1 (4-pound) chicken
- 1 bunch sage, divided
- 1 lemon, zest and juice
- salt and freshly ground black pepper

Directions:
1. Preheat the toaster oven to 350°F and pour a little water into the bottom of the air fryer oven. (This will help prevent the grease that drips into the bottom drawer from burning and smoking.)
2. Run your fingers between the skin and flesh of the chicken breasts and thighs. Push a couple of sage leaves up underneath the skin of the chicken on each breast and each thigh.
3. Push some of the lemon zest up under the skin of the chicken next to the sage. Sprinkle some of the zest inside the chicken cavity, and reserve any leftover zest. Squeeze the lemon juice all over the chicken and in the cavity as well.
4. Season the chicken, inside and out, with the salt and freshly ground black pepper. Set a few sage leaves aside for the final garnish. Crumple up the remaining sage leaves and push them into the cavity of the chicken, along with one of the squeezed lemon halves.
5. Place the chicken breast side up into the air fryer oven and air-fry for 20 minutes at 350°F. Flip the chicken over so that it is breast side down and continue to air-fry for another 20 minutes. Return the chicken to breast side up and finish air-frying for 20 more minutes. The internal temperature of the chicken should register 165°F in the thickest part of the thigh when fully cooked. Remove the chicken from the air fryer oven and let it rest on a cutting board for at least 5 minutes.
6. Cut the rested chicken into pieces, sprinkle with the reserved lemon zest and garnish with the reserved sage leaves.

Crispy Curry Chicken Tenders

Servings: 4
Cooking Time: 14 Minutes
Ingredients:
- 1 pound boneless skinless chicken tenders
- ¼ cup plain yogurt
- 2 tablespoons thai red curry paste
- 1½ teaspoons salt, divided
- ½ teaspoon pepper
- 1¾ cups panko breadcrumbs
- 1 teaspoon granulated garlic
- 1 teaspoon granulated onion
- Olive oil or avocado oil spray

Directions:
1. Whisk together the yogurt, curry paste, 1 teaspoon of salt, and pepper in a large bowl. Add the chicken tenders and

toss to coat. Cover bowl with plastic wrap and marinate in the fridge for 6-8 hours.

2. Combine the panko breadcrumbs, ½ teaspoon salt, garlic, and onion. Remove chicken tenders from the marinade and coat individually in the panko mixture.
3. Preheat the toaster oven to 430°F.
4. Spray both sides of each chicken tender well with olive oil or avocado oil spray, then place into the fry basket.
5. Insert the fry basket at mid position in the preheated oven.
6. Select the Air Fry and Shake functions, adjust time to 14 minutes, and press Start/Pause.
7. Flip chicken tenders halfway through cooking. The Shake Reminder will let you know when.
8. Remove when chicken tenders are golden and crispy.

Chicken Cutlets With Broccoli Rabe And Roasted Peppers

Servings: 2
Cooking Time: 10 Minutes

Ingredients:

- ½ bunch broccoli rabe
- olive oil, in a spray bottle
- salt and freshly ground black pepper
- ⅔ cup roasted red pepper strips
- 2 (4-ounce) boneless, skinless chicken breasts
- 2 tablespoons all-purpose flour
- 1 egg, beaten
- ⅓ cup seasoned breadcrumbs
- 2 slices aged provolone cheese

Directions:

1. Bring a medium saucepot of salted water to a boil on the stovetop. Blanch the broccoli rabe for 3 minutes in the boiling water and then drain. When it has cooled a little, squeeze out as much water as possible, drizzle a little olive oil on top, season with salt and black pepper and set aside. Dry the roasted red peppers with a clean kitchen towel and set them aside as well.
2. Place each chicken breast between 2 pieces of plastic wrap. Use a meat pounder to flatten the chicken breasts to about ½-inch thick. Season the chicken on both sides with salt and pepper.
3. Preheat the toaster oven to 400°F.
4. Set up a dredging station with three shallow dishes. Place the flour in one dish, the egg in a second dish and the breadcrumbs in a third dish. Coat the chicken on all sides with the flour. Shake off any excess flour and dip the chicken into the egg. Let the excess egg drip off and coat both sides of the chicken in the breadcrumbs. Spray the chicken with olive oil on both sides and transfer to the air fryer oven.
5. Air-fry the chicken at 400°F for 5 minutes. Turn the chicken over and air-fry for another minute. Then, top the chicken breast with the broccoli rabe and roasted peppers. Place a slice of the provolone cheese on top and secure it with a toothpick or two.
6. Air-fry at 360° for 3 to 4 minutes to melt the cheese and warm everything together.

Sesame Chicken Breasts

Servings: 2
Cooking Time: 20 Minutes

Ingredients:

- Mixture:
- 2 tablespoons sesame oil
- 2 teaspoons soy sauce
- 2 teaspoons balsamic vinegar
- 2 skinless, boneless chicken breast filets
- 3 tablespoons sesame seeds

Directions:

1. Combine the mixture ingredients in a small bowl and brush the filets liberally. Reserve the mixture. Place the filets on a broiling rack with a pan underneath.
2. BROIL 15 minutes, or until the meat is tender and the juices, when the meat is pierced, run clear. Remove from the oven and brush the filets with the remaining mixture. Place the sesame seeds on a plate and press the chicken breast halves into the seeds, coating well.
3. BROIL for 5 minutes, or until the sesame seeds are browned.

Chicken Fajitas

Servings: 4
Cooking Time: 15 Minutes

Ingredients:

- FOR THE FAJITAS
- ½ teaspoon ground cumin
- ½ teaspoon garlic powder
- ¼ teaspoon smoked paprika
- ¼ teaspoon onion powder
- ¼ teaspoon chili powder
- 1 pound boneless, skinless chicken breast, cut into ¼-inch strips
- 1 red bell pepper, cut into thin slices
- 1 green bell pepper, cut into thin slices
- 1 small red onion, cut into thin slices
- 2 tablespoons olive oil
- 8 (6-inch) tortillas
- OPTIONAL TOPPINGS
- Salsa
- Sour cream
- Pickled jalapeños
- Shredded lettuce

Directions:

1. Preheat the toaster oven to 375°F on AIR FRY for 5 minutes.
2. Place the air-fryer basket in the baking tray.
3. In a large bowl, stir the cumin, garlic powder, paprika, onion powder, and chili powder until well mixed. Add the chicken, bell peppers, onion, and oil, and toss to coat evenly.
4. Spread the chicken and veggies on the baking sheet.
5. In position 2, air fry for 15 minutes, tossing them halfway through, until cooked and the vegetables are lightly browned.
6. Serve tucked into the tortillas with your favorite toppings.

Peanut Butter-barbeque Chicken

Servings: 4
Cooking Time: 20 Minutes
Ingredients:

- 1 pound boneless, skinless chicken thighs
- salt and pepper
- 1 large orange
- ½ cup barbeque sauce
- 2 tablespoons smooth peanut butter
- 2 tablespoons chopped peanuts for garnish (optional)
- cooking spray

Directions:

1. Season chicken with salt and pepper to taste. Place in a shallow dish or plastic bag.
2. Grate orange peel, squeeze orange and reserve 1 tablespoon of juice for the sauce.
3. Pour remaining juice over chicken and marinate for 30 minutes.
4. Mix together the reserved 1 tablespoon of orange juice, barbeque sauce, peanut butter, and 1 teaspoon grated orange peel.
5. Place ¼ cup of sauce mixture in a small bowl for basting. Set remaining sauce aside to serve with cooked chicken.
6. Preheat the toaster oven to 360°F. Spray air fryer oven with nonstick cooking spray.
7. Remove chicken from marinade, letting excess drip off. Place in air fryer oven and air-fry for 5 minutes. Turn chicken over and cook 5 minutes longer.
8. Brush both sides of chicken lightly with sauce.
9. Cook chicken 5 minutes, then turn thighs one more time, again brushing both sides lightly with sauce. Air-fry for 5 more minutes or until chicken is done and juices run clear.
10. Serve chicken with remaining sauce on the side and garnish with chopped peanuts if you like.

Sweet-and-sour Chicken

Servings: 6
Cooking Time: 10 Minutes
Ingredients:

- 1 cup pineapple juice
- 1 cup plus 3 tablespoons cornstarch, divided
- ¼ cup sugar
- ¼ cup ketchup
- ¼ cup apple cider vinegar
- 2 tablespoons soy sauce or tamari
- 1 teaspoon garlic powder, divided
- ¼ cup flour
- 1 tablespoon sesame seeds
- ½ teaspoon salt
- ¼ teaspoon ground black pepper
- 2 large eggs
- 2 pounds chicken breasts, cut into 1-inch cubes
- 1 red bell pepper, cut into 1-inch pieces
- 1 carrot, sliced into ¼-inch-thick rounds

Directions:

1. In a medium saucepan, whisk together the pineapple juice, 3 tablespoons of the cornstarch, the sugar, the ketchup, the apple cider vinegar, the soy sauce or tamari, and ½ teaspoon of the garlic powder. Cook over medium-low heat, whisking occasionally as the sauce thickens, about 6 minutes. Stir and set aside while preparing the chicken.
2. Preheat the toaster oven to 370°F.
3. In a medium bowl, place the remaining 1 cup of cornstarch, the flour, the sesame seeds, the salt, the remaining ½ teaspoon of garlic powder, and the pepper.
4. In a second medium bowl, whisk the eggs.
5. Working in batches, place the cubed chicken in the cornstarch mixture to lightly coat; then dip it into the egg mixture, and return it to the cornstarch mixture. Shake off the excess and place the coated chicken in the air fryer oven. Spray with cooking spray and air-fry for 5 minutes, and spray with more cooking spray. Cook an additional 3 to 5 minutes, or until completely cooked and golden brown.
6. On the last batch of chicken, add the bell pepper and carrot to the air fryer oven and cook with the chicken.
7. Place the cooked chicken and vegetables into a serving bowl and toss with the sweet-and-sour sauce to serve.

Chicken Pot Pie

Servings: 4
Cooking Time: 65 Minutes
Ingredients:

- ¼ cup salted butter
- 1 small sweet onion, chopped
- 1 carrot, chopped
- 1 teaspoon minced garlic
- ¼ cup all-purpose flour
- 1 cup low-sodium chicken broth
- ¼ cup heavy (whipping) cream
- 2 cups diced store-bought rotisserie chicken
- 1 cup frozen peas
- Sea salt, for seasoning
- Freshly ground black pepper, for seasoning
- 1 unbaked store-bought pie crust

Directions:

1. Place the rack in position 1 and preheat the toaster oven to 350°F on BAKE for 5 minutes.
2. Melt the butter in a large saucepan over medium-high heat. Sauté the onion, carrot, and garlic until softened, about 12 minutes. Whisk in the flour to form a thick paste and whisk for 1 minute to cook.
3. Add the broth and whisk until thickened, about 2 minutes. Add the heavy cream, whisking to combine. Add the chicken and peas, and season with salt and pepper.
4. Transfer the filling to a 1½-quart casserole dish and top with the pie crust, tucking the edges into the sides of the casserole dish to completely enclose the filling. Cut 4 or 5 slits in the top of the crust.
5. Bake for 50 minutes until the crust is golden brown and the filling is bubbly. Serve.

Jerk Chicken Drumsticks

Servings: 2
Cooking Time: 20 Minutes
Ingredients:

- 1 or 2 cloves garlic
- 1 inch of fresh ginger
- 2 serrano peppers, (with seeds if you like it spicy, seeds removed for less heat)
- 1 teaspoon ground allspice
- 1 teaspoon ground nutmeg
- 1 teaspoon chili powder
- ½ teaspoon dried thyme
- ½ teaspoon ground cinnamon
- ½ teaspoon paprika
- 1 tablespoon brown sugar
- 1 teaspoon soy sauce
- 2 tablespoons vegetable oil
- 6 skinless chicken drumsticks

Directions:

1. Combine all the ingredients except the chicken in a small chopper or blender and blend to a paste. Make slashes into the meat of the chicken drumsticks and rub the spice blend all over the chicken (a pair of plastic gloves makes this really easy). Transfer the rubbed chicken to a non-reactive covered container and let the chicken marinate for at least 30 minutes or overnight in the refrigerator.
2. Preheat the toaster oven to 400°F.
3. Transfer the drumsticks to the air fryer oven. Air-fry for 10 minutes. Turn the drumsticks over and air-fry for another 10 minutes. Serve warm with some rice and vegetables or a green salad.

Tandoori Chicken Legs

Servings: 2
Cooking Time: 30 Minutes
Ingredients:

- 1 cup plain yogurt
- 2 cloves garlic, minced
- 1 tablespoon grated fresh ginger
- 2 teaspoons paprika
- 2 teaspoons ground coriander
- 1 teaspoon ground turmeric
- 1 teaspoon salt
- ¼ teaspoon ground cayenne pepper
- juice of 1 lime
- 2 bone-in, skin-on chicken legs
- fresh cilantro leaves

Directions:

1. Make the marinade by combining the yogurt, garlic, ginger, spices and lime juice. Make slashes into the chicken legs to help the marinade penetrate the meat. Pour the marinade over the chicken legs, cover and let the chicken marinate for at least an hour or overnight in the refrigerator.
2. Preheat the toaster oven oven to 380°F.
3. Transfer the chicken legs from the marinade to the air fryer oven, reserving any extra marinade. Air-fry for 15 minutes. Flip the chicken over and pour the remaining marinade over the top. Air-fry for another 15 minutes, watching to make sure it doesn't brown too much. If it does start to get too brown, you can loosely tent the chicken with aluminum foil, tucking the ends of the foil under the chicken to stop it from blowing around.
4. Serve over rice with some fresh cilantro on top.

Jerk Turkey Meatballs

Servings: 7
Cooking Time: 8 Minutes
Ingredients:

- 1 pound lean ground turkey
- ¼ cup chopped onion
- 1 teaspoon minced garlic
- ½ teaspoon dried thyme
- ¼ teaspoon ground cinnamon
- 1 teaspoon cayenne pepper
- ½ teaspoon paprika
- ½ teaspoon salt
- ⅛ teaspoon black pepper
- ¼ teaspoon red pepper flakes
- 2 teaspoons brown sugar
- 1 large egg, whisked
- ⅓ cup panko breadcrumbs
- 2⅓ cups cooked brown Jasmine rice
- 2 green onions, chopped
- ¾ cup sweet onion dressing

Directions:

1. Preheat the toaster oven to 350°F.
2. In a medium bowl, mix the ground turkey with the onion, garlic, thyme, cinnamon, cayenne pepper, paprika, salt, pepper, red pepper flakes, and brown sugar. Add the whisked egg and stir in the breadcrumbs until the turkey starts to hold together.
3. Using a 1-ounce scoop, portion the turkey into meatballs. You should get about 28 meatballs.
4. Spray the air fryer oven with olive oil spray.
5. Place the meatballs into the air fryer oven and air-fry for 5 minutes, rotate the meatball, and cook another 2 to 4 minutes (or until the internal temperature of the meatballs reaches 165°F).
6. Remove the meatballs from the air fryer oven and repeat for the remaining meatballs.
7. Serve warm over a bed of rice with chopped green onions and spicy Caribbean jerk dressing.

Harissa Lemon Whole Chicken

Servings: 6
Cooking Time: 60 Minutes
Ingredients:

- 2 teaspoons kosher salt
- ½ teaspoon freshly ground black pepper
- ½ teaspoon ground cumin
- 2 garlic cloves
- 6 tablespoons harissa paste
- ½ lemon, juiced
- 1 whole lemon, zested
- 1 (5 pound) whole chicken

Directions:

1. Place salt, pepper, cumin, garlic cloves, harissa paste, lemon juice, and lemon zest in a food processor and pulse until they form a smooth puree.
2. Rub the puree all over the chicken, especially inside the cavity, and cover with plastic wrap.
3. Marinate for 1 hour at room temperature.
4. Preheat the toaster oven to 350°F.
5. Place the marinated chicken on the food tray, then insert the tray at low position in the preheated oven.
6. Select the Roast function, then press Start/Pause.
7. Remove when done, tent chicken with foil, and allow it to rest for 20 minutes before serving.

Fish And Seafood

Shrimp Patties

Servings: 4
Cooking Time: 10 Minutes
Ingredients:

- ½ pound shelled and deveined raw shrimp
- ¼ cup chopped red bell pepper
- ¼ cup chopped green onion
- ¼ cup chopped celery
- 2 cups cooked sushi rice
- ½ teaspoon garlic powder
- ½ teaspoon Old Bay Seasoning
- ½ teaspoon salt
- 2 teaspoons Worcestershire sauce
- ½ cup plain breadcrumbs
- oil for misting or cooking spray

Directions:

1. Finely chop the shrimp. You can do this in a food processor, but it takes only a few pulses. Be careful not to overprocess into mush.
2. Place shrimp in a large bowl and add all other ingredients except the breadcrumbs and oil. Stir until well combined.
3. Preheat the toaster oven to 390°F.
4. Shape shrimp mixture into 8 patties, no more than ½-inch thick. Roll patties in breadcrumbs and mist with oil or cooking spray.
5. Place 4 shrimp patties in air fryer oven and air-fry at 390°F for 10 minutes, until shrimp cooks through and outside is crispy.
6. Repeat step 5 to cook remaining shrimp patties.

Flounder Fillets

Servings: 4
Cooking Time: 8 Minutes
Ingredients:

- 1 egg white
- 1 tablespoon water
- 1 cup panko breadcrumbs
- 2 tablespoons extra-light virgin olive oil
- 4 4-ounce flounder fillets
- salt and pepper
- oil for misting or cooking spray

Directions:

1. Preheat the toaster oven to 390°F.
2. Beat together egg white and water in shallow dish.
3. In another shallow dish, mix panko crumbs and oil until well combined and crumbly (best done by hand).
4. Season flounder fillets with salt and pepper to taste. Dip each fillet into egg mixture and then roll in panko crumbs, pressing in crumbs so that fish is nicely coated.
5. Spray air fryer oven with nonstick cooking spray and add fillets. Air-fry at 390°F for 3 minutes.
6. Spray fish fillets but do not turn. Cook 5 minutes longer or until golden brown and crispy. Using a spatula, carefully remove fish from air fryer oven and serve.

Tuna Nuggets In Hoisin Sauce

Servings: 4
Cooking Time: 7 Minutes
Ingredients:

- ½ cup hoisin sauce
- 2 tablespoons rice wine vinegar
- 2 teaspoons sesame oil
- 1 teaspoon garlic powder
- 2 teaspoons dried lemongrass
- ¼ teaspoon red pepper flakes
- ½ small onion, quartered and thinly sliced
- 8 ounces fresh tuna, cut into 1-inch cubes
- cooking spray
- 3 cups cooked jasmine rice

Directions:

1. Mix the hoisin sauce, vinegar, sesame oil, and seasonings together.
2. Stir in the onions and tuna nuggets.
3. Spray air fryer oven baking pan with nonstick spray and pour in tuna mixture.
4. Air-fry at 390°F for 3 minutes. Stir gently.
5. Cook 2 minutes and stir again, checking for doneness. Tuna should be barely cooked through, just beginning to flake and still very moist. If necessary, continue cooking and stirring in 1-minute intervals until done.
6. Serve warm over hot jasmine rice.

Garlic-lemon Shrimp Skewers

Servings: 2
Cooking Time: 8 Minutes
Ingredients:

- Juice and zest of 1 lemon
- 1 tablespoon olive oil
- ½ teaspoon garlic puree
- ¼ teaspoon smoked paprika
- 12 large shrimp, peeled and deveined
- Oil spray (hand-pumped)
- Sea salt, for seasoning
- Freshly ground black pepper, for seasoning
- 1 tablespoon chopped fresh parsley

Directions:

1. Preheat the toaster oven to 350°F on AIR FRY for 5 minutes.
2. In a medium bowl, stir the lemon juice, lemon zest, olive oil, garlic, and paprika.
3. Add the shrimp and toss to combine. Cover, refrigerate, and let marinate for 30 minutes.
4. Soak 4 wooden skewers in water while the shrimp marinate.
5. Place the air-fryer basket in the baking tray and spray it generously with the oil.
6. Thread 3 shrimp on each skewer and place them in the basket. Discard any remaining marinade.
7. In position 2, air fry for 8 minutes, turning halfway through, until just cooked.
8. Season with the salt and pepper and serve topped with the parsley.

Fish Tacos With Jalapeño-lime Sauce

Servings: 4
Cooking Time: 7 Minutes
Ingredients:

- Fish Tacos
- 1 pound fish fillets
- ¼ teaspoon cumin
- ¼ teaspoon coriander
- ⅛ teaspoon ground red pepper
- 1 tablespoon lime zest
- ¼ teaspoon smoked paprika
- 1 teaspoon oil
- cooking spray
- 6–8 corn or flour tortillas (6-inch size)
- Jalapeño-Lime Sauce
- ½ cup sour cream
- 1 tablespoon lime juice
- ¼ teaspoon grated lime zest
- ½ teaspoon minced jalapeño (flesh only)
- ¼ teaspoon cumin
- Napa Cabbage Garnish
- 1 cup shredded Napa cabbage
- ¼ cup slivered red or green bell pepper
- ¼ cup slivered onion

Directions:

1. Slice the fish fillets into strips approximately ½-inch thick.
2. Put the strips into a sealable plastic bag along with the cumin, coriander, red pepper, lime zest, smoked paprika, and oil. Massage seasonings into the fish until evenly distributed.
3. Spray air fryer oven with nonstick cooking spray and place seasoned fish inside.
4. Air-fry at 390°F for approximately 5 minutes. Distribute fish. Cook an additional 2 minutes, until fish flakes easily.
5. While the fish is cooking, prepare the Jalapeño-Lime Sauce by mixing the sour cream, lime juice, lime zest, jalapeño, and cumin together to make a smooth sauce. Set aside.
6. Mix the cabbage, bell pepper, and onion together and set aside.
7. To warm refrigerated tortillas, wrap in damp paper towels and microwave for 30 to 60 seconds.
8. To serve, spoon some of fish into a warm tortilla. Add one or two tablespoons Napa Cabbage Garnish and drizzle with Jalapeño-Lime Sauce.

Baked Clam Appetizers

Servings: 12
Cooking Time: 10 Minutes
Ingredients:

- 1 6-ounce can minced clams, well drained
- 1 cup multigrain bread crumbs
- 1 tablespoon minced onion
- 1 teaspoon garlic powder
- 1 teaspoon Worcestershire sauce
- 1 tablespoon chopped fresh parsley
- 2 tablespoons olive oil

- Salt and freshly ground black pepper
- Lemon wedges

Directions:

1. Preheat the toaster oven to 450° F.
2. Combine all the ingredients in a medium bowl and fill 12 scrubbed clamshells or small baking dishes with equal portions of the mixture. Place in an 8½ × 8½ × 2-inch oiled or nonstick square (cake) pan.
3. BAKE for 10 minutes, or until lightly browned.

Shrimp & Grits

Servings: 4
Cooking Time: 5 Minutes

Ingredients:

- 1 pound raw shelled shrimp, deveined (26–30 count or smaller)
- Marinade
- 2 tablespoons lemon juice
- 2 tablespoons Worcestershire sauce
- 1 tablespoon olive oil
- 1 teaspoon Old Bay Seasoning
- ½ teaspoon hot sauce
- Grits
- ¾ cup quick cooking grits (not instant)
- 3 cups water
- ½ teaspoon salt
- 1 tablespoon butter
- ½ cup chopped green bell pepper
- ½ cup chopped celery
- ½ cup chopped onion
- ½ teaspoon oregano
- ¼ teaspoon Old Bay Seasoning
- 2 ounces sharp Cheddar cheese, grated

Directions:

1. Stir together all marinade ingredients. Pour marinade over shrimp and set aside.
2. For grits, heat water and salt to boil in saucepan on stovetop. Stir in grits, lower heat to medium-low, and cook about 5 minutes or until thick and done.
3. Place butter, bell pepper, celery, and onion in air fryer oven baking pan. Air-fry at 390°F for 2 minutes and stir. Cook 6 or 7 minutes longer, until crisp tender.
4. Add oregano and 1 teaspoon Old Bay to cooked vegetables. Stir in grits and cheese and air-fry at 390°F for 1 minute. Stir and cook 1 to 2 minutes longer to melt cheese.
5. Remove baking pan from air fryer oven. Cover with plate to keep warm while shrimp cooks.
6. Drain marinade from shrimp. Place shrimp in air fryer oven and air-fry at 360°F for 3 minutes. Cook 2 more minutes, until done.
7. To serve, spoon grits onto plates and top with shrimp.

Light Trout Amandine

Servings: 4
Cooking Time: 15 Minutes

Ingredients:

- 1 tablespoon margarine
- ½ cup sliced almonds
- 1 tablespoon lemon juice
- 1 teaspoon Worcestershire sauce
- Salt and freshly ground black pepper
- 4 6-ounce trout fillets
- 2 tablespoons chopped fresh parsley

Directions:

1. Combine the margarine and almonds in an oiled or nonstick 8½ × 8½ × 2-inch square baking (cake) pan.
2. BROIL for 5 minutes, or until the margarine is melted. Remove the pan from the oven and add the lemon juice and Worcestershire sauce. Season to taste with salt and pepper, and stir again to blend well. Add the trout fillets and spoon the mixture over them to coat well.
3. BROIL for 10 minutes, or until the almonds and fillets are lightly browned. Garnish with the chopped parsley before serving.

Fish And "chips"

Servings: 2
Cooking Time: 10 Minutes

Ingredients:

- ½ cup flour
- ½ teaspoon paprika
- ¼ teaspoon ground white pepper (or freshly ground black pepper)
- 1 egg
- ¼ cup mayonnaise
- 2 cups salt & vinegar kettle cooked potato chips, coarsely crushed
- 12 ounces cod
- tartar sauce
- lemon wedges

Directions:

1. Set up a dredging station. Combine the flour, paprika and pepper in a shallow dish. Combine the egg and mayonnaise in a second shallow dish. Place the crushed potato chips in a third shallow dish.
2. Cut the cod into 6 pieces. Dredge each piece of fish in the flour, then dip it into the egg mixture and then place it into the crushed potato chips. Make sure all sides of the fish are covered and pat the chips gently onto the fish so they stick well.
3. Preheat the toaster oven to 370°F.
4. Place the coated fish fillets into the air fry oven. (It is ok if a couple of pieces slightly overlap or rest on top of other fillets in order to fit everything in the air fryer oven.)
5. Air-fry for 10 minutes, gently turning the fish over halfway through the cooking time.
6. Transfer the fish to a platter and serve with tartar sauce and lemon wedges.

Ginger Miso Calamari

Servings: 4
Cooking Time: 10 Minutes

Ingredients:

- 15 ounces calamari, cleaned
- Sauce:
- 2 tablespoons dry white wine
- 2 tablespoons white miso

- 1 tablespoon balsamic vinegar
- 1 teaspoon honey
- 1 teaspoon toasted sesame oil
- 1 teaspoon olive oil
- 1 tablespoon grated fresh ginger
- Salt and white pepper to taste

Directions:

1. Slice the calamari bodies into ½-inch rings, leaving the tentacles uncut. Set aside.
2. Whisk together the sauce ingredients in a bowl. Transfer the mixture to a baking pan and add the calamari, mixing well to coat.
3. BROIL for 20 minutes, turning with tongs every 5 minutes, or until cooked but not rubbery. Serve with the sauce.

Shrimp Po'boy With Remoulade Sauce

Servings: 6
Cooking Time: 8 Minutes
Ingredients:

- ½ cup all-purpose flour
- ½ teaspoon paprika
- 1 teaspoon garlic powder
- ½ teaspoon black pepper
- ¼ teaspoon salt
- 2 eggs, whisked
- 1½ cups panko breadcrumbs
- 1 pound small shrimp, peeled and deveined
- Six 6-inch French rolls
- 2 cups shredded lettuce
- 12 ⅛-inch tomato slices
- ¾ cup Remoulade Sauce (see the following recipe)

Directions:

1. Preheat the toaster oven to 360°F.
2. In a medium bowl, mix the flour, paprika, garlic powder, pepper, and salt.
3. In a shallow dish, place the eggs.
4. In a third dish, place the panko breadcrumbs.
5. Covering the shrimp in the flour, dip them into the egg, and coat them with the breadcrumbs. Repeat until all shrimp are covered in the breading.
6. Liberally spray the metal trivet that fits inside the air fryer oven with olive oil spray. Place the shrimp onto the trivet, leaving space between the shrimp to flip. Air-fry for 4 minutes, flip the shrimp, and cook another 4 minutes. Repeat until all the shrimp are cooked.
7. Slice the rolls in half. Stuff each roll with shredded lettuce, tomato slices, breaded shrimp, and remoulade sauce. Serve immediately.

Crispy Smelts

Servings: 3
Cooking Time: 20 Minutes
Ingredients:

- 1 pound Cleaned smelts
- 3 tablespoons Tapioca flour
- Vegetable oil spray
- To taste Coarse sea salt or kosher salt

Directions:

1. Preheat the toaster oven to 400°F.
2. Toss the smelts and tapioca flour in a large bowl until the little fish are evenly coated.
3. Lay the smelts out on a large cutting board. Lightly coat both sides of each fish with vegetable oil spray.
4. When the machine is at temperature, set the smelts close together in the air fryer oven, with a few even overlapping on top. Air-fry undisturbed for 20 minutes, until lightly browned and crisp.
5. Remove from the machine and turn out the fish onto a wire rack. The smelts will most likely come out as one large block, or maybe in a couple of large pieces. Cool for a minute or two, then sprinkle the smelts with salt and break the block(s) into much smaller sections or individual fish to serve.

Fish With Sun-dried Tomato Pesto

Servings: 4
Cooking Time: 31 Minutes
Ingredients:

- Tomato sauce:
- ¼ cup chopped sun-dried tomatoes
- 2 tablespoons chopped fresh basil
- ⅔ cup dry white wine
- 2 tablespoons grated Parmesan cheese
- 2 tablespoons olive oil
- 1 tablespoon pine nuts
- 2 garlic cloves
- Salt and freshly ground black pepper to taste
- 4 6-ounce fish fillets (trout, catfish, flounder, or tilapia)
- 1 tablespoon reduced-fat mayonnaise
- 2 tablespoons chopped fresh cilantro Olive oil

Directions:

1. Preheat the toaster oven to 400° F.
2. Process the tomato sauce ingredients in a blender or food processor until smooth.
3. Layer the fish fillets in an oiled or nonstick 8½ × 8½ × 2-inch square baking (cake) pan. Spoon the sauce over the fish, spreading evenly.
4. BAKE, uncovered, for 25 minutes, or until the fish flakes easily with a fork. Remove from the oven, spread the mayonnaise on top of the fish, and garnish with the cilantro.
5. BROIL for 6 minutes, or until lightly browned.

Shrimp With Jalapeño Dip

Servings: 4
Cooking Time: 10 Minutes
Ingredients:

- Seasonings:
- 1 teaspoon ground cumin
- 1 tablespoon minced garlic
- 1 teaspoon paprika
- 1 teaspoon chili powder
- Pinch of cayenne
- Salt to taste
- 1½ pounds large shrimp, peeled and deveined

Directions:

1. Combine the seasonings in a plastic bag, add the shrimp, and shake well to coat. Transfer the shrimp to an oiled or nonstick 8½ × 8½ × 2-inch square baking (cake) pan.
2. BROIL for 5 minutes. Remove the pan from the oven and turn the shrimp with tongs. Broil 5 minutes again, or until the shrimp are cooked (they should be firm but not rubbery.) Serve with Jalapeño Dip.

Broiled Lemon Coconut Shrimp

Servings: 4
Cooking Time: 10 Minutes
Ingredients:
- Brushing mixture:
- 2 tablespoons lemon juice
- 4 tablespoons olive oil
- 1 tablespoon grated lemon zest
- Salt to taste
- 1 pound fresh shrimp, peeled, deveined, and butterflied
- ½ cup grated unsweetened coconut

Directions:
1. Combine the brushing mixture ingredients in a small bowl. Add the shrimp and toss to coat well. Set aside.
2. Place the coconut on a plate, spreading it out evenly.
3. Press each shrimp into the coconut, coating well on all sides. Place the shrimp in an 8½ × 8½ × 2-inch oiled or nonstick square (cake) pan.
4. BROIL the shrimp for 5 minutes, turn with tongs, and broil for 5 more minutes, or until browned lightly.

Sea Bass With Potato Scales And Caper Aïoli

Servings: 2
Cooking Time: 10 Minutes
Ingredients:
- 2 (6- to 8-ounce) fillets of sea bass
- salt and freshly ground black pepper
- ¼ cup mayonnaise
- 2 teaspoons finely chopped lemon zest
- 1 teaspoon chopped fresh thyme
- 2 fingerling potatoes, very thinly sliced into rounds
- olive oil
- ½ clove garlic, crushed into a paste
- 1 tablespoon capers, drained and rinsed
- 1 tablespoon olive oil
- 1 teaspoon lemon juice, to taste

Directions:
1. Preheat the toaster oven to 400°F.
2. Season the fish well with salt and freshly ground black pepper. Mix the mayonnaise, lemon zest and thyme together in a small bowl. Spread a thin layer of the mayonnaise mixture on both fillets. Start layering rows of potato slices onto the fish fillets to simulate the fish scales. The second row should overlap the first row slightly. Dabbing a little more mayonnaise along the upper edge of the row of potatoes where the next row overlaps will help the potato slices stick. Press the potatoes onto the fish to secure them well and season again with salt. Brush or spray the potato layer with olive oil.
3. Transfer the fish to the air fryer oven and air-fry for 8 to 10 minutes, depending on the thickness of your fillets. 1-inch of fish should take 10 minutes at 400°F.
4. While the fish is cooking, add the garlic, capers, olive oil and lemon juice to the remaining mayonnaise mixture to make the caper aïoli.
5. Serve the fish warm with a dollop of the aïoli on top or on the side.

Cajun Flounder Fillets

Servings: 2
Cooking Time: 5 Minutes
Ingredients:
- 2 4-ounce skinless flounder fillet(s)
- 2 teaspoons Peanut oil
- 1 teaspoon Purchased or homemade Cajun dried seasoning blend

Directions:
1. Preheat the toaster oven to 400°F.
2. Oil the fillet(s) by drizzling on the peanut oil, then gently rubbing in the oil with your clean, dry fingers. Sprinkle the seasoning blend evenly over both sides of the fillet(s).
3. When the machine is at temperature, set the fillet(s) in the air fryer oven. If working with more than one fillet, they should not touch, although they may be quite close together, depending on the air fryer oven's size. Air-fry undisturbed for 5 minutes, or until lightly browned and cooked through.
4. Use a nonstick-safe spatula to transfer the fillets to a serving platter or plate(s). Serve at once.

Blackened Red Snapper

Servings: 4
Cooking Time: 8 Minutes
Ingredients:
- 1½ teaspoons black pepper
- ¼ teaspoon thyme
- ¼ teaspoon garlic powder
- ⅛ teaspoon cayenne pepper
- 1 teaspoon olive oil
- 4 4-ounce red snapper fillet portions, skin on
- 4 thin slices lemon
- cooking spray

Directions:
1. Mix the spices and oil together to make a paste. Rub into both sides of the fish.
2. Spray air fryer oven with nonstick cooking spray and lay snapper steaks in air fryer oven, skin-side down.
3. Place a lemon slice on each piece of fish.
4. Air-fry at 390°F for 8 minutes. The fish will not flake when done, but it should be white through the center.

Broiled Dill And Lemon Salmon

Servings: 25
Cooking Time: 2 Minutes
Ingredients:
- Brushing mixture:
- 2 tablespoons lemon juice
- 2 tablespoons olive oil

- 1 tablespoon soy sauce
- 1 teaspoon dried dill or dill weed
- ½ teaspoon garlic powder
- 1 teaspoon soy sauce
- 2 6-ounce salmon steaks

Directions:

1. Combine the brushing mixture ingredients in a small bowl and brush the salmon steak tops, skin side down, liberally, reserving the remaining mixture. Let the steaks sit at room temperature for 10 minutes, then place on a broiling rack with a pan underneath.
2. BROIL 15 minutes, remove from the oven, and brush the steaks with the remaining mixture. Broil again for 5 minutes, or until the meat flakes easily with a fork.

Crunchy And Buttery Cod With Ritz® Cracker Crust

Servings: 2
Cooking Time: 10 Minutes
Ingredients:

- 4 tablespoons butter, melted
- 8 to 10 RITZ® crackers, crushed into crumbs
- 2 (6-ounce) cod fillets
- salt and freshly ground black pepper
- 1 lemon

Directions:

1. Preheat the toaster oven to 380°F.
2. Melt the butter in a small saucepan on the stovetop or in a microwavable dish in the microwave, and then transfer the butter to a shallow dish. Place the crushed RITZ® crackers into a second shallow dish.
3. Season the fish fillets with salt and freshly ground black pepper. Dip them into the butter and then coat both sides with the RITZ® crackers.
4. Place the fish into the air fryer oven and air-fry at 380°F for 10 minutes, flipping the fish over halfway through the cooking time.
5. Serve with a wedge of lemon to squeeze over the top.

Roasted Fish With Provençal Crumb Topping

Servings: 3
Cooking Time: 25 Minutes
Ingredients:

- 1 tablespoon olive oil, plus more for greasing
- ⅓ cup finely chopped onion
- 1 clove garlic, minced
- ¾ cup fresh bread crumbs
- 2 tablespoons chopped fresh flat-leaf (Italian) parsley
- 1 teaspoon fresh thyme leaves
- 3 (5-ounce) cod fillets, or other white-fleshed, mild-flavored fish, patted dry (about 1 ¼ inches thick)
- 2 tablespoons dry white wine
- 2 teaspoons fresh lemon juice

Directions:

1. Preheat the toaster oven to 400°F. Lightly grease the baking pan with olive oil.
2. Heat the tablespoon of olive oil in a small skillet over medium-high heat. Add the onion and cook, stirring frequently, for 3 to 4 minutes, or until tender. Add the garlic and cook for 30 seconds. Remove the skillet from the heat. Stir in the bread crumbs, parsley, and thyme.
3. Place the fish in the prepared pan. Drizzle with the wine. Divide the crumb mixture evenly over the top of each fish fillet, and press onto the fillets. Roast for 20 to 25 minutes, or until the top is brown and the fish is opaque and flakes easily when tested with a fork. Sprinkle the lemon juice evenly over the fish.

Fried Shrimp

Servings: 3
Cooking Time: 7 Minutes
Ingredients:

- 1 Large egg white
- 2 tablespoons Water
- 1 cup Plain dried bread crumbs (gluten-free, if a concern)
- ¼ cup All-purpose flour or almond flour
- ¼ cup Yellow cornmeal
- 1 teaspoon Celery salt
- 1 teaspoon Mild paprika
- Up to ½ teaspoon Cayenne (optional)
- ¾ pound Large shrimp (20–25 per pound), peeled and deveined
- Vegetable oil spray

Directions:

1. Preheat the toaster oven to 400°F.
2. Set two medium or large bowls on your counter. In the first, whisk the egg white and water until foamy. In the second, stir the bread crumbs, flour, cornmeal, celery salt, paprika, and cayenne (if using) until well combined.
3. Pour all the shrimp into the egg white mixture and stir gently until all the shrimp are coated. Use kitchen tongs to pick them up one by one and transfer them to the bread-crumb mixture. Turn each in the bread-crumb mixture to coat it evenly and thoroughly on all sides before setting it on a cutting board. When you're done coating the shrimp, coat them all on both sides with the vegetable oil spray.
4. Set the shrimp in as close to one layer in the air fryer oven as you can. Some may overlap. Air-fry for 7 minutes, gently rearranging the shrimp at the 4-minute mark to get covered surfaces exposed, until golden brown and firm but not hard.
5. Use kitchen tongs to gently transfer the shrimp to a wire rack. Cool for only a minute or two before serving.

Crab-stuffed Peppers

Servings: 4
Cooking Time: 45 Minutes
Ingredients:

- Filling:
- 1½ cups fresh crabmeat, chopped, or 2 6-ounce cans lump crabmeat, drained
- 4 plum tomatoes, chopped
- 2 4-ounce cans sliced mushrooms, drained well
- 4 tablespoons pitted and sliced black olives
- 2 tablespoons olive oil

- 2 garlic cloves, minced
- ½ teaspoon ground cumin
- Salt and freshly ground black pepper to taste
- 4 large bell peppers, tops cut off, seeds and membrane removed
- ½ cup shredded low-fat mozzarella cheese

Directions:

1. Preheat the toaster oven to 375° F.
2. Combine the filling ingredients in a bowl and adjust the seasonings. Spoon the mixture to generously fill each pepper. Place the peppers upright in an 8½ × 8½ × 2-inch oiled or nonstick square (cake) pan.
3. BAKE for 40 minutes, or until the peppers are tender. Remove from the oven and sprinkle the cheese in equal portions on top of the peppers.
4. BROIL 5 minutes, or until the cheese is melted.

Fried Scallops

Servings: 3
Cooking Time: 6 Minutes

Ingredients:

- ½ cup All-purpose flour or tapioca flour
- 1 Large egg(s), well beaten
- 2 cups Corn flake crumbs (gluten-free, if a concern)
- Up to 2 teaspoons Cayenne
- 1 teaspoon Celery seeds
- 1 teaspoon Table salt
- 1 pound Sea scallops
- Vegetable oil spray

Directions:

1. Preheat the toaster oven to 400°F.
2. Set up and fill three shallow soup plates or small pie plates on your counter: one for the flour; one for the beaten egg(s); and one for the corn flake crumbs, stirred with the cayenne, celery seeds, and salt until well combined.
3. One by one, dip a scallop in the flour, turning it every way to coat it thoroughly. Gently shake off any excess flour, then dip the scallop in the egg(s), turning it again to coat all sides. Let any excess egg slip back into the rest, then set the scallop in the corn flake mixture. Turn it several times, pressing gently to get an even coating on the scallop all around. Generously coat the scallop with vegetable oil spray, then set it aside on a cutting board. Coat the remaining scallops in the same way.
4. Set the scallops in the air fryer oven with as much air space between them as possible. They should not touch. Air-fry undisturbed for 6 minutes, or until lightly browned and firm.
5. Use kitchen tongs to gently transfer the scallops to a wire rack. Cool for only a minute or two before serving.

Stuffed Baked Red Snapper

Servings: 2
Cooking Time: 30 Minutes

Ingredients:

- Stuffing mixture:
- 12 medium shrimp, cooked, peeled, and chopped
- 2 tablespoons multigrain bread crumbs
- 1 teaspoon anchovy paste
- ¼ teaspoon paprika
- Salt to taste
- 2 6-ounce red snapper fillets
- 1 egg
- ½ cup fat-free half-and-half
- 2 tablespoons cooking sherry

Directions:

1. Preheat the toaster oven to 350° F.
2. Combine all the stuffing mixture ingredients in a medium bowl and place a mound of mixture on one end of each fillet. Fold over the other fillet end, skewering the edge with toothpicks.
3. Place the rolled fillets in an oiled or nonstick 8½ × 8½ × 2-inch square baking (cake) pan.
4. Whisk the egg in a small bowl until light in color, then whisk in the half-and-half and sherry. Pour over the fillets. Cover the pan with aluminum foil.
5. BAKE for 30 minutes.

Roasted Garlic Shrimp

Servings: 4
Cooking Time: 12 Minutes

Ingredients:

- Nonstick cooking spray
- ¼ cup unsalted butter, melted
- 2 cloves garlic, minced
- 1 teaspoon grated lemon zest
- ½ teaspoon dried thyme leaves
- ¼ teaspoon freshly ground black pepper
- Kosher salt
- 1 pound uncooked large shrimp, fresh or frozen and thawed, peeled and deveined
- 1 ½ tablespoons fresh lemon juice
- Optional: Minced fresh flat-leaf (Italian) parsley

Directions:

1. Preheat the toaster oven to 400°F. Spray a 12 x 12-inch baking pan with nonstick cooking spray.
2. Mix the melted butter, garlic, lemon zest, thyme, and pepper in a small bowl. Season with salt. Set aside.
3. Arrange the shrimp in a single layer in the prepared pan. Pour the butter mixture over the shrimp, then stir gently to coat the shrimp.
4. Roast, uncovered, for 10 to 12 minutes or until the shrimp turn pink. Drizzle with the lemon juice. Transfer to a serving platter and spoon any collected drippings over the shrimp. Garnish, if desired, with minced parsley.

Almond-crusted Fish

Servings: 4
Cooking Time: 10 Minutes

Ingredients:

- 4 4-ounce fish fillets
- ¾ cup breadcrumbs
- ¼ cup sliced almonds, crushed
- 2 tablespoons lemon juice
- ⅛ teaspoon cayenne
- salt and pepper
- ¾ cup flour

- 1 egg, beaten with 1 tablespoon water
- oil for misting or cooking spray

Directions:

1. Split fish fillets lengthwise down the center to create 8 pieces.
2. Mix breadcrumbs and almonds together and set aside.
3. Mix the lemon juice and cayenne together. Brush on all sides of fish.
4. Season fish to taste with salt and pepper.
5. Place the flour on a sheet of wax paper.
6. Roll fillets in flour, dip in egg wash, and roll in the crumb mixture.
7. Mist both sides of fish with oil or cooking spray.
8. Spray air fryer oven and lay fillets inside.
9. Air-fry at 390°F for 5 minutes, turn fish over, and air-fry for an additional 5 minutes or until fish is done and flakes easily.

Snapper With Capers And Olives

Servings: 2

Cooking Time: 10 Minutes

Ingredients:

- 2 tablespoons capers
- ¼ cup pitted and sliced black olives
- 2 tablespoons olive oil
- ½ teaspoon dried oregano
- Salt and freshly ground black pepper to taste
- 2 6-ounce red snapper fillets
- 1 tomato, cut into wedges

Directions:

1. Combine the capers, olives, olive oil, and seasonings in a bowl.
2. Place the fillets in an oiled or nonstick 8½ × 8½ × 2-inch square baking (cake) pan and spoon the caper mixture over them.
3. BROIL for 10 minutes, or until the fish flakes easily with a fork. Serve with the tomato wedges.

Oven-poached Salmon

Servings: 2

Cooking Time: 20 Minutes

Ingredients:

- Poaching liquid:
- 1 cup dry white wine
- 2 bay leaves
- 1 tablespoon mustard seed
- Salt and freshly ground black pepper to taste
- 2 6-ounce salmon steaks
- 2 tablespoons fresh watercress, rinsed, drained, and chopped (for serving hot)
- 1 lemon, cut into small wedges (for serving hot)
- Cucumber Sauce (recipe follows)

Directions:

1. Preheat the toaster oven to 350° F.
2. Combine the poaching liquid ingredients with 1 cup water in a small bowl and set aside.
3. Place the salmon steaks in an oiled or nonstick 8½ × 8½ × 2-inch square baking (cake) pan and pour enough poaching liquid over the steaks to barely cover them. Adjust the seasonings to taste.
4. BAKE, uncovered, for 20 minutes, or until the fish feels springy to the touch. Remove the bay leaves and serve the fish hot with watercress and lemon or cold with Cucumber Sauce.

Almond Crab Cakes

Servings: 4

Cooking Time: 10 Minutes

Ingredients:

- 1 pound cooked lump crabmeat, drained and picked over
- ¼ cup ground almonds
- 1 tablespoon Dijon mustard
- 1 scallion, white and green parts, finely chopped
- ½ red bell pepper, finely chopped
- 1 large egg
- 1 teaspoon lemon zest
- Oil spray (hand-pumped)
- 3 tablespoons almond flour

Directions:

1. Preheat the toaster oven to 375°F on AIR FRY for 5 minutes.
2. In a medium bowl, mix the crab meat, almonds, mustard, scallion, bell pepper, egg, and lemon zest until well combined and the mixture holds together when pressed. If the crab cakes do not stick together, add more ground almond.
3. Divide the crab mixture into 8 patties and press them to about 1 inch thick. Place them on a plate, cover, and chill for 30 minutes.
4. Place the air-fryer basket in the baking tray and generously spray with the oil.
5. Place the almond flour on a plate and dredge the crab cakes until they are lightly coated.
6. Place them in the basket and lightly spray both sides with the oil.
7. In position 2, air fry for 10 minutes, turning halfway through, until golden brown. Serve.

Maple Balsamic Glazed Salmon

Servings: 4

Cooking Time: 10 Minutes

Ingredients:

- 4 (6-ounce) fillets of salmon
- salt and freshly ground black pepper
- vegetable oil
- ¼ cup pure maple syrup
- 3 tablespoons balsamic vinegar
- 1 teaspoon Dijon mustard

Directions:

1. Preheat the toaster oven to 400°F.
2. Season the salmon well with salt and freshly ground black pepper. Spray or brush the bottom of the air fryer oven with vegetable oil and place the salmon fillets inside. Air-fry the salmon for 5 minutes.
3. While the salmon is air-frying, combine the maple syrup, balsamic vinegar and Dijon mustard in a small saucepan

over medium heat and stir to blend well. Let the mixture simmer while the fish is cooking. It should start to thicken slightly, but keep your eye on it so it doesn't burn.

4. Brush the glaze on the salmon fillets and air-fry for an additional 5 minutes. The salmon should feel firm to the touch when finished and the glaze should be nicely browned on top. Brush a little more glaze on top before removing and serving with rice and vegetables, or a nice green salad.

Tortilla-crusted Tilapia

Servings: 4
Cooking Time: 12 Minutes
Ingredients:

- 4 (5-ounce) tilapia fillets
- ½ teaspoon ground cumin
- Sea salt, for seasoning
- 1 cup tortilla chips, coarsely crushed
- Oil spray (hand-pumped)
- 1 lime, cut into wedges

Directions:

1. Preheat the toaster oven to 375°F on BAKE for 5 minutes.
2. Line the baking tray with parchment paper.
3. Lightly season the fish with the cumin and salt.
4. Press the tortilla chips onto the top of the fish fillets and place them on the baking sheet.
5. Lightly spray the fish with oil.
6. In position 2, bake until golden and just cooked through, about 12 minutes in total.
7. Serve with the lime wedges.

Coconut-shrimp Po' Boys

Servings: 4
Cooking Time: 5 Minutes
Ingredients:

- ½ cup cornstarch
- 2 eggs
- 2 tablespoons milk
- ¾ cup shredded coconut
- ½ cup panko breadcrumbs
- 1 pound (31–35 count) shrimp, peeled and deveined
- Old Bay Seasoning
- oil for misting or cooking spray
- 2 large hoagie rolls
- honey mustard or light mayonnaise
- 1½ cups shredded lettuce
- 1 large tomato, thinly sliced

Directions:

1. Place cornstarch in a shallow dish or plate.
2. In another shallow dish, beat together eggs and milk.
3. In a third dish mix the coconut and panko crumbs.
4. Sprinkle shrimp with Old Bay Seasoning to taste.
5. Dip shrimp in cornstarch to coat lightly, dip in egg mixture, shake off excess, and roll in coconut mixture to coat well.
6. Spray both sides of coated shrimp with oil or cooking spray.
7. Cook half the shrimp in a single layer at 390°F for 5 minutes.
8. Repeat to cook remaining shrimp.
9. To Assemble
10. Split each hoagie lengthwise, leaving one long edge intact.
11. Place in air fryer oven and air-fry at 390°F for 1 to 2 minutes or until heated through.
12. Remove buns, break apart, and place on 4 plates, cut side up.
13. Spread with honey mustard and/or mayonnaise.
14. Top with shredded lettuce, tomato slices, and coconut shrimp.

Coconut Shrimp

Servings: 4
Cooking Time: 15 Minutes
Ingredients:

- ¼ cup cassava flour
- 1 teaspoon sugar
- ¼ teaspoon black pepper
- ½ teaspoon salt
- 2 large eggs
- 1 cup shredded coconut flakes, unsweetened
- ½ pound deveined, tail-off large shrimp

Directions:

1. Preheat the toaster oven to 330°F. Spray the air fryer oven with olive oil spray. Set aside.
2. In a small bowl, mix the flour, sugar, pepper, and salt.
3. In a separate bowl, whisk the eggs.
4. In a third bowl, place the coconut flakes.
5. Place 1 shrimp at a time in the flour mixture, then wash with the eggs, and cover with coconut flakes.
6. Liberally spray the metal trivet that fits inside the air fryer oven with olive oil spray. Place the shrimp onto the metal trivet and air-fry for 15 minutes, flipping halfway through. Repeat until all shrimp are cooked.
7. Serve immediately with desired sauce.

Sweet Chili Shrimp

Servings: 4
Cooking Time: 6 Minutes
Ingredients:

- 1 pound jumbo shrimp, peeled and deveined
- ¼ cup sweet chili sauce
- 1 lime, zested and juiced
- 1 tablespoon soy sauce
- 1 tablespoon honey
- 1 tablespoon olive oil
- 1 large garlic clove, minced
- ½ teaspoon salt
- ¼ teaspoon pepper
- 1 green onion, thinly sliced, for garnish

Directions:

1. Place the shrimp in a large bowl. Whisk all the remaining ingredients except the green onion in a separate bowl.
2. Pour sauce over the shrimp and toss to coat.

3. Preheat the toaster Oven to 430°F.
4. Line the food tray with foil, place shrimp on the tray, then insert at top position in the preheated oven.
5. Select the Air Fry function, adjust time to 6 minutes, and press Start/Pause.
6. Remove shrimp and garnish with sliced green onions.

Molasses-glazed Salmon

Servings: 4
Cooking Time: 15 Minutes
Ingredients:

- Oil spray (hand-pumped)
- 4 (5-ounce) salmon fillets
- Sea salt, for seasoning
- ¼ cup molasses
- 1 teaspoon fresh ginger, peeled and grated

Directions:

1. Preheat the toaster oven to 350°F on CONVECTION BAKE for 5 minutes.
2. Place the air-fryer basket in the baking tray. Generously spray the basket with the oil.
3. Pat the salmon dry with paper towels, season lightly with salt, and place on the baking tray.
4. In a small bowl, stir the molasses and ginger until well blended.
5. Spread the molasses mixture on the fish fillets.
6. Place the baking tray in position 2 and bake for 15 minutes until just cooked through. Serve.

Crunchy Clam Strips

Servings: 3
Cooking Time: 8 Minutes
Ingredients:

- ½ pound Clam strips, drained
- 1 Large egg, well beaten
- ½ cup All-purpose flour
- ½ cup Yellow cornmeal
- 1½ teaspoons Table salt
- 1½ teaspoons Ground black pepper
- Up to ¾ teaspoon Cayenne
- Vegetable oil spray

Directions:

1. Preheat the toaster oven to 400°F.
2. Toss the clam strips and beaten egg in a bowl until the clams are well coated.
3. Mix the flour, cornmeal, salt, pepper, and cayenne in a large zip-closed plastic bag until well combined. Using a flatware fork or small kitchen tongs, lift the clam strips one by one out of the egg, letting any excess egg slip back into the rest. Put the strips in the bag with the flour mixture. Once all the strips are in the bag, seal it until the strips are well coated.
4. Use kitchen tongs to pick out the clam strips and lay them on a cutting board (leaving any extra flour mixture in the bag to be discarded). Coat the strips on both sides with vegetable oil spray.
5. When the machine is at temperature, spread the clam strips in the air fryer oven in one layer. They may touch in places, but try to leave as much air space as possible around them. Air-fry undisturbed for 8 minutes, or until brown and crunchy.
6. Gently dump the contents of the air fryer oven onto a serving platter. Cool for just a minute or two before serving hot.

Marinated Catfish

Servings: 4
Cooking Time: 10 Minutes
Ingredients:

- Marinade:
- 1 tablespoon olive oil
- 1 tablespoon lemon juice
- ¼ dry white wine
- 1 tablespoon garlic powder
- 1 tablespoon soy sauce
- 4 6-ounce catfish fillets

Directions:

1. Combine the marinade ingredients in an 8½ × 8½ × 4-inch ovenproof baking dish. Add the fillets and let stand for 10 minutes, spooning the marinade over the fillets every 2 minutes.
2. BROIL the fillets for 15 minutes, or until the fish flakes easily with a fork.

Tilapia Teriyaki

Servings: 3
Cooking Time: 10 Minutes
Ingredients:

- 4 tablespoons teriyaki sauce
- 1 tablespoon pineapple juice
- 1 pound tilapia fillets
- cooking spray
- 6 ounces frozen mixed peppers with onions, thawed and drained
- 2 cups cooked rice

Directions:

1. Mix the teriyaki sauce and pineapple juice together in a small bowl.
2. Split tilapia fillets down the center lengthwise.
3. Brush all sides of fish with the sauce, spray air fryer oven with nonstick cooking spray, and place fish in the air fryer oven.
4. Stir the peppers and onions into the remaining sauce and spoon over the fish. Save any leftover sauce for drizzling over the fish when serving.
5. Air-fry at 360°F for 10 minutes, until fish flakes easily with a fork and is done in center.
6. Divide into 3 or 4 servings and serve each with approximately ½ cup cooked rice.

Beer-battered Cod

Servings: 3
Cooking Time: 12 Minutes
Ingredients:

- 1½ cups All-purpose flour
- 3 tablespoons Old Bay seasoning
- 1 Large egg(s)
- ¼ cup Amber beer, pale ale, or IPA

- 3 4-ounce skinless cod fillets
- Vegetable oil spray

Directions:

1. Preheat the toaster oven to 400°F.
2. Set up and fill two shallow soup plates or small pie plates on your counter: one with the flour, whisked with the Old Bay until well combined; and one with the egg(s), whisked with the beer until foamy and uniform.
3. Dip a piece of cod in the flour mixture, turning it to coat on all sides (not just the top and bottom). Gently shake off any excess flour and dip the fish in the egg mixture, turning it to coat. Let any excess egg mixture slip back into the rest, then set the fish back in the flour mixture and coat it again, then back in the egg mixture for a second wash, then back in the flour mixture for a third time. Coat the fish on all sides with vegetable oil spray and set it aside. "Batter" the remaining piece(s) of cod in the same way.
4. Set the coated cod fillets in the air fryer oven with as much space between them as possible. They should not touch. Air-fry undisturbed for 12 minutes, or until brown and crisp.
5. Use kitchen tongs to gently transfer the fish to a wire rack. Cool for only a couple of minutes before serving.

Tex-mex Fish Tacos

Servings: 3

Cooking Time: 7 Minutes

Ingredients:

- ¾ teaspoon Chile powder
- ¼ teaspoon Ground cumin
- ¼ teaspoon Dried oregano
- 3 5-ounce skinless mahi-mahi fillets
- Vegetable oil spray
- 3 Corn or flour tortillas
- 6 tablespoons Diced tomatoes
- 3 tablespoons Regular, low-fat, or fat-free sour cream

Directions:

1. Preheat the toaster oven to 400°F.
2. Stir the chile powder, cumin, and oregano in a small bowl until well combined.
3. Coat each piece of fish all over (even the sides and ends) with vegetable oil spray. Sprinkle the spice mixture evenly over all sides of the fillets. Lightly spray them again.
4. When the machine is at temperature, set the fillets in the air fryer oven with as much air space between them as possible. Air-fry undisturbed for 7 minutes, until lightly browned and firm but not hard.
5. Use a nonstick-safe spatula to transfer the fillets to a wire rack. Microwave the tortillas on high for a few seconds, until supple. Put a fillet in each tortilla and top each with 2 tablespoons diced tomatoes and 1 tablespoon sour cream.

Baked Parsley Mussels With Zucchini

Servings: 6

Cooking Time: 40 Minutes

Ingredients:

- 2 pounds (approximately 40) mussels, cooked, shells discarded
- 4 small zucchini squash, scrubbed, halved, and cut lengthwise into ½-inch-wide strips
- ½ cup dry white wine
- 1 tablespoon chopped fresh oregano or 1 teaspoon dried oregano
- 2 garlic cloves, minced
- ¼ cup chopped fresh Italian parsley
- 2 tablespoons olive oil
- Freshly ground black pepper to taste
- ¼ cup grated low-fat Parmesan cheese

Directions:

1. Preheat the toaster oven to 350° F.
2. Combine all the ingredients except the Parmesan cheese in a 1-quart 8½ × 8½ × 4-inch ovenproof baking dish, mixing well. Adjust the seasonings to taste and cover with aluminum foil.
3. BAKE for 35 minutes, or until the zucchini is tender. Uncover and sprinkle with Parmesan cheese.
4. BROIL for 5 minutes, or until the cheese is melted and the top is lightly browned.

Catfish Kebabs

Servings: 4

Cooking Time: 20 Minutes

Ingredients:

- Marinade:
- 3 tablespoons lemon juice
- 3 tablespoons tomato juice
- 2 garlic cloves, minced
- 2 tablespoons olive oil
- 1 teaspoon soy sauce
- 4 5-ounce catfish fillets
- 4 9-inch metal skewers
- 2 plum tomatoes, quartered
- 1 onion, cut into 1 × 1-inch pieces

Directions:

1. Combine the marinade ingredients in a small bowl. Set aside.
2. Cut the fillets into 2 by 3-inch strips and place in a shallow glass or ceramic dish. Add the marinade and refrigerate, covered, for at least 20 minutes. Remove the strips from the marinade, roll, and skewer, alternating the rolled strips with the tomatoes and onion.
3. Brush the kebabs with marinade, reserving the remaining marinade for brushing again later. Place the skewers on a broiling rack with a pan underneath.
4. Broil for 10 minutes, then remove the pan from the oven and carefully turn the skewers. Brush the kebabs with the marinade and broil again for 10 minutes, or until browned.

Best-dressed Trout

Servings: 2

Cooking Time: 25 Minutes

Ingredients:

- 2 dressed trout
- 1 egg, beaten
- 2 tablespoons finely ground almonds
- 2 tablespoons unbleached flour

- 1 teaspoon paprika or smoked paprika
- Pinch of salt (optional)
- 4 lemon slices, approximately ¼ inch thick
- 1 teaspoon lemon juice

Directions:

1. Preheat the toaster oven to 400° F.
2. Brush the trout (both sides) with the beaten egg. Blend the almonds, flour, paprika, and salt in a bowl and sprinkle both sides of the trout. Insert 2 lemon slices in each trout cavity and place the trout in an oiled or nonstick 8½ × 8½ × 2-inch square baking (cake) pan.
3. BAKE for 20 minutes, or until the meat is white and firm. Remove from the oven and turn the trout carefully with a spatula.
4. BROIL for 5 minutes, or until the trout is lightly browned.

Spicy Fish Street Tacos With Sriracha Slaw

Servings: 2
Cooking Time: 5 Minutes

Ingredients:

- Sriracha Slaw:
- ½ cup mayonnaise
- 2 tablespoons rice vinegar
- 1 teaspoon sugar
- 2 tablespoons sriracha chili sauce
- 5 cups shredded green cabbage
- ¼ cup shredded carrots
- 2 scallions, chopped
- salt and freshly ground black pepper
- Tacos:
- ½ cup flour
- 1 teaspoon chili powder
- ½ teaspoon ground cumin
- 1 teaspoon salt
- freshly ground black pepper
- ½ teaspoon baking powder
- 1 egg, beaten
- ¼ cup milk
- 1 cup breadcrumbs
- 1 pound mahi-mahi or snapper fillets
- 1 tablespoon canola or vegetable oil
- 6 (6-inch) flour tortillas
- 1 lime, cut into wedges

Directions:

1. Start by making the sriracha slaw. Combine the mayonnaise, rice vinegar, sugar, and sriracha sauce in a large bowl. Mix well and add the green cabbage, carrots, and scallions. Toss until all the vegetables are coated with the dressing and season with salt and pepper. Refrigerate the slaw until you are ready to serve the tacos.
2. Combine the flour, chili powder, cumin, salt, pepper and baking powder in a bowl. Add the egg and milk and mix until the batter is smooth. Place the breadcrumbs in shallow dish.
3. Cut the fish fillets into 1-inch wide sticks, approximately 4-inches long. You should have about 12 fish sticks total. Dip the fish sticks into the batter, coating all sides. Let the excess batter drip off the fish and then roll them in the breadcrumbs, patting the crumbs onto all sides of the fish sticks. Set the coated fish on a plate or baking sheet until all the fish has been coated.
4. Preheat the toaster oven to 400°F.
5. Spray the coated fish sticks with oil on all sides. Spray or brush the inside of the air fryer oven with oil and transfer the fish to the air fryer oven. Place as many sticks as you can in one layer, leaving a little room around each stick. Place any remaining sticks on top, perpendicular to the first layer.
6. Air-fry the fish for 3 minutes. Turn the fish sticks over and air-fry for an additional 2 minutes.
7. While the fish is air-frying, warm the tortilla shells either in a 350°F oven wrapped in foil or in a skillet with a little oil over medium-high heat for a couple minutes. Fold the tortillas in half and keep them warm until the remaining tortillas and fish are ready.
8. To assemble the tacos, place two pieces of the fish in each tortilla shell and top with the sriracha slaw. Squeeze the lime wedge over top and dig in.

Bacon-wrapped Scallops

Servings: 4
Cooking Time: 8 Minutes

Ingredients:

- 16 large scallops
- 8 bacon strips
- ½ teaspoon black pepper
- ¼ teaspoon smoked paprika

Directions:

1. Pat the scallops dry with a paper towel. Slice each of the bacon strips in half. Wrap 1 bacon strip around 1 scallop and secure with a toothpick. Repeat with the remaining scallops. Season the scallops with pepper and paprika.
2. Preheat the toaster oven to 350°F.
3. Place the bacon-wrapped scallops in the air fryer oven and air-fry for 4 minutes. Cook another 6 to 7 minutes. When the bacon is crispy, the scallops should be cooked through and slightly firm, but not rubbery. Serve immediately.

Better Fish Sticks

Servings: 3
Cooking Time: 8 Minutes

Ingredients:

- ¾ cup Seasoned Italian-style dried bread crumbs (gluten-free, if a concern)
- 3 tablespoons (about ½ ounce) Finely grated Parmesan cheese
- 10 ounces Skinless cod fillets, cut lengthwise into 1-inch-wide pieces
- 3 tablespoons Regular or low-fat mayonnaise (not fat-free; gluten-free, if a concern)
- Vegetable oil spray

Directions:

1. Preheat the toaster oven to 400°F.

2. Mix the bread crumbs and grated Parmesan in a shallow soup bowl or a small pie plate.
3. Smear the fish fillet sticks completely with the mayonnaise, then dip them one by one in the bread-crumb mixture, turning and pressing gently to make an even and thorough coating. Coat each stick on all sides with vegetable oil spray.
4. Set the fish sticks in the air fryer oven with at least ¼ inch between them. Air-fry undisturbed for 8 minutes, or until golden brown and crisp.
5. Use a nonstick-safe spatula to gently transfer them from the air fryer oven to a wire rack. Cool for only a minute or two before serving.

Pecan-topped Sole

Servings: 4
Cooking Time: 12 Minutes
Ingredients:

- 4 (4-ounce) sole fillets
- Sea salt, for seasoning
- Freshly ground black pepper, for seasoning
- 1 cup crushed pecans
- ½ cup seasoned bread crumbs
- 1 large egg
- 2 tablespoons water
- Oil spray (hand-pumped)

Directions:

1. Preheat the toaster oven to 375°F on BAKE for 5 minutes.
2. Line the baking tray with parchment paper.
3. Pat the fish dry with paper towels and lightly season with salt and pepper.
4. In a small bowl, stir the pecans and bread crumbs.
5. In another small bowl, beat the egg and water until well blended.
6. Dredge the fish in the egg mixture, shaking off any excess, then in the nut mixture.
7. Place the fish in the baking sheet and repeat with the remaining fish.
8. Lightly spray the fillets with the oil on both sides.
9. In position 2, bake until golden and crispy, turning halfway, for 12 minutes in total. Serve.

Lobster Tails

Servings: 4
Cooking Time: 10 Minutes
Ingredients:

- Brushing mixture:
- 2 tablespoons lemon juice
- 2 tablespoons olive oil
- ½ teaspoon garlic powder
- ¼ teaspoon ground thyme
- 4 6-ounce lobster tails

Directions:

1. Whisk together the brushing mixture ingredients in a small bowl and set aside. CUT the top of each lobster shell lengthwise from the top edge to the tail with a sharp scissors. Place the lobster tails, cut side down, on a broiling rack with a pan underneath. Brush with the brushing mixture.
2. BROIL for 5 minutes. Remove from the oven and brush again. Broil for 5 minutes, or until the lobster flesh turns from translucent to opaque.

Popcorn Crawfish

Servings: 4
Cooking Time: 18 Minutes
Ingredients:

- ½ cup flour, plus 2 tablespoons
- ½ teaspoon garlic powder
- 1½ teaspoons Old Bay Seasoning
- ½ teaspoon onion powder
- ½ cup beer, plus 2 tablespoons
- 12-ounce package frozen crawfish tail meat, thawed and drained
- oil for misting or cooking spray
- Coating
- 1½ cups panko crumbs
- 1 teaspoon Old Bay Seasoning
- ½ teaspoon ground black pepper

Directions:

1. In a large bowl, mix together the flour, garlic powder, Old Bay Seasoning, and onion powder. Stir in beer to blend.
2. Add crawfish meat to batter and stir to coat.
3. Combine the coating ingredients in food processor and pulse to finely crush the crumbs. Transfer crumbs to shallow dish.
4. Preheat the toaster oven to 390°F.
5. Pour the crawfish and batter into a colander to drain. Stir with a spoon to drain excess batter.
6. Working with a handful of crawfish at a time, roll in crumbs and place on a cookie sheet. It's okay if some of the smaller pieces of crawfish meat stick together.
7. Spray breaded crawfish with oil or cooking spray and place all at once into air fryer oven.
8. Air-fry at 390°F for 5 minutes. Stir and mist again with olive oil or spray. Cook 5 more minutes, stir again, and mist lightly again. Continue cooking 5 more minutes, until browned and crispy.

Oysters Broiled In Wine Sauce

Servings: 2
Cooking Time: 20 Minutes
Ingredients:

- Sauce:
- 2 tablespoons margarine, at room temperature
- 1 cup dry white wine
- 3 garlic cloves, minced
- Salt and freshly ground black pepper to taste
- 24 fresh oysters, shucked and drained

Directions:

1. Combine the sauce ingredients in a 1-quart 8½ × 8½ × 4-inch ovenproof baking dish and adjust the seasonings to taste.
2. BROIL the sauce for 5 minutes, remove the pan from the oven, and stir. Return to the oven and broil for another 5 minutes, or until the sauce begins to bubble. Remove from the oven and cool for 5 minutes. Add the oysters, spooning the sauce over them to cover thoroughly.

3. BROIL for 5 minutes, or until the oysters are just cooked.

Lightened-up Breaded Fish Filets

Servings: 4
Cooking Time: 10 Minutes
Ingredients:

- ½ cup all-purpose flour
- ½ teaspoon cayenne pepper
- 1 teaspoon garlic powder
- ½ teaspoon black pepper
- ¼ teaspoon salt
- 2 eggs, whisked
- 1½ cups panko breadcrumbs
- 1 pound boneless white fish filets
- 1 cup tartar sauce
- 1 lemon, sliced into wedges

Directions:

1. In a medium bowl, mix the flour, cayenne pepper, garlic powder, pepper, and salt.
2. In a shallow dish, place the eggs.
3. In a third dish, place the breadcrumbs.
4. Cover the fish in the flour, dip them in the egg, and coat them with panko. Repeat until all fish are covered in the breading.
5. Liberally spray the metal trivet that fits inside the air fryer oven with olive oil mist. Place the fish onto the trivet, leaving space between the filets to flip. Air-fry for 5 minutes, flip the fish, and cook another 5 minutes. Repeat until all the fish is cooked.
6. Serve warm with tartar sauce and lemon wedges.

Crab Cakes

Servings: 4
Cooking Time: 9 Minutes
Ingredients:

- 1 pound lump crab meat, checked for shells
- ⅓ cup breadcrumbs
- ¼ cup finely chopped onions
- ¼ cup finely chopped red bell peppers
- ¼ cup finely chopped parsley
- ¼ teaspoon sea salt
- 2 eggs, whisked
- ¾ cup mayonnaise, divided
- ¼ cup sour cream
- 1 lemon, divided
- ¼ cup sweet pickle relish
- 1 tablespoon prepared mustard

Directions:

1. In a large bowl, mix together the crab meat, breadcrumbs, onions, bell peppers, parsley, sea salt, eggs, and ¼ cup of the mayonnaise.
2. Preheat the toaster oven to 380°F.
3. Form 8 patties with the crab cake mixture. Line the air fryer oven with parchment paper and place the crab cakes on the parchment paper. Spray with cooking spray. Air-fry for 4 minutes, turn over the crab cakes, spray with cooking spray, and air-fry for an additional 3 to 5 minutes, or until golden brown and the edges are crispy. Cook in batches as needed.
4. Meanwhile, make the sauce. In a small bowl, mix together the remaining ½ cup of mayonnaise, the sour cream, the juice from ½ of the lemon, the pickle relish, and the mustard.
5. Place the cooked crab cakes on a serving platter and serve with the remaining ½ lemon cut into wedges and the dipping sauce.

Scallops In Orange Sauce

Servings: 4
Cooking Time: 3 Minutes
Ingredients:

- Broiling mixture:
- 1 cup orange juice
- 1 teaspoon soy sauce
- 2 garlic cloves, finely minced
- 1 teaspoon grated orange zest
- 1½ pounds (3 cups) bay scallops, rinsed and drained
- 1 7-ounce can sliced water chestnuts, drained well
- 2 tablespoons chopped watercress

Directions:

1. Whisk together the broiling mixture ingredients in a small bowl and transfer to an 8½ × 8½ × 2-inch oiled or nonstick square (cake) pan.
2. BROIL the sauce for 10 minutes to reduce the liquid and meld the flavors. Remove the pan from the oven and add the scallops, spooning the sauce over them.
3. BROIL for 3 minutes, or until opaque. Serve the scallops with the sauce and garnish with the sliced water chestnuts and chopped watercress.

Sesame-crusted Tuna Steaks

Servings: 3
Cooking Time: 13 Minutes
Ingredients:

- ½ cup Sesame seeds, preferably a blend of white and black
- 1½ tablespoons Toasted sesame oil
- 3 6-ounce skinless tuna steaks

Directions:

1. Preheat the toaster oven to 400°F.
2. Pour the sesame seeds on a dinner plate. Use ½ tablespoon of the sesame oil as a rub on both sides and the edges of a tuna steak. Set it in the sesame seeds, then turn it several times, pressing gently, to create an even coating of the seeds, including around the steak's edge. Set aside and continue coating the remaining steak(s).
3. When the machine is at temperature, set the steaks in the air fryer oven with as much air space between them as possible. Air-fry undisturbed for 10 minutes for medium-rare (not USDA-approved), or 12 to 13 minutes for cooked through (USDA-approved).
4. Use a nonstick-safe spatula to transfer the steaks to serving plates. Serve hot.

Garlic And Dill Salmon

Servings: 2
Cooking Time: 8 Minutes

Ingredients:

- 12 ounces salmon filets with skin
- 2 tablespoons melted butter
- 1 tablespoon extra-virgin olive oil
- 2 garlic cloves, minced
- 1 tablespoon fresh dill
- ½ teaspoon sea salt
- ½ lemon

Directions:

1. Pat the salmon dry with paper towels.
2. In a small bowl, mix together the melted butter, olive oil, garlic, and dill.
3. Sprinkle the top of the salmon with sea salt. Brush all sides of the salmon with the garlic and dill butter.
4. Preheat the toaster oven to 350°F.
5. Place the salmon, skin side down, in the air fryer oven. Air-fry for 6 to 8 minutes, or until the fish flakes in the center.
6. Remove the salmon and plate on a serving platter. Squeeze fresh lemon over the top of the salmon. Serve immediately.

Lemon-dill Salmon Burgers

Servings: 4
Cooking Time: 8 Minutes

Ingredients:

- 2 (6-ounce) fillets of salmon, finely chopped by hand or in a food processor
- 1 cup fine breadcrumbs
- 1 teaspoon freshly grated lemon zest
- 2 tablespoons chopped fresh dill weed
- 1 teaspoon salt
- freshly ground black pepper
- 2 eggs, lightly beaten
- 4 brioche or hamburger buns
- lettuce, tomato, red onion, avocado, mayonnaise or mustard, to serve

Directions:

1. Preheat the toaster oven to 400°F.
2. Combine all the ingredients in a bowl. Mix together well and divide into four balls. Flatten the balls into patties, making an indentation in the center of each patty with your thumb (this will help the burger stay flat as it cooks) and flattening the sides of the burgers so that they fit nicely into the air fryer oven.
3. Transfer the burgers to the air fryer oven and air-fry for 4 minutes. Flip the burgers over and air-fry for another 3 to 4 minutes, until nicely browned and firm to the touch.
4. Serve on soft brioche buns with your choice of topping – lettuce, tomato, red onion, avocado, mayonnaise or mustard.

Fried Oysters

Servings: 12
Cooking Time: 8 Minutes

Ingredients:

- 1½ cups All-purpose flour
- 1½ cups Yellow cornmeal
- 1½ tablespoons Cajun dried seasoning blend
- 1¼ cups, plus more if needed Amber beer, pale ale, or IPA
- 12 Large shucked oysters, any liquid drained off
- Vegetable oil spray

Directions:

1. Preheat the toaster oven to 400°F.
2. Whisk ⅔ cup of the flour, ½ cup of the cornmeal, and the seasoning blend in a bowl until uniform. Set aside.
3. Whisk the remaining ⅓ cup flour and the remaining ½ cup cornmeal with the beer in a second bowl, adding more beer in dribs and drabs until the mixture is the consistency of pancake batter.
4. Using a fork, dip a shucked oyster in the beer batter, coating it thoroughly. Gently shake off any excess batter, then set the oyster in the dry mixture and turn gently to coat well and evenly. Set the coated oyster on a cutting board and continue dipping and coating the remainder of the oysters.
5. Coat the oysters with vegetable oil spray, then set them in the air fryer oven with as much air space between them as possible. Air-fry undisturbed for 8 minutes, or until lightly browned and crisp.
6. Use a nonstick-safe spatula to transfer the oysters to a wire rack. Cool for a couple of minutes before serving.

Crispy Pecan Fish

Servings: 4
Cooking Time: 20 Minutes

Ingredients:

- 3 tablespoons multigrain bread crumbs
- 3 tablespoons ground pecans
- 4 6-ounce fish fillets, approximately ¼ inch thick
- 1 egg white, whisked until frothy
- 1 tablespoon olive oil
- Salt and freshly ground black pepper to taste

Directions:

1. Combine the bread crumbs and pecans in a small bowl and transfer to a platter or plate.
2. Brush both sides of the fillets with egg white and dredge in the bread crumb/pecan mixture. Transfer the fillets to an oiled or nonstick 8½ × 8½ × 2-inch square baking (cake) pan.
3. BROIL for 10 minutes. Remove from the oven and carefully turn the fillets with a spatula. Broil again for 10 minutes, or until the fillets are lightly browned. Season to taste with the salt and pepper.

Coconut Jerk Shrimp

Servings: 3
Cooking Time: 8 Minutes
Ingredients:

- 1 Large egg white(s)
- 1 teaspoon Purchased or homemade jerk dried seasoning blend
- ¾ cup Plain panko bread crumbs (gluten-free, if a concern)
- ¾ cup Unsweetened shredded coconut
- 12 Large shrimp (20–25 per pound), peeled and deveined
- Coconut oil spray

Directions:

1. Preheat the toaster oven to 375°F .
2. Whisk the egg white(s) and seasoning blend in a bowl until foamy. Add the shrimp and toss well to coat evenly.
3. Mix the bread crumbs and coconut on a dinner plate until well combined. Use kitchen tongs to pick up a shrimp, letting the excess egg white mixture slip back into the rest. Set the shrimp in the bread-crumb mixture. Turn several times to coat evenly and thoroughly. Set on a cutting board and continue coating the remainder of the shrimp.
4. Lightly coat all the shrimp on both sides with the coconut oil spray. Set them in the air fryer oven in one layer with as much space between them as possible. (You can even stand some up along the air fryer oven's wall in some models.) Air-fry undisturbed for 6 minutes, or until the coating is lightly browned. If the air fryer oven is at 360°F, you may need to add 2 minutes to the cooking time.
5. Use clean kitchen tongs to transfer the shrimp to a wire rack. Cool for only a minute or two before serving.

Snacks Appetizers And Sides

Shrimp Pirogues

Servings: 8
Cooking Time: 5 Minutes
Ingredients:

- 12 ounces small, peeled, and deveined raw shrimp
- 3 ounces cream cheese, room temperature
- 2 tablespoons plain yogurt
- 1 teaspoon lemon juice
- 1 teaspoon dried dill weed, crushed
- salt
- 4 small hothouse cucumbers, each approximately 6 inches long

Directions:

1. Pour 4 tablespoons water in bottom of air fryer oven.
2. Place shrimp in air fryer oven in single layer and air-fry at 390°F for 5 minutes, just until done. Watch carefully because shrimp cooks quickly, and overcooking makes it tough.
3. Chop shrimp into small pieces, no larger than ½ inch. Refrigerate while mixing the remaining ingredients.
4. With a fork, mash and whip the cream cheese until smooth.
5. Stir in the yogurt and beat until smooth. Stir in lemon juice, dill weed, and chopped shrimp.
6. Taste for seasoning. If needed, add ¼ to ½ teaspoon salt to suit your taste.
7. Store in refrigerator until serving time.
8. When ready to serve, wash and dry cucumbers and split them lengthwise. Scoop out the seeds and turn cucumbers upside down on paper towels to drain for 10 minutes.
9. Just before filling, wipe centers of cucumbers dry. Spoon the shrimp mixture into the pirogues and cut in half crosswise. Serve immediately.

Crab Rangoon

Servings: 18
Cooking Time: 6 Minutes
Ingredients:

- 4½ tablespoons (a little more than ¼ pound) Crabmeat, preferably backfin or claw, picked over for shells and cartilage
- 1½ ounces (3 tablespoons) Regular or low-fat cream cheese (not fat-free), softened to room temperature
- 1½ tablespoons Minced scallion
- 1½ teaspoons Minced garlic
- 1½ teaspoons Worcestershire sauce
- 18 Wonton wrappers (thawed, if necessary)
- Vegetable oil spray

Directions:

1. Preheat the toaster oven to 400°F.
2. Gently stir the crab, cream cheese, scallion, garlic, and Worcestershire sauce in a medium bowl until well combined.
3. Set a bowl of water on a clean, dry work surface or next to a large cutting board. Set one wonton wrapper on the surface, then put a teaspoonful of the crab mixture in the

center of the wrapper. Dip your clean finger in the water and run it around the edge of the wrapper. Bring all four sides up to the center and over the filling, and pinch them together in the middle to seal without covering all of the filling. The traditional look is for the corners of the filled wonton to become four open "flower petals" radiating out from the filled center. Set the filled wonton aside and continue making more as needed. (If you want a video tutorial on filling these, see ours at our YouTube channel, Cooking with Bruce and Mark.)

4. Generously coat the filled wontons with vegetable oil spray. Set them sealed side up in the air fryer oven with a little room among them. Air-fry undisturbed for 6 minutes, or until golden brown and crisp.

5. Use a nonstick-safe spatula to gently transfer the wontons to a wire rack. Cool for 5 minutes before serving warm.

Caramelized Onion Dip

Servings: 2

Cooking Time: 20 Minutes

Ingredients:

- 1 tablespoon unsalted butter
- 1 tablespoon olive oil
- 1 large sweet onion, quartered and very thinly sliced crosswise
- Kosher salt
- 1 clove garlic, minced
- 3 tablespoons dry white wine
- ½ teaspoon dried thyme leaves
- ½ teaspoon freshly ground black pepper
- 1 baguette, thinly sliced
- Nonstick cooking spray
- 1 cup shredded Gruyère or Swiss cheese
- ½ cup sour cream
- ½ cup mayonnaise
- ¼ cup shredded Parmesan cheese
- 3 strips bacon, cooked until crisp and crumbled

Directions:

1. Melt the butter and olive oil in a large skillet over medium heat. Add the onion and season with salt. Cook, stirring frequently, for 3 minutes. Reduce the heat to low and cook, stirring occasionally, for 20 to 25 minutes, or until the onions are a deep golden brown color.
2. Increase the heat to medium. Stir in the garlic, wine, thyme, and pepper. Cook, stirring frequently, for 3 minutes or until the wine has mostly evaporated. Remove from the heat.
3. Meanwhile, toast the baguette slices in the toaster oven until golden brown and crisp; set aside.
4. Preheat the toaster oven to 350°F. Spray a 1-quart casserole with nonstick cooking spray.
5. Stir the Gruyère, sour cream, mayonnaise, Parmesan, and bacon into the onions. Spoon the mixture into the prepared casserole dish. Cover and bake for 20 minutes or until hot and the cheese is melted. Allow to stand for 5 to 10 minutes before serving. To serve, spoon the warm onion-cheese mixture onto the toast.

Fried Mozzarella Sticks

Servings: 7

Cooking Time: 5 Minutes

Ingredients:

- 7 1-ounce string cheese sticks, unwrapped
- ½ cup All-purpose flour or tapioca flour
- 2 Large egg(s), well beaten
- 2¼ cups Seasoned Italian-style dried bread crumbs (gluten-free, if a concern)
- Olive oil spray

Directions:

1. Unwrap the string cheese and place the pieces in the freezer for 20 minutes (but not longer, or they will be too frozen to soften in the time given in the air fryer oven).
2. Preheat the toaster oven to 400°F.
3. Set up and fill three shallow soup plates or small pie plates on your counter: one for the flour, one for the egg(s), and one for the bread crumbs.
4. Dip a piece of cold string cheese in the flour until well coated (keep the others in the freezer). Gently tap off any excess flour, then set the stick in the egg(s). Roll it around to coat, let any excess egg mixture slip back into the rest, and set the stick in the bread crumbs. Gently roll it around to coat it evenly, even the ends. Now dip it back in the egg(s), then again in the bread crumbs, rolling it to coat well and evenly. Set the stick aside on a cutting board and coat the remaining pieces of string cheese in the same way.
5. Lightly coat the sticks all over with olive oil spray. Place them in the air fryer oven in one layer and air-fry undisturbed for 5 minutes, or until golden brown and crisp.
6. Remove from the machine and cool for 5 minutes. Use a nonstick-safe spatula to transfer the mozzarella sticks to a serving platter. Serve hot.

Avocado Fries

Servings: 8

Cooking Time: 8 Minutes

Ingredients:

- 2 medium avocados, firm but ripe
- 1 large egg
- ½ teaspoon garlic powder
- ¼ teaspoon cayenne pepper
- ¼ teaspoon salt
- ¾ cup almond flour
- ½ cup finely grated Parmesan cheese
- ½ cup gluten-free breadcrumbs

Directions:

1. Preheat the toaster oven to 370°F.
2. Rinse the outside of the avocado with water. Slice the avocado in half, slice it in half again, and then slice it in half once more to get 8 slices. Remove the outer skin. Repeat for the other avocado. Set the avocado slices aside.
3. In a small bowl, whisk the egg, garlic powder, cayenne pepper, and salt in a small bowl. Set aside.
4. In a separate bowl, pour the almond flour.
5. In a third bowl, mix the Parmesan cheese and breadcrumbs.

6. Carefully roll the avocado slices in the almond flour, then dip them in the egg wash, and coat them in the cheese and breadcrumb topping. Repeat until all 16 fries are coated.
7. Liberally spray the air fryer oven with olive oil spray and place the avocado fries into the air fryer oven, leaving a little space around the sides between fries. Depending on the size of your air fryer oven, you may need to cook these in batches.
8. Cook fries for 8 minutes, or until the outer coating turns light brown.
9. Carefully remove, repeat with remaining slices, and then serve warm.

Zucchini Fries With Roasted Garlic Aïoli

Servings: 4
Cooking Time: 12 Minutes
Ingredients:

- Roasted Garlic Aïoli:
- 1 teaspoon roasted garlic
- ½ cup mayonnaise
- 2 tablespoons olive oil
- juice of ½ lemon
- salt and pepper
- Zucchini Fries:
- ½ cup flour
- 2 eggs, beaten
- 1 cup seasoned breadcrumbs
- salt and pepper
- 1 large zucchini, cut into ½-inch sticks
- olive oil in a spray bottle, can or mister

Directions:

1. To make the aïoli, combine the roasted garlic, mayonnaise, olive oil and lemon juice in a bowl and whisk well. Season the aïoli with salt and pepper to taste.
2. Prepare the zucchini fries. Create a dredging station with three shallow dishes. Place the flour in the first shallow dish and season well with salt and freshly ground black pepper. Put the beaten eggs in the second shallow dish. In the third shallow dish, combine the breadcrumbs, salt and pepper. Dredge the zucchini sticks, coating with flour first, then dipping them into the eggs to coat, and finally tossing in breadcrumbs. Shake the dish with the breadcrumbs and pat the crumbs onto the zucchini sticks gently with your hands so they stick evenly.
3. Place the zucchini fries on a flat surface and let them sit at least 10 minutes before air-frying to let them dry out a little. Preheat the toaster oven oven to 400°F.
4. Spray the zucchini sticks with olive oil, and place them into the air fryer oven. You can air-fry the zucchini in two layers, placing the second layer in the opposite direction to the first. Air-fry for 12 minutes turning and rotating the fries halfway through the cooking time. Spray with additional oil when you turn them over.
5. Serve zucchini fries warm with the roasted garlic aïoli.

Cauliflower-crust Pizza

Servings: 3
Cooking Time: 14 Minutes
Ingredients:

- 1 pound 2 ounces Riced cauliflower
- 1 plus 1 large egg yolk Large egg(s)
- 3 tablespoons (a little more than ½ ounce) Finely grated Parmesan cheese
- 1½ tablespoons Potato starch
- ¾ teaspoon Dried oregano
- ¾ teaspoon Table salt
- Vegetable oil spray
- 3 tablespoons Purchased pizza sauce
- 6 tablespoons (about 1½ ounces) Shredded semi-firm mozzarella

Directions:

1. Pour the riced cauliflower into a medium microwave-safe bowl. Microwave on high for 4 minutes. Stir well, then cool for 15 minutes.
2. Preheat the toaster oven to 400°F.
3. Pour the riced cauliflower into a clean kitchen towel or a large piece of cheesecloth. Gather the towel or cheesecloth together. Working over the sink, squeeze the moisture out of the cauliflower, getting out as much of the liquid as you can.
4. Pour the squeezed cauliflower back into that same medium bowl and stir in the egg, egg yolk (if using), cheese, potato starch, oregano, and salt to form a loose, uniform "dough."
5. Cut a piece of aluminum foil or parchment paper into a 6-inch circle for a small pizza, a 7-inch circle for a medium one, or an 8-inch circle for a large one. Coat the circle with vegetable oil spray, then place it in the air-fryer oven. Using a small offset spatula or the back of a flatware tablespoon, spread and smooth the cauliflower mixture onto the circle right to the edges. Air-fry undisturbed for 10 minutes.
6. Remove the pan from the air fryer oven. Reduce the machine's temperature to 350°F .
7. Using a large nonstick-safe spatula, flip over the cauliflower circle along with its foil or parchment paper right in the air fryer oven. Peel off and discard the foil or parchment paper. Spread the pizza sauce evenly over the crust and sprinkle with the cheese.
8. Air-fry undisturbed for 4 minutes, or until the cheese has melted and begun to bubble. Remove the pan from the machine and cool for 5 minutes. Use the same spatula to transfer the pizza to a wire rack to cool for 5 minutes more before cutting the pie into wedges to serve.

Bacon Corn Muffins

Servings: 6
Cooking Time: 17 Minutes
Ingredients:

- 1 1/4 cups self rising cornmeal mix
- 3/4 cup buttermilk
- 1/3 cup chopped cooked bacon
- 1/4 cup butter, melted
- 1 large egg, slightly beaten

Directions:

1. Preheat toaster oven to 425°F on CONVECTION setting.
2. Stir cornmeal mix, buttermilk, bacon, butter and egg until blended.

3. Spoon batter into lightly greased muffin pan, filling 3/4 full.
4. Bake 15 to 17 minutes until toothpick inserted in center comes out clean.
5. Cool 10 minutes on wire rack; remove.

Ham And Cheese Palmiers

Servings: 30
Cooking Time: 60 Minutes
Ingredients:

- 1 (9½ by 9-inch) sheet puff pastry, thawed
- 2 tablespoons Dijon mustard
- 2 teaspoons minced fresh thyme
- 2 ounces Parmesan cheese, grated (1 cup)
- 4 ounces thinly sliced deli ham

Directions:

1. Roll puff pastry into 12-inch square on lightly floured counter. Brush evenly with mustard; sprinkle with thyme and Parmesan; pressing gently to adhere, and lay ham evenly over top. Roll up opposite sides of pastry until they meet in middle. Wrap pastry log in plastic wrap and refrigerate until firm, about 1 hour.
2. Adjust toaster oven rack to middle position, select air-fry or convection setting, and preheat the toaster oven to 400 degrees. Line large and small rimmed baking sheets with parchment paper. Using sharp knife, trim ends of log, then slice into ⅓-inch-thick pieces. Space desired number of palmiers at least 1 inch apart on prepared small sheet; space remaining palmiers evenly on prepared large sheet. Re-shape palmiers as needed.
3. Bake small sheet of palmiers until golden brown and crisp, 15 to 25 minutes. Transfer palmiers to wire rack and let cool for 15 minutes before serving. (Palmiers can be held at room temperature for up to 6 hours before serving.)
4. Freeze remaining large sheet of palmiers until firm, about 1 hour. Transfer palmiers to 1-gallon zipper-lock bag and freeze for up to 1 month. Cook frozen palmiers as directed; do not thaw.

Pizza Bagel Bites

Servings: 2
Cooking Time: 5 Minutes
Ingredients:

- 2 Mini bagel(s), split into two rings
- ¼ cup Purchased pizza sauce
- ½ cup Finely grated or shredded cheese, such as Parmesan cheese, semi-firm mozzarella, fontina, or (preferably) a cheese blend

Directions:

1. Preheat the toaster oven to 375°F .
2. Spread the cut side of each bagel half with 1 tablespoon pizza sauce; top each half with 2 tablespoons shredded cheese.
3. When the machine is at temperature, put the bagels cheese side up in the air fryer oven in one layer. Air-fry undisturbed for 4 minutes, or until the cheese has melted and is gooey. You may need to air-fry the pizza bagel bites for 1 minute extra if the temperature is at 360°F.
4. Use a nonstick-safe spatula to transfer the topped bagel halves to a wire rack. Cool for at least 5 minutes before serving.

Potato Samosas

Servings: 12
Cooking Time: 10 Minutes
Ingredients:

- ¾ cup Instant mashed potato flakes
- ¾ cup Boiling water
- ⅓ cup Plain full-fat or low-fat yogurt (not Greek yogurt or fat-free yogurt)
- 1 teaspoon Yellow curry powder, purchased or homemade
- ½ teaspoon Table salt
- 1½ Purchased refrigerated pie crust(s), from a minimum 14.1-ounce box
- All-purpose flour
- Vegetable oil spray

Directions:

1. Put the potato flakes in a medium bowl and pour the boiling water over them. Stir well to form a mixture like thick mashed potatoes. Cool for 15 minutes.
2. Preheat the toaster oven to 400°F.
3. Stir the yogurt, curry powder, and salt into the potato mixture until smooth and uniform.
4. Unwrap and unroll the sheet(s) of pie crust dough onto a clean, dry work surface. Cut out as many 4-inch circles as you can with a big cookie cutter or a giant sturdy water glass, or even by tracing the circle with the rim of a 4-inch plate. Gather up the scraps of dough. Lightly flour your work surface and set the scraps on top. Roll them together into a sheet that matches the thickness of the original crusts and cut more circles until you have the number you need—8 circles for the small batch, 12 for the medium batch, or 16 for the large.
5. Pick up one of the circles and create something like an ice cream cone by folding and sealing the circle together so that it is closed at the bottom and flared open at the top, in a conical shape. Put 1 tablespoon of the potato filling into the open cone, then push the filling into the cone toward the point. Fold the top over the filling and press to seal the dough into a triangular shape with corners, taking care to seal those corners all around. Set aside and continue forming and filling the remainder of the dough circles as directed.
6. Lightly coat the filled dough pockets with vegetable oil spray on all sides. Set them in the air fryer oven in one layer and air-fry undisturbed for 10 minutes, or until lightly browned and crisp.
7. Gently turn the contents of the air fryer oven out onto a wire rack. Use kitchen tongs to gently set all the samosas seam side up. Cool for 10 minutes before serving.

Elote

Servings: 2
Cooking Time: 45 Minutes
Ingredients:

- 2 ears corn, husks and silk removed, stalks left intact
- 1 teaspoon extra-virgn olive oil
- 3 tablespoons mayonnaise
- 1 tablespoon crumbled queso fresco
- 1 tablespoon minced fresh cilantro
- 1 teaspoon lime juice, plus lime wedges for serving
- 1 small garlic clove, minced
- ¼ teaspoon chili powder
- Pinch table salt

Directions:

1. Adjust toaster oven rack to middle position, select broiler function, and heat broiler. Brush corn all over with oil and transfer to small aluminum foil–lined rimmed baking sheet. Broil corn until well browned on 1 side, 15 to 20 minutes. Flip corn and broil until browned on opposite side, 15 to 20 minutes.
2. Meanwhile, whisk mayonnaise, queso fresco, cilantro, lime juice, garlic, chili powder, and salt in bowl until incorporated. Remove corn from oven and brush evenly on all sides with mayonnaise mixture. Season with salt and pepper to taste. Serve corn with lime wedges and any extra mayonnaise mixture.

Crab Rangoon Dip With Wonton Chips

Servings: 6
Cooking Time: 18 Minutes
Ingredients:

- Wonton Chips:
- 1 (12-ounce) package wonton wrappers
- vegetable oil
- sea salt
- Crab Rangoon Dip:
- 8 ounces cream cheese, softened
- ¾ cup sour cream
- 1 teaspoon Worcestershire sauce
- 1½ teaspoons soy sauce
- 1 teaspoon sesame oil
- ⅛ teaspoon ground cayenne pepper
- ¼ teaspoon salt
- freshly ground black pepper
- 8 ounces cooked crabmeat
- 1 cup grated white Cheddar cheese
- ⅓ cup chopped scallions
- paprika (for garnish)

Directions:

1. Cut the wonton wrappers in half diagonally to form triangles. Working in batches, lay the wonton triangles on a flat surface and brush or spray both sides with vegetable oil.
2. Preheat the toaster oven to 370°F.
3. Place about 10 to 12 wonton triangles in the air fryer oven, letting them overlap slightly. Air-fry for just 2 minutes. Transfer the wonton chips to a large bowl and season immediately with sea salt. (You'll hear the chips start to spin around in the air fryer oven when they are almost done.) Repeat with the rest of wontons (keeping those fishing hands at bay!).
4. To make the dip, combine the cream cheese, sour cream, Worcestershire sauce, soy sauce, sesame oil, cayenne pepper, salt, and freshly ground black pepper in a bowl. Mix well and then fold in the crabmeat, Cheddar cheese, and scallions.
5. Transfer the dip to a 7-inch ceramic baking pan or shallow casserole dish. Sprinkle paprika on top and cover the dish with aluminum foil. Lower the dish into the air fryer oven using a sling made of aluminum foil (fold a piece of aluminum foil into a strip about 2-inches wide by 24-inches long). Air-fry for 11 minutes. Remove the aluminum foil and air-fry for another 5 minutes to finish cooking and brown the top. Serve hot with the wonton chips.

Roasted Brussels Sprouts

Servings: 2
Cooking Time: 30 Minutes
Ingredients:

- 12 ounces brussels sprouts, trimmed and halved
- 4 teaspoons water
- 1 tablespoon extra-virgin olive oil
- ⅛ teaspoon table salt
- Pinch pepper
- Lemon wedges

Directions:

1. Adjust toaster oven rack to middle position and preheat the toaster oven to 450 degrees. Toss brussels sprouts, water, oil, salt, and pepper together on small rimmed baking sheet, then arrange cut side down on sheet in even layer.
2. Cover sheet tightly with aluminum foil and roast for 10 minutes. Remove foil and continue to roast until sprouts are browned and tender, 10 to 15 minutes. Season with salt and pepper. Serve with lemon wedges.

Foolproof Baked White Rice

Servings: 2
Cooking Time: 45 Minutes
Ingredients:

- 1¾ cups boiling water
- 1 cup long-grain white rice, rinsed
- 1 teaspoon extra-virgin olive oil
- ¼ teaspoon table salt

Directions:

1. Adjust toaster oven rack to middle position and preheat the toaster oven to 450 degrees. Combine all ingredients in 8-inch square baking dish or pan. Cover dish tightly with aluminum foil and bake until liquid is absorbed and rice is tender, 20 to 30 minutes, rotating dish halfway through baking.
2. Remove dish from oven, uncover, and fluff rice with fork, scraping up any rice that has stuck to bottom. Re-cover dish with foil and let rice sit for 10 minutes. Season with salt and pepper to taste. Serve.

Rumaki

Servings: 24
Cooking Time: 12 Minutes
Ingredients:

- 10 ounces raw chicken livers
- 1 can sliced water chestnuts, drained
- ¼ cup low-sodium teriyaki sauce
- 12 slices turkey bacon
- toothpicks

Directions:

1. Cut livers into 1½-inch pieces, trimming out tough veins as you slice.
2. Place livers, water chestnuts, and teriyaki sauce in small container with lid. If needed, add another tablespoon of teriyaki sauce to make sure livers are covered. Refrigerate for 1 hour.
3. When ready to cook, cut bacon slices in half crosswise.
4. Wrap 1 piece of liver and 1 slice of water chestnut in each bacon strip. Secure with toothpick.
5. When you have wrapped half of the livers, place them in the air fryer oven in a single layer.
6. Air-fry at 390°F for 12 minutes, until liver is done and bacon is crispy.
7. While first batch cooks, wrap the remaining livers. Repeat step 6 to cook your second batch.

Baba Ghanouj

Servings: 2
Cooking Time: 40 Minutes
Ingredients:

- 2 Small (12-ounce) purple Italian eggplant(s)
- ¼ cup Olive oil
- ¼ cup Tahini
- ½ teaspoon Ground black pepper
- ¼ teaspoon Onion powder
- ¼ teaspoon Mild smoked paprika (optional)
- Up to 1 teaspoon Table salt

Directions:

1. Preheat the toaster oven to 400°F.
2. Prick the eggplant(s) on all sides with a fork. When the machine is at temperature, set the eggplant(s) in the air fryer oven in one layer. Air-fry undisturbed for 40 minutes, or until blackened and soft.
3. Remove from the machine. Cool the eggplant(s) in the air fryer oven for 20 minutes.
4. Use a nonstick-safe spatula, and perhaps a flatware tablespoon for balance, to gently transfer the eggplant(s) to a bowl. The juices will run out. Make sure the bowl is close to the air fryer oven. Split the eggplant(s) open.
5. Scrape the soft insides of half an eggplant into a food processor. Repeat with the remaining piece(s). Add any juices from the bowl to the eggplant in the food processor, but discard the skins and stems.
6. Add the olive oil, tahini, pepper, onion powder, and smoked paprika (if using). Add about half the salt, then cover and process until smooth, stopping the machine at least once to scrape down the inside of the canister. Check the spread for salt and add more as needed. Scrape the baba ghanouj into a bowl and serve warm, or set aside at room temperature for up to 2 hours, or cover and store in the refrigerator for up to 4 days.

Crispy Wontons

Servings: 8
Cooking Time: 10 Minutes
Ingredients:

- ½ cup refried beans
- 3 tablespoons salsa
- ¼ cup canned artichoke hearts, drained and patted dry
- ¼ cup frozen spinach, defrosted and squeezed dry
- 2 ounces cream cheese
- 1½ teaspoons dried oregano, divided
- ¼ teaspoon garlic powder
- ¼ teaspoon onion powder
- ½ teaspoon salt
- ¼ cup chopped pepperoni
- ¼ cup grated mozzarella cheese
- 1 tablespoon grated Parmesan
- 2 ounces cream cheese
- ½ teaspoon dried oregano
- 32 wontons
- 1 cup water

Directions:

1. Preheat the toaster oven to 370°F.
2. In a medium bowl, mix together the refried beans and salsa.
3. In a second medium bowl, mix together the artichoke hearts, spinach, cream cheese, oregano, garlic powder, onion powder, and salt.
4. In a third medium bowl, mix together the pepperoni, mozzarella cheese, Parmesan cheese, cream cheese, and the remaining ½ teaspoon of oregano.
5. Get a towel lightly damp with water and ring it out. While working with the wontons, leave the unfilled wontons under the damp towel so they don't dry out.
6. Working with 8 wontons at a time, place 2 teaspoons of one of the fillings into the center of the wonton, rotating among the different fillings (one filling per wonton). Working one at a time, use a pastry brush, dip the pastry brush into the water, and brush the edges of the dough with the water. Fold the dough in half to form a triangle and set aside. Continue until 8 wontons are formed. Spray the wontons with cooking spray and cover with a dry towel. Repeat until all 32 wontons have been filled.
7. Place the wontons into the air fryer oven, leaving space between the wontons, and air-fry for 5 minutes. Turn over and check for brownness, and then air-fry for another 5 minutes.

Oven-fried Barbecue Chicken Wings

Servings: 2
Cooking Time: 90 Minutes
Ingredients:

- WINGS
- 1¾ pounds chicken wings, halved at joints, wingtips discarded
- 1½ teaspoons baking powder
- ¼ teaspoon table salt

- BARBECUE SAUCE
- 2 tablespoons ketchup
- 2 tablespoons water
- 2 teaspoons molasses
- 1½ teaspoons cider vinegar
- 1½ teaspoons minced canned chipotle chile in adobo sauce
- ⅛ teaspoon liquid smoke

Directions:

1. For the wings Adjust toaster oven rack to middle position and preheat the toaster oven to 250 degrees. Set small wire rack in small aluminum foil–lined rimmed baking sheet and spray rack with vegetable oil spray. Pat wings dry with paper towels. Combine baking powder and salt in large bowl, add wings, and toss to coat evenly.
2. Arrange wings skin side up in single layer on prepared wire rack. Bake wings for 30 minutes. Increase oven temperature to 450 degrees, rotate sheet, and continue to bake wings until golden brown and crisp, 25 to 30 minutes. Remove sheet from oven and let sit for 5 minutes.
3. For the barbecue sauce Meanwhile, whisk all ingredients together in clean large bowl. Add wings and toss to coat. Serve.

White Bean Gratin With Rosemary And Parmesan

Servings: 4
Cooking Time: 30 Minutes

Ingredients:

- 1 onion, chopped fine
- 2 tablespoons extra-virgin olive oil
- 3 garlic cloves, minced
- 1 teaspoon minced fresh rosemary or ¼ teaspoon dried
- 2 (15-ounce) cans white or cannellini beans, rinsed, divided
- ½ cup chicken broth
- 2 ounces Parmesan cheese, grated (1 cup)

Directions:

1. Microwave onion, oil, garlic, and rosemary in medium bowl, stirring occasionally, until onion is softened, about 5 minutes.
2. Adjust toaster oven rack to middle position, select broiler function, and heat broiler. Add ⅔ cup beans to bowl with onion mixture and mash with potato masher until smooth. Stir in broth and remaining whole beans until combined. Transfer mixture to 8-inch square broiler-safe baking dish or pan and sprinkle evenly with Parmesan. Broil until mixture is bubbling around edges and cheese is golden brown, 5 to 7 minutes. Transfer dish to wire rack and let cool slightly before serving.

Crispy Chili Kale Chips

Servings: 4
Cooking Time: 10 Minutes

Ingredients:

- 2 cups kale, stemmed and torn into 2-inch pieces
- 1 tablespoon extra-virgin olive oil
- ½ teaspoon chipotle chili powder
- Sea salt, for seasoning

Directions:

1. Preheat the toaster oven to 350°F on AIR FRY for 5 minutes.
2. Dry the kale with paper towels. Transfer the kale to a medium bowl and add the olive oil and chili powder. Toss the kale using your hands to evenly coat the leaves with the oil.
3. Place the air-fryer basket in the baking sheet and spread the kale in a single layer in the basket. You might have to cook two batches.
4. Air fry in position 2 for 5 minutes, until the leaves are crispy.
5. Transfer the kale chips to a large bowl and repeat with the remaining kale. Season the chips with salt and serve immediately.

Pork Belly Scallion Yakitori

Servings: 3
Cooking Time: 10 Minutes

Ingredients:

- ¼ cup soy sauce
- 1 tablespoons sake
- 2 tablespoons mirin
- 2 teaspoons rice wine vinegar
- 2 tablespoons dark brown sugar
- ½ teaspoon onion powder
- ¼ teaspoon garlic powder
- ¼ teaspoon kosher salt
- 1½ inch piece of ginger, peeled and roughly sliced
- 1 pound of ½-inch thick sliced pork belly, cut into 2-inch pieces
- 6 scallions
- Lemon wedges, for serving

Directions:

1. Combine soy sauce, sake, mirin, rice wine vinegar, dark brown sugar, onion powder, garlic powder, kosher salt, and ginger in a bowl.
2. Add the pork belly to the marinade and massage the marinade into the meat.
3. Cover and place into the refrigerator for 5 hours.
4. Remove from the fridge and pat the pork belly dry with paper towels. Set aside and allow to sit at room temperature for 1 hour.
5. Cut off the thinner dark green part of the scallion and discard.
6. Cut the trimmed scallions into thirds.
7. Skewer a piece of pork belly, followed by a piece of scallion, then repeat until the skewer is filled. Place the skewers onto the food tray.
8. Preheat the toaster oven to 450°F.
9. Insert the food tray with yakitori at top position in the preheated oven.
10. Select the Broil and Shake functions, then press Start/Pause.
11. Flip the yakitori halfway through cooking. The Shake Reminder will let you know when.
12. Remove when done and serve with a wedge of lemon.

Arancini With Sun-dried Tomatoes And Mozzarella

Servings: 6
Cooking Time: 15 Minutes

Ingredients:

- 1 tablespoon olive oil
- ½ small onion, finely chopped
- 1 cup Arborio rice
- ¼ cup white wine or dry vermouth
- 1 cup vegetable or chicken stock
- 1½ cups water
- 1 teaspoon salt
- freshly ground black pepper
- ⅓ cup grated Parmigiano-Reggiano cheese
- 2 to 3 ounces mozzarella cheese
- 2 eggs, lightly beaten
- ¼ cup chopped oil-packed sun-dried tomatoes
- 1½ cups Italian seasoned breadcrumbs, divided
- olive oil
- marinara sauce, for serving

Directions:

1. .Start by cooking the Arborio rice.
2. Stovetop Method: Preheat a medium saucepan over medium heat. Add the olive oil and sauté the onion until it starts to become tender – about 5 minutes. Add the rice and stir well to coat all the grains of rice. Add the white wine or vermouth. Let this simmer and get absorbed by the rice. Then add the stock and water, cover, reduce the heat to low and simmer for 20 minutes.
3. Pressure-Cooker Method: Preheat the pressure cooker using the BROWN setting. Add the oil and cook the onion for a few minutes. Add the rice, wine, stock, water, salt and freshly ground black pepper, give everything one good stir and lock the lid in place. Pressure cook on HIGH for 7 minutes. Reduce the pressure with the QUICK-RELEASE method and carefully remove the lid.
4. Taste the rice to make sure it is tender. Season with salt and freshly ground black pepper and stir in the grated Parmigiano-Reggiano cheese. Spread the rice out onto a baking sheet to cool.
5. While the rice is cooling, cut the mozzarella into ¾-inch cubes.
6. Once the rice has cooled, combine the rice with the eggs, sun-dried tomatoes and ½ cup of the breadcrumbs. Place the remaining breadcrumbs in a shallow dish. Shape the rice mixture into 12 balls. Press a hole in the rice ball with your finger and push one or two cubes of mozzarella cheese into the hole. Mold the rice back into a ball, enclosing the cheese. Roll the finished rice balls in the breadcrumbs and place them on a baking sheet while you make the remaining rice balls. Spray or brush the rice balls with olive oil.
7. Preheat the toaster oven to 380°F.
8. Cook 6 arancini at a time. Air-fry for 10 minutes. Gently turn the arancini over, brush or spray with oil again and air-fry for another 5 minutes. Serve warm with the marinara sauce.

Parmesan Crisps

Servings: 6
Cooking Time: 7 Minutes

Ingredients:

- 6 tablespoons shredded Parmesan cheese

Directions:

1. Preheat the toaster oven to 350°F on BAKE for 10 minutes.
2. Line the baking tray with a silicone mat or parchment paper.
3. Place the Parmesan by tablespoons about 2 inches apart on the tray, spreading the cheese out in an even layer about 2½ inches in diameter.
4. Place the try in position 2 and bake for 7 minutes until the edges are browned, and the cheese is no longer bubbling.
5. Remove from the oven and allow to cool on the rack for 10 minutes before serving.

Sesame Green Beans

Servings: 4
Cooking Time: 8 Minutes

Ingredients:

- 1 pound green beans, stems trimmed
- 1 tablespoon olive oil
- 1 teaspoon sesame oil
- 1 tablespoon sesame seeds
- Pinch sea salt

Directions:

1. Preheat the toaster oven to 350°F on AIR FRY for 5 minutes.
2. In a large bowl, toss the green beans, olive oil, and sesame oil.
3. Place the air-fryer basket in the baking tray and spread the beans in the basket.
4. Place the tray in position 2 and air fry for 8 minutes, shaking the basket at the halfway point. The beans should be lightly golden and fragrant.
5. Transfer the beans to a serving plate and serve topped with the sesame seeds and seasoned with salt.

Fried Wontons

Servings: 24
Cooking Time: 6 Minutes

Ingredients:

- 6 ounces Lean ground beef, pork, or turkey
- 1 tablespoon Regular or reduced-sodium soy sauce or tamari sauce
- 1½ teaspoons Minced garlic
- ¾ teaspoon Ground dried ginger
- ½ teaspoon Ground white pepper
- 24 Wonton wrappers (thawed, if necessary)
- Vegetable oil spray

Directions:

1. Preheat the toaster oven to 350°F .
2. Stir the ground meat, soy or tamari sauce, garlic, ginger, and white pepper in a bowl until the spices are uniformly distributed in the mixture.
3. Set a small bowl of water on a clean, dry surface or next to a clean, dry cutting board. Set one wonton wrapper on the

surface. Dip your clean finger in the water, then run it along the edges of the wrapper. Set 1 teaspoon of the ground meat mixture in the center of the wrapper. Fold it over, corner to corner, to create a filled triangle. Press to seal the edges, then pull the corners on the longest side up and together over the filling to create the classic wonton shape. Press the corners together to seal. Set aside and continue filling and making more filled wontons.
4. Generously coat the filled wontons on all sides with vegetable oil spray. Arrange them in the air fryer oven in one layer and air-fry for 6 minutes, at the 2- and 4-minute marks to rearrange the wontons (but always making sure they're still in one layer), until golden brown and crisp.
5. Pour the wontons in the pan onto a wire rack or even into a serving bowl. Cool for 2 or 3 minutes (but not much longer) and serve hot.

Buffalo Chicken Dip

Servings: 6
Cooking Time: 60 Minutes
Ingredients:
- 1 pound cream cheese
- ¾ cup Frank's RedHot Original Cayenne Pepper Sauce
- 3 cups shredded cooked chicken
- 1 cup ranch dressing
- 4 ounces blue cheese, crumbled (1 cup)
- 2 teaspoons Worcestershire sauce
- 4 ounces sharp cheddar cheese, shredded (1 cup)
- 2 scallions, sliced thin

Directions:
1. Adjust toaster oven rack to middle position and preheat the toaster oven to 350 degrees. Combine cream cheese and hot sauce in medium bowl and microwave until cream cheese is very soft, about 2 minutes, whisking halfway through microwaving. Whisk until smooth and no lumps of cream cheese remain. Stir in chicken, dressing, blue cheese, and Worcestershire until combined (visible bits of blue cheese are OK).
2. Transfer mixture to 2-quart baking dish and smooth top with rubber spatula. Bake for 20 minutes. Remove dish from toaster oven, stir dip, and sprinkle with cheddar. Return dish to oven and continue to bake until cheddar is melted and dip is bubbling around edges, 15 to 20 minutes longer. Transfer dish to wire rack and let cool for 10 minutes. Sprinkle with scallions and serve.

Baked Spinach + Artichoke Dip

Servings: 5
Cooking Time: 40 Minutes
Ingredients:
- Nonstick cooking spray
- 2 tablespoons unsalted butter
- ½ medium onion, chopped
- 2 cloves garlic, minced
- 5 ounces frozen, chopped loose-pack spinach (about 1 ¾ cups), thawed and squeezed dry
- 1 (13.75-ounce) can quartered artichoke hearts, drained and chopped
- 1 (8-ounce) package cream cheese, cut into cubes and softened
- ½ cup mayonnaise
- Kosher salt and freshly ground black pepper
- 2 cups shredded Colby Jack or Mexican blend cheese
- ¾ cup shredded Parmesan cheese
- Tortilla chips, pita bread triangles, carrot or celery sticks, broccoli or cauliflower florets, for dipping

Directions:
1. Preheat the toaster oven to 350°F. Spray a 2-quart casserole dish with nonstick cooking spray.
2. Melt the butter in a large skillet over medium-high heat. Add the onion and cook, stirring frequently, until tender, 3 to 5 minutes. Add the garlic and cook, stirring frequently, for 30 seconds. Remove from the heat.
3. Stir in the spinach, artichokes, cream cheese, and mayonnaise. Season with salt and pepper. Blend in the Colby Jack and Parmesan cheeses. Spoon the mixture into the prepared casserole dish. Cover and bake for 20 minutes. Stir the dip and bake, covered, for an additional 10 to 15 minutes, or until hot and melted. Serve with any of the dipping choices.

French Fries

Servings: 4
Cooking Time: 40 Minutes
Ingredients:
- 1 pound russet potatoes, scrubbed
- 2 tablespoons olive oil
- Sea salt, for seasoning
- Oil spray (hand-pumped)

Directions:
1. Cut the potatoes lengthwise into ¼-inch-wide batons (fries). Place the fries in a large bowl and cover them with cold water and set aside in the refrigerator for 1 hour.
2. Preheat the toaster oven on AIR FRY to 375°F for 5 minutes.
3. Drain the fries and pat them thoroughly with paper towels to get them as dry as possible.
4. Place the fries in a large bowl and add the olive oil. Generously season with salt.
5. Place the air-fryer basket in the baking sheet and generously spray it with oil.
6. Spread the fries in a single layer in the basket. You will have to do this in two batches. Cover the first batch loosely with foil to keep it warm while you cook the second batch.
7. In position 2, air fry for 10 minutes, then toss and cook for an additional 5 minutes until golden and crispy. If the fries are not crispy enough, cook for 5 additional minutes.
8. Repeat with the remaining fries. Serve immediately.

Spanakopita Spinach, Feta And Pine Nut Phyllo Bites

Servings: 8
Cooking Time: 10 Minutes

Ingredients:

- ½ (10-ounce) package frozen spinach, thawed and squeezed dry (about 1 cup)
- ¾ cup crumbled feta cheese
- ¼ cup grated Parmesan cheese
- ¼ cup pine nuts, toasted
- ⅛ teaspoon ground nutmeg
- 1 egg, lightly beaten
- ½ teaspoon salt
- freshly ground black pepper
- 6 sheets phyllo dough
- ½ cup butter, melted

Directions:

1. Combine the spinach, cheeses, pine nuts, nutmeg and egg in a bowl. Season with salt and freshly ground black pepper.
2. While building the phyllo triangles, always keep the dough sheets you are not working with covered with plastic wrap and a damp clean kitchen towel. Remove one sheet of the phyllo and place it on a flat surface. Brush the phyllo sheet with melted butter and then layer another sheet of phyllo on top. Brush the second sheet of phyllo with butter. Cut the layered phyllo sheets into 6 strips, about 2½- to 3-inches wide.
3. Place a heaping tablespoon of the spinach filling at the end of each strip of dough. Fold the bottom right corner of the strip over the filling towards the left edge of the strip to make a triangle. Continue to fold the phyllo dough around the spinach as you would fold a flag, making triangle after triangle. Brush the outside of the phyllo triangle with more melted butter and set it aside until you've finished the 6 strips of dough, making 6 triangles.
4. Preheat the toaster oven to 350°F.
5. Transfer the first six phyllo triangles to the air fryer oven and air-fry for 5 minutes. Turn the triangles over and air-fry for another 5 minutes.
6. While the first batch of triangles is air-frying, build another set of triangles and air-fry in the same manner. You should do three batches total. These can be warmed in the air fryer oven for a minute or two just before serving if you like.

Fried Apple Wedges

Servings: 4
Cooking Time: 9 Minutes

Ingredients:

- ¼ cup panko breadcrumbs
- ¼ cup pecans
- 1½ teaspoons cinnamon
- 1½ teaspoons brown sugar
- ¼ cup cornstarch
- 1 egg white
- 2 teaspoons water
- 1 medium apple
- oil for misting or cooking spray

Directions:

1. In a food processor, combine panko, pecans, cinnamon, and brown sugar. Process to make small crumbs.
2. Place cornstarch in a plastic bag or bowl with lid. In a shallow dish, beat together the egg white and water until slightly foamy.
3. Preheat the toaster oven to 390°F.
4. Cut apple into small wedges. The thickest edge should be no more than ⅜- to ½-inch thick. Cut away the core, but do not peel.
5. Place apple wedges in cornstarch, reseal bag or bowl, and shake to coat.
6. Dip wedges in egg wash, shake off excess, and roll in crumb mixture. Spray with oil.
7. Place apples in air fryer oven in single layer and air-fry for 5 minutes.Break apart any apples that have stuck together. Mist lightly with oil and cook 4 minutes longer, until crispy.

Thick-crust Pepperoni Pizza

Servings: 2
Cooking Time: 10 Minutes

Ingredients:

- 10 ounces Purchased fresh pizza dough (not a prebaked crust)
- Olive oil spray
- ¼ cup Purchased pizza sauce
- 10 slices Sliced pepperoni
- ⅓ cup Purchased shredded Italian 3- or 4-cheese blend

Directions:

1. Preheat the toaster oven to 400°F.
2. Generously coat the inside of a 6-inch round cake pan for a small air fryer oven, a 7-inch round cake pan for a medium air fryer oven, or an 8-inch round cake pan for a large model with olive oil spray.
3. Set the dough in the pan and press it to fill the bottom in an even, thick layer. Spread the sauce over the dough, then top with the pepperoni and cheese.
4. When the machine is at temperature, set the pan in the air fryer oven and air-fry undisturbed for 10 minutes, or until puffed, brown, and bubbling.
5. Use kitchen tongs to transfer the cake pan to a wire rack. Cool for only a minute or so. Use a spatula to loosen the pizza from the pan and lift it out and onto the rack. Continue cooling for a few minutes before cutting into wedges to serve.

Sweet And Salty Roasted Nuts

Servings: 4
Cooking Time: 20 Minutes

Ingredients:

- 1 large egg white
- 1 tablespoon water
- 3 cups raw mixed nuts (almonds, cashews, hazelnuts, pecan halves, or walnut halves)
- ¼ cup granulated sugar
- ½ teaspoon chili powder
- ¼ teaspoon ground cinnamon

- ⅛ teaspoon cayenne powder

Directions:

1. Preheat the toaster oven to 325°F on AIR FRY for 5 minutes.
2. In a medium bowl, whisk the egg white and the water until frothy.
3. Add the nuts to the bowl and toss to coat.
4. In a small bowl, stir the sugar, chili powder, cinnamon, and cayenne until well mixed. Add the sugar mixture to the nuts and toss to coat them thoroughly.
5. Place the air-fryer basket in the baking tray and spread the nuts out evenly in a single layer. Air fry in position 2 for 20 minutes, shaking the basket after 10 minutes until the nuts are golden brown and dry.
6. Cool the nuts completely on the tray and serve.

Roasted Fennel With Wine + Parmesan

Servings: 3

Cooking Time: 26 Minutes

Ingredients:

- 3 medium fennel bulbs, trimmed, cored, and cut horizontally into ⅓-inch-thick slices, reserving 2 teaspoons fronds (leaves)
- 2 ½ tablespoons olive oil, plus more for greasing
- Kosher salt and freshly ground black pepper
- 2 tablespoons dry white wine
- 3 tablespoons shredded Parmesan cheese

Directions:

1. Preheat the toaster oven to 425 °F. Lightly oil a 12 x 12-inch baking pan.
2. Arrange the fennel in a single layer on the prepared pan. Drizzle the olive oil evenly over and season with salt and pepper. Stir to blend well and arrange in a single layer. Roast for 12 minutes. Stir and roast for an additional 10 to 12 minutes, or until the fennel is brown and crisp around the edges and the largest piece is tender when pierced with the tip of a knife.
3. Carefully remove the pan from the oven. Drizzle the wine over the cooked fennel and sprinkle with the Parmesan cheese. Return to the oven and bake for an additional 2 minutes or until the cheese is melted. Sprinkle with the reserved fronds before serving warm.

Cajun Roasted Okra

Servings: 4-6

Cooking Time: 40 Minutes

Ingredients:

- 1 pound okra, tops removed and sliced in half lengthwise
- 2 Tablespoons olive oil
- 1 teaspoon Cajun seasoning
- 1/2 teaspoon black pepper
- Sea salt to taste
- Cajun Dipping Sauce

Directions:

1. Preheat the toaster oven to 450°F.
2. Line a 15X9X1-inch baking pan with aluminum foil and spray with nonstick cooking spray.
3. Place okra, olive oil, Cajun seasoning, pepper and salt in prepared pan; stir until well coated.
4. Bake 35 to 40 minutes or until okra is crisp.
5. Serve with Cajun Dipping Sauce.

Middle Eastern Phyllo Rolls

Servings: 6

Cooking Time: 5 Minutes

Ingredients:

- 6 ounces Lean ground beef or ground lamb
- 3 tablespoons Sliced almonds
- 1 tablespoon Chutney (any variety), finely chopped
- ¼ teaspoon Ground cinnamon
- ¼ teaspoon Ground coriander
- ¼ teaspoon Ground cumin
- ¼ teaspoon Ground dried turmeric
- ¼ teaspoon Table salt
- ¼ teaspoon Ground black pepper
- 6 18 × 14-inch phyllo sheets (thawed, if necessary)
- Olive oil spray

Directions:

1. Set a medium skillet over medium heat for a minute or two, then crumble in the ground meat. Air-fry for 3 minutes, stirring often, or until well browned. Stir in the almonds, chutney, cinnamon, coriander, cumin, turmeric, salt, and pepper until well combined. Remove from the heat, scrape the cooked ground meat mixture into a bowl, and cool for 15 minutes.
2. Preheat the toaster oven to 400°F.
3. Place one sheet of phyllo dough on a clean, dry work surface. (Keep the others covered.) Lightly coat it with olive oil spray, then fold it in half by bringing the short ends together. Place about 3 tablespoons of the ground meat mixture along one of the longer edges, then fold both of the shorter sides of the dough up and over the meat to partially enclose it (and become a border along the sheet of dough). Roll the dough closed, coat it with olive oil spray on all sides, and set it aside seam side down. Repeat this filling and spraying process with the remaining phyllo sheets.
4. Set the rolls seam side down in the air fryer oven in one layer with some air space between them. Air-fry undisturbed for 5 minutes, or until very crisp and golden brown.
5. Use kitchen tongs to transfer the rolls to a wire rack. Cool for only 2 or 3 minutes before serving hot.

Crispy Tofu Bites

Servings: 4

Cooking Time: 20 Minutes

Ingredients:

- 1 pound Extra firm unflavored tofu
- Vegetable oil spray

Directions:

1. Wrap the piece of tofu in a triple layer of paper towels. Place it on a wooden cutting board and set a large pot on top of it to press out excess moisture. Set aside for 10 minutes.
2. Preheat the toaster oven to 400°F.
3. Remove the pot and unwrap the tofu. Cut it into 1-inch cubes. Place these in a bowl and coat them generously with

vegetable oil spray. Toss gently, then spray generously again before tossing, until all are glistening.
4. Gently pour the tofu pieces into the air fryer oven, spread them into as close to one layer as possible, and air-fry for 20 minutes, using kitchen tongs to gently rearrange the pieces at the 7- and 14-minute marks, until light brown and crisp.
5. Gently pour the tofu pieces onto a wire rack. Cool for 5 minutes before serving warm.

Cranberry Pecan Rice Pilaf

Servings: 8
Cooking Time: 75 Minutes
Ingredients:

- Nonstick cooking spray
- 2 tablespoons unsalted butter
- 1 shallot, chopped
- ⅔ cup long-grain brown rice, rinsed and drained
- ¼ cup chopped pecans
- 1 (14.5-ounce) can reduced-sodium chicken broth
- ½ cup dried sweetened cranberries
- 2 tablespoons minced fresh flat-leaf (Italian) parsley
- 1 tablespoon minced fresh rosemary leaves or 1 teaspoon dried rosemary leaves, crumbled
- Kosher salt and freshly ground black pepper

Directions:

1. Preheat the toaster oven to 375°F. Spray a 2-quart casserole with nonstick cooking spray.
2. Melt the butter in a large skillet over medium-high heat. Add the shallot and cook, stirring frequently, for 3 minutes. Stir in the rice and cook, stirring frequently, until the rice is beginning to toast. Stir in the pecans and cook until the rice is golden brown and the pecans are toasted. Stir in the broth and ⅓ cup water. Heat until it just begins to boil. Remove from the heat and stir in the cranberries, parsley, and rosemary. Season with salt and pepper. Spoon the rice mixture into the prepared casserole dish.
3. Cover and bake for 70 to 75 minutes or until the rice is tender.

Bagel Chips

Servings: 2
Cooking Time: 4 Minutes
Ingredients:

- Sweet
- 1 large plain bagel
- 2 teaspoons sugar
- 1 teaspoon ground cinnamon
- butter-flavored cooking spray
- Savory
- 1 large plain bagel
- 1 teaspoon Italian seasoning
- ½ teaspoon garlic powder
- oil for misting or cooking spray

Directions:

1. Preheat the toaster oven to 390°F.
2. Cut bagel into ¼-inch slices or thinner.
3. Mix the seasonings together.
4. Spread out the slices, mist with oil or cooking spray, and sprinkle with half of the seasonings.
5. Turn over and repeat to coat the other side with oil or cooking spray and seasonings.
6. Place in air fryer oven and air-fry for 2 minutes. Stir a little and continue cooking for 2 minutes or until toasty brown and crispy.

Fried Green Tomatoes

Servings: 4
Cooking Time: 15 Minutes
Ingredients:

- 2 eggs
- ¼ cup buttermilk
- ½ cup cornmeal
- ½ cup breadcrumbs
- ¼ teaspoon salt
- 1½ pounds firm green tomatoes, cut in ¼-inch slices
- oil for misting or cooking spray
- Horseradish Drizzle
- ¼ cup mayonnaise
- ¼ cup sour cream
- 2 teaspoons prepared horseradish
- ½ teaspoon Worcestershire sauce
- ½ teaspoon lemon juice
- ⅛ teaspoon black pepper

Directions:

1. Mix all ingredients for Horseradish Drizzle together and chill while you prepare the green tomatoes.
2. Preheat the toaster oven to 390°F.
3. Beat the eggs and buttermilk together in a shallow bowl.
4. Mix cornmeal, breadcrumbs, and salt together in a plate or shallow dish.
5. Dip 4 tomato slices in the egg mixture, then roll in the breadcrumb mixture.
6. Mist one side with oil and place in air fryer oven, oil-side down, in a single layer.
7. Mist the top with oil.
8. Air-fry for 15 minutes, turning once, until brown and crispy.
9. Repeat steps 5 through 8 to cook remaining tomatoes.
10. Drizzle horseradish sauce over tomatoes just before serving.

Pork Pot Stickers With Yum Yum Sauce

Servings: 48
Cooking Time: 8 Minutes
Ingredients:

- 1 pound ground pork
- 2 cups shredded green cabbage
- ¼ cup shredded carrot
- ½ cup finely chopped water chestnuts
- 2 teaspoons minced fresh ginger
- ¼ cup hoisin sauce
- 2 tablespoons soy sauce
- 1 tablespoon sesame oil
- freshly ground black pepper

- 3 scallions, minced
- 48 round dumpling wrappers (or wonton wrappers with the corners cut off to make them round)
- 1 tablespoon vegetable oil
- soy sauce, for serving
- Yum Yum Sauce:
- 1½ cups mayonnaise
- 2 tablespoons sugar
- 3 tablespoons rice vinegar
- 1 teaspoon soy sauce
- 2 tablespoons ketchup
- 1½ teaspoons paprika
- ¼ teaspoon ground cayenne pepper
- ¼ teaspoon garlic powder

Directions:

1. Preheat a large sauté pan over medium-high heat. Add the ground pork and brown for a few minutes. Remove the cooked pork to a bowl using a slotted spoon and discard the fat from the pan. Return the cooked pork to the sauté pan and add the cabbage, carrots and water chestnuts. Sauté for a minute and then add the fresh ginger, hoisin sauce, soy sauce, sesame oil, and freshly ground black pepper. Sauté for a few more minutes, just until cabbage and carrots are soft. Then stir in the scallions and transfer the pork filling to a bowl to cool.
2. Make the pot stickers in batches of 1 Place 12 dumpling wrappers on a flat surface. Brush a little water around the perimeter of the wrappers. Place a rounded teaspoon of the filling into the center of each wrapper. Fold the wrapper over the filling, bringing the edges together to form a half moon, sealing the edges shut. Brush a little more water on the top surface of the sealed edge of the pot sticker. Make pleats in the dough around the sealed edge by pinching the dough and folding the edge over on itself. You should have about 5 to 6 pleats in the dough. Repeat this three times until you have 48 pot stickers. Freeze the pot stickers for 2 hours (or as long as 3 weeks in an airtight container).
3. Preheat the toaster oven to 400°F.
4. Air-fry the pot stickers in batches of 16. Brush or spray the pot stickers with vegetable oil just before putting them in the air fryer oven. Air-fry for 8 minutes, turning the pot stickers once or twice during the cooking process.
5. While the pot stickers are cooking, combine all the ingredients for the Yum Yum sauce in a bowl. Serve the pot stickers warm with the Yum Yum sauce and soy sauce for dipping.

Sweet Chili– Glazed Wings

Servings: 4
Cooking Time: 27 Minutes

Ingredients:

- 1 pound chicken wing drumettes
- ½ cup reduced-sodium soy sauce
- 3 tablespoons honey
- 3 tablespoons unseasoned rice vinegar
- 1 tablespoon sesame oil
- 1 ½ teaspoons chili garlic paste
- ¼ teaspoon freshly ground black pepper
- ¼ cup jarred Asian sweet chili sauce

Directions:

1. Place the chicken drumettes in a deep bowl. Stir the soy sauce, honey, rice vinegar, sesame oil, chili garlic paste, and pepper in a small bowl. Pour the soy sauce mixture over the chicken. Cover the bowl and refrigerate for several hours or overnight.
2. Preheat the toaster oven to 375°F. Line a 12 x 12-inch baking pan with aluminum foil.
3. Drain and discard the marinade. Pat the chicken dry and arrange in a single layer in the prepared pan. Bake, uncovered, for 18 to 20 minutes or until lightly browned and almost done.
4. Brush the chicken with the sweet chili sauce, turning to coat evenly. Bake for 6 to 7 minutes or until the chicken is done, a meat thermometer registers 165°F, and the edges are beginning to crisp.

Cheesy Zucchini Squash Casserole

Servings: 12-14
Cooking Time: 30 Minutes

Ingredients:

- 1 Tablespoon olive oil
- 1 medium sweet onion, halved and thinly sliced
- 1 garlic clove, minced
- 1 pound zucchini, thinly sliced
- 1 pound yellow squash, thinly sliced
- 1 large egg
- 1/2 cup sour cream
- 1 cup shredded Cheddar cheese
- 1 cup shredded Swiss cheese
- 1 teaspoon thyme
- 1 teaspoon salt
- 1/2 teaspoon black pepper
- 3/4 cup seasoned panko crumbs
- 1 Tablespoon butter, melted

Directions:

1. Preheat the toaster oven to 350°F.
2. Heat olive oil in large skillet over medium-high heat. Add onion and garlic; cook 2 minutes. Stir in zucchini and yellow squash, cooking an additional 4 minutes or until squash is tender.
3. Beat egg and sour cream in large bowl until well blended. Stir in squash mixture, cheeses, thyme, salt and pepper. Pour into 8x8-inch baking dish.
4. Stir crumbs and butter in small bowl. Sprinkle over squash mixture.
5. Bake 25 to 30 minutes or until crumbs are golden brown and mixture is heated through.

Loaded Cauliflower Casserole

Servings: 6
Cooking Time: 35 Minutes

Ingredients:

- Nonstick cooking spray
- 1 cup heavy cream
- 4 tablespoons unsalted butter
- 3 cloves garlic, minced

- 1 teaspoon fresh thyme leaves
- ¾ teaspoon kosher salt
- ¼ teaspoon freshly ground black pepper
- 6 cups cauliflower florets (a medium head)
- ½ cup finely chopped sweet or yellow onion
- 2 cups shredded white cheddar cheese
- 1 ½ cups fresh coarse bread crumbs
- 2 tablespoons sesame seeds
- 3 tablespoons unsalted butter, melted

Directions:

1. Preheat the toaster oven to 425 ºF. Spray a 9-inch deep-dish pie plate or 9-inch cake pan with nonstick cooking spray.
2. Bring the cream, butter, garlic, thyme, salt, and pepper to a simmer in a small saucepan over medium heat. Remove from the heat.
3. Place half of the cauliflower into the prepared pan. Sprinkle with half of the onion and half of the cheese. Repeat with the remaining cauliflower, onion, and cheese. Pour the cream mixture over all. Cover and bake until the cauliflower is tender and cooked through, about 20 minutes.
4. Remove the foil and bake for an additional 15 minutes, or until the top is bubbly and beginning to turn golden.
5. Combine the bread crumbs, sesame seeds, and melted butter in a small bowl. Sprinkle over the top and bake for an additional 15 minutes or until golden.

Sausage Cheese Pinwheels

Servings: 16
Cooking Time: 22 Minutes

Ingredients:

- 1 sheet frozen puff pastry, about 9 inches square, thawed (½ of a 17.3-ounce package)
- ½ pound bulk sausage
- ¾ cup shredded cheddar cheese

Directions:

1. Preheat the toaster oven to 400°F. Grease a 12 x 12-inch baking pan.
2. Unfold the puff pastry on a lightly floured surface and roll into a 10 x 12-inch rectangle. Carefully spread the sausage over the surface of the rectangle to within ½ inch of all four edges. Sprinkle the cheese evenly over the sausage. Starting with the long side, roll up tightly and press the edges to seal.
3. Using a serrated knife, slice the roll into ½-inch-thick pieces. You will get about 16 slices. Place the slices, cut side up, in the prepared baking pan. Bake for 18 to 22 minutes or until golden and the sausage is cooked through.
4. Serve warm or at room temperature.

Cheese Straws

Servings: 8
Cooking Time: 7 Minutes

Ingredients:

- For dusting All-purpose flour
- Two quarters of one thawed sheet (that is, a half of the sheet cut into two even pieces; wrap and refreeze the remainder) A 17.25-ounce box frozen puff pastry
- 1 Large egg(s)
- 2 tablespoons Water
- ¼ cup (about ¾ ounce) Finely grated Parmesan cheese
- up to 1 teaspoon Ground black pepper

Directions:

1. Preheat the toaster oven to 400°F.
2. Dust a clean, dry work surface with flour. Set one of the pieces of puff pastry on top, dust the pastry lightly with flour, and roll with a rolling pin to a 6-inch square.
3. Whisk the egg(s) and water in a small or medium bowl until uniform. Brush the pastry square(s) generously with this mixture. Sprinkle each square with 2 tablespoons grated cheese and up to ½ teaspoon ground black pepper.
4. Cut each square into 4 even strips. Grasp each end of 1 strip with clean, dry hands; twist it into a cheese straw. Place the twisted straws on a baking sheet.
5. Lay as many straws as will fit in the air-fryer oven—as a general rule, 4 of them in a small machine, 5 in a medium model, or 6 in a large. There should be space for air to circulate around the straws. Set the baking sheet with any remaining straws in the fridge.
6. Air-fry undisturbed for 7 minutes, or until puffed and crisp. Use tongs to transfer the cheese straws to a wire rack, then make subsequent batches in the same way (keeping the baking sheet with the remaining straws in the fridge as each batch cooks). Serve warm.

Creamy Scalloped Potatoes

Servings: 4
Cooking Time: 58 Minutes

Ingredients:

- Oil spray (hand-pumped)
- 2 tablespoons salted butter
- 1 small onion, finely chopped
- 1 teaspoon minced garlic
- 2 tablespoons all-purpose flour
- 1 cup whole milk
- ½ cup low-sodium chicken broth
- ¼ teaspoon ground nutmeg
- ⅛ teaspoon sea salt
- ⅛ teaspoon freshly ground black pepper
- 1½ pounds russet potatoes, cut into ⅛-inch-thick slices

Directions:

1. Place the rack on position 1 and preheat the toaster oven on BAKE to 350°F for 5 minutes.
2. Lightly spray an 8-inch-square baking dish with oil and set aside.
3. Melt the butter in a medium saucepan over medium-high heat. Sauté the onion and garlic in the butter until softened, about 4 minutes. Add the flour and cook, whisking, for 1 minute.
4. Whisk in the milk and chicken broth until well blended and cook, whisking constantly, until thickened, about 3 minutes. Remove the sauce from the heat and whisk in the nutmeg, salt, and pepper. Set aside.
5. Layer one-third of the potato slices in the baking dish and top with one-third of the sauce. Repeat the layering in thirds, ending with the cream sauce.
6. Cover the dish with aluminum foil and bake for 25 minutes. Remove the foil and bake for an additional 25

minutes until golden brown and the potatoes are tender. Serve.

Roasted Pumpkin Seeds

Servings: 2-4
Cooking Time: 50 Minutes
Ingredients:

- 1 medium pumpkin
- 1 tablespoon vegetable oil
- Salt

Directions:

1. Preheat the toaster oven to 300°F. Line a baking sheet with parchment paper. Set aside.
2. Cut the top from the pumpkin. Using a large spoon, scrape out the pulp and seeds from the pumpkin and place in a colander or strainer.
3. Separate the pulp and strings from seeds. Rinse seeds and pat dry with paper towels.
4. Spread the seeds on the prepared baking sheet.
5. Bake until the seeds are dry, about 30 minutes.
6. In a small bowl, toss seeds with oil and salt. Bake until seeds are toasted, an additional 15 to 20 minutes.

Cherry Chipotle Bbq Chicken Wings

Servings: 2
Cooking Time: 12 Minutes
Ingredients:

- 1 teaspoon smoked paprika
- ½ teaspoon dry mustard powder
- 1 teaspoon dried oregano
- 1 teaspoon dried thyme
- ½ teaspoon chili powder
- 1 teaspoon salt
- 2 pounds chicken wings
- vegetable oil or spray
- salt and freshly ground black pepper
- 1 to 2 tablespoons chopped chipotle peppers in adobo sauce
- ⅓ cup cherry preserves ¼ cup tomato ketchup

Directions:

1. Combine the first six ingredients in a large bowl. Prepare the chicken wings by cutting off the wing tips and discarding (or freezing for chicken stock). Divide the drumettes from the win-gettes by cutting through the joint. Place the chicken wing pieces in the bowl with the spice mix. Toss or shake well to coat.
2. Preheat the toaster oven to 400°F.
3. Spray the wings lightly with the vegetable oil and air-fry the wings in two batches for 10 minutes per batch. When both batches are done, toss all the wings back into the air fryer oven for another 2 minutes to heat through and finish cooking.
4. While the wings are air-frying, combine the chopped chipotle peppers, cherry preserves and ketchup in a bowl.
5. Remove the wings from the air fryer oven, toss them in the cherry chipotle BBQ sauce and serve with napkins!

Rosemary Roasted Vegetables

Servings: 4
Cooking Time: 25 Minutes
Ingredients:

- 3 tablespoons olive oil
- Grated zest and juice of 1 lemon
- 2 tablespoons chopped fresh rosemary leaves
- 4 cloves garlic, minced
- Kosher salt and freshly ground black pepper
- 6 cups vegetables, diced, such as bell peppers, onions, zucchini, mushrooms, cherry tomatoes, potatoes, and eggplant

Directions:

1. Preheat the toaster oven to 425 ºF.
2. Stir the olive oil, lemon zest, lemon juice, rosemary, and garlic in a small bowl. Season with salt and pepper. Place the vegetables into a large bowl and drizzle the olive oil mixture over all. Stir gently to coat.
3. Arrange the vegetables in a single layer in a 12 x 12-inch baking pan. Roast for 10 minutes. Stir and roast for an additional 10 to 15 minutes, or until the vegetables are tender.

All-purpose Cornbread

Servings: 6
Cooking Time: 60 Minutes
Ingredients:

- 1½ cups (7½ ounces) all-purpose flour
- 1 cup (5 ounces) cornmeal
- 2 teaspoons baking powder
- ¼ teaspoon baking soda
- ¾ teaspoon table salt
- ¼ cup packed (1¾ ounces) light brown sugar
- ¾ cup frozen corn, thawed
- 1 cup buttermilk
- 2 large eggs
- 8 tablespoons unsalted butter, melted and cooled

Directions:

1. Adjust toaster oven rack to middle position and preheat the toaster oven to 400 degrees. Spray 8-inch square baking dish or pan with vegetable oil spray. Whisk flour, cornmeal, baking powder, baking soda, and salt together in medium bowl; set aside.
2. Process sugar, corn, and buttermilk in food processor until combined, about 5 seconds. Add eggs and process until well combined (corn lumps will remain), about 5 seconds.
3. Using rubber spatula, make well in center of dry ingredients; pour wet ingredients into well. Begin folding dry ingredients into wet, giving mixture only a few turns to barely combine. Add melted butter and continue to fold until dry ingredients are just moistened. Transfer batter to prepared dish and smooth top.
4. Bake until deep golden brown and toothpick inserted in center comes out clean, 25 to 35 minutes. Let cornbread cool in dish on wire rack for 10 minutes. Remove bread from dish and let cool until just warm, about 10 minutes longer. Serve. (Cornbread can be wrapped in aluminum foil and reheated in 350-degree oven for 10 to 15 minutes.)

Creamy Crab Dip

Servings: 4
Cooking Time: 20 Minutes

Ingredients:

- 6 ounces cream cheese, room temperature
- ½ cup sour cream
- ½ cup grated Parmesan cheese
- ½ cup shredded cheddar cheese
- Juice of ½ lemon
- ½ teaspoon garlic powder
- Dash hot sauce
- 1 (6-ounce) can crab meat, drained
- Sea salt, for seasoning
- Freshly ground black pepper, for seasoning
- Baguette, cut into ¼-inch-wide rounds, for serving

Directions:

1. Place the rack on position 1 and preheat the toaster oven on BAKE to 400°F for 5 minutes.
2. In a medium bowl, stir the cream cheese, sour cream, Parmesan, cheddar, lemon juice, garlic powder, and hot sauce until well blended.
3. Fold in the crab and season with salt and pepper.
4. Spoon the dip into a shallow heatproof 4-cup bowl.
5. Bake for 20 minutes until golden and bubbling.
6. Serve with baguette slices.

Wonton Cups

Servings: 6
Cooking Time: 10 Minutes

Ingredients:

- 6 wonton wrappers (3-inch squares)
- 2 Tablespoons melted butter
- Filling of choice

Directions:

1. Preheat toaster oven to 350°F.
2. Carefully press and fold one wonton wrapper in each cup of a 6-cup muffin pan.
3. Very lightly brush edges of wrappers with butter.
4. Bake 8 to 10 minutes or until golden brown.

Broiled Maryland Crabcakes With Creamy Herb Sauce

Servings: 8-9
Cooking Time: 8 Minutes

Ingredients:

- 1 large egg
- 3 Tablespoons mayonnaise
- 1 Tablespoon brown mustard
- 1 Tablespoon all-purpose flour
- 1 teaspoon seafood seasoning
- 1/2 teason salt
- 1/4 teaspoon ground black pepper
- 1 pound lump crabmeat
- 1/4 cup chopped parsley
- 1 small shallot, minced
- 1 garlic clove, minced
- Creamy Herb Sauce

Directions:

1. In a medium bowl, mix egg, mayonnaise, mustard, flour, seafood seasoning, salt and pepper until well blended.
2. Stir in crabmeat, parsley, shallots and garlic until crab is coated with mayonnaise mixture.
3. Place 1/4 cup crab mixture on broiler pan; lightly press down. Repeat with remaining mixture.
4. Set toaster oven on BROIL. Broil crabcakes 8 minutes, without turning.
5. Serve with Creamy Herb Sauce.

Firecracker Bites

Servings: 20
Cooking Time: 15 Minutes

Ingredients:

- 1 sleeve saltine crackers (about 43)
- ¼ cup canola or vegetable oil
- 1 tablespoon dried parsley flakes
- 1 teaspoon dried dill
- 1 teaspoon garlic powder or granulated garlic
- 1 teaspoon onion powder
- ½ teaspoon freshly ground black pepper
- ½ teaspoon seasoned salt
- 2 teaspoons red pepper flakes

Directions:

1. Place the crackers in a zip-top bag.
2. Combine the canola oil, parsley, dill, garlic powder, onion powder, pepper, salt, and red pepper flakes in a small bowl. Pour the oil-seasoning mixture over the crackers and turn the bag over to allow the mixture to permeate all the crackers. Turn the bag frequently for about 15 minutes.
3. Preheat the toaster oven to 250°F.
4. Place the crackers evenly in a 12 x 12-inch baking pan. Bake for 15 minutes. Let the crackers cool completely. These will keep for several weeks in a sealed container.

Breaded Zucchini

Servings: 4
Cooking Time: 10 Minutes

Ingredients:

- 1 cup all-purpose flour
- 2 large eggs
- 1½ cups panko bread crumbs
- ½ cup grated Parmesan cheese
- Sea salt, for seasoning
- Freshly ground black pepper, for seasoning
- Oil spray (hand-pumped)
- 2 zucchini, cut into ¼-inch slices

Directions:

1. Preheat the toaster oven on AIR FRY to 350°F for 5 minutes.
2. Sprinkle the flour onto a plate.
3. In a small bowl, beat the eggs and place the bowl next to the flour.
4. In a medium bowl, stir the bread crumbs and cheese and season the mixture with salt and pepper. Place the bowl next to the eggs.
5. Place the air-fryer basket on the baking sheet and generously spray the rack with oil.

6. Dredge a zucchini slice in the flour, then the eggs, then the bread crumb mixture until well coated. Place the slice in the basket and repeat with the remaining zucchini slices. Spray the slices on both sides with oil.
7. In position 2, air fry for 10 minutes, turning once at 5 minutes, until golden brown and crispy. Serve immediately.

Cauliflower "tater" Tots

Servings: 6
Cooking Time: 10 Minutes
Ingredients:

- 1 head of cauliflower
- 2 eggs
- ¼ cup all-purpose flour
- ½ cup grated Parmesan cheese
- 1 teaspoon salt
- freshly ground black pepper
- vegetable or olive oil, in a spray bottle

Directions:
1. Grate the head of cauliflower with a box grater or finely chop it in a food processor. You should have about 3½ cups. Place the chopped cauliflower in the center of a clean kitchen towel and twist the towel tightly to squeeze all the water out of the cauliflower. (This can be done in two batches to make it easier to drain all the water from the cauliflower.)
2. Place the squeezed cauliflower in a large bowl. Add the eggs, flour, Parmesan cheese, salt and freshly ground black pepper. Shape the cauliflower into small cylinders or "tater tot" shapes, rolling roughly one tablespoon of the mixture at a time. Place the tots on a cookie sheet lined with paper towel to absorb any residual moisture. Spray the cauliflower tots all over with oil.
3. Preheat the toaster oven to 400°F.
4. Air-fry the tots at 400°F, one layer at a time for 10 minutes, turning them over for the last few minutes of the cooking process for even browning. Season with salt and black pepper. Serve hot with your favorite dipping sauce.

Sweet Potato Casserole

Servings: 4
Cooking Time: 90 Minutes
Ingredients:

- 2 tablespoons packed brown sugar, divided
- ½ teaspoon grated orange zest, divided, plus 1 tablespoon juice
- 1½ pounds sweet potatoes, peeled and cut into 1½-inch pieces
- 2 tablespoons unsalted butter, cut into 4 pieces
- 2 tablespoons heavy cream
- ½ teaspoon table salt
- ¼ teaspoon ground cinnamon
- ⅛ teaspoon pepper
- Pinch cayenne pepper

Directions:
1. Adjust toaster oven rack to middle position and preheat the toaster oven to 400 degrees. Mix 4 teaspoons sugar and ¼ teaspoon orange zest in small bowl until thoroughly combined; set aside.
2. Toss sweet potatoes and remaining 2 teaspoons sugar together in bowl, then spread into even layer on aluminum foil–lined small rimmed baking sheet. Cover sheet tightly with foil and roast until sweet potatoes are tender, 45 to 60 minutes, rotating sheet halfway through roasting. Remove sheet from oven, select broiler function, and heat broiler.
3. Transfer potatoes and any accumulated liquid to food processor. Add butter, cream, salt, cinnamon, pepper, cayenne, remaining ¼ teaspoon orange zest, and orange juice and process until completely smooth, 30 to 60 seconds, scraping down sides of bowl as needed.
4. Transfer potato puree to 8-inch square broiler-safe baking dish or pan and sprinkle evenly with reserved sugar-zest mixture. Broil sweet potatoes until topping is melted and beginning to caramelize, 10 to 12 minutes. Transfer dish to wire rack and let cool for 10 minutes. Serve.

Buffalo Cauliflower

Servings: 4
Cooking Time: 30 Minutes
Ingredients:

- 1 cup gluten free panko breadcrumbs
- 1 teaspoon ground paprika
- ½ teaspoon garlic powder
- ¼ teaspoon onion powder
- ½ teaspoon cayenne pepper
- 1 teaspoon kosher salt
- ½ teaspoon freshly ground black pepper
- 1 head cauliflower, cut into florets
- 2 tablespoons cornstarch
- 3 eggs, beaten
- Cooking spray
- ¾ cup buffalo wing sauce, warm
- Ranch or bleu cheese dressing, for serving

Directions:
1. Combine panko breadcrumbs, paprika, garlic powder, onion powder, cayenne pepper, kosher salt, and black pepper in a large bowl. Set aside.
2. Toss together cauliflower and cornstarch until the cauliflower is lightly coated.
3. Shake any excess cornstarch off the cauliflower, then dip into beaten eggs, then into seasoned breadcrumbs.
4. Spray the breaded cauliflower with cooking spray, place into the fry basket, and set aside. You may need to work in batches.
5. Preheat the toaster oven to 380°F.
6. Insert the fry basket with the cauliflower at top position in the preheated oven.
7. Select the Air Fry and Shake functions, adjust time to 30 minutes, and press Start/Pause.
8. Flip the cauliflower halfway through cooking. The Shake Reminder will let you know when.
9. Remove when done and place into a large bowl.
10. Toss the cauliflower in the buffalo wing sauce until they are well coated.
11. Serve with a side of ranch or blue cheese dressing.

Cuban Sliders

Servings: 8
Cooking Time: 8 Minutes
Ingredients:

- 8 slices ciabatta bread, ¼-inch thick
- cooking spray
- 1 tablespoon brown mustard
- 6-8 ounces thin sliced leftover roast pork
- 4 ounces thin deli turkey
- ⅓ cup bread and butter pickle slices
- 2–3 ounces Pepper Jack cheese slices

Directions:

1. Spray one side of each slice of bread with butter or olive oil cooking spray.
2. Spread brown mustard on other side of each slice.
3. Layer pork roast, turkey, pickles, and cheese on 4 of the slices. Top with remaining slices.
4. Air-fry at 390°F for approximately 8 minutes. The sandwiches should be golden brown.
5. Cut each slider in half to make 8 portions.

Vegetables And Vegetarian

Roasted Herbed Shiitake Mushrooms

Servings: 5
Cooking Time: 4 Minutes
Ingredients:

- 8 ounces shiitake mushrooms, stems removed and caps roughly chopped
- 1 tablespoon olive oil
- ½ teaspoon salt
- freshly ground black pepper
- 1 teaspoon chopped fresh thyme leaves
- 1 teaspoon chopped fresh oregano
- 1 tablespoon chopped fresh parsley

Directions:

1. Preheat the toaster oven to 400°F.
2. Toss the mushrooms with the olive oil, salt, pepper, thyme and oregano. Air-fry for 5 minutes. The mushrooms will still be somewhat chewy with a meaty texture. If you'd like them a little more tender, add a couple of minutes to this cooking time.
3. Once cooked, add the parsley to the mushrooms and toss. Season again to taste and serve.

Crunchy Roasted Potatoes

Servings: 5
Cooking Time: 25 Minutes
Ingredients:

- 2 pounds Small (1- to 1½-inch-diameter) red, white, or purple potatoes
- 2 tablespoons Olive oil
- 2 teaspoons Table salt
- ¾ teaspoon Garlic powder
- ½ teaspoon Ground black pepper

Directions:

1. Preheat the toaster oven to 400°F.
2. Toss the potatoes, oil, salt, garlic powder, and pepper in a large bowl until the spuds are evenly and thoroughly coated.
3. When the machine is at temperature, pour the potatoes into the air fryer oven, spreading them into an even layer (although they may be stacked on top of each other). Air-fry for 25 minutes, tossing twice, until the potatoes are tender but crunchy.
4. Pour the contents of the air fryer oven into a serving bowl. Cool for 5 minutes before serving.

Glazed Carrots

Servings: 4
Cooking Time: 10 Minutes
Ingredients:

- 2 teaspoons honey
- 1 teaspoon orange juice
- ½ teaspoon grated orange rind
- ⅛ teaspoon ginger
- 1 pound baby carrots
- 2 teaspoons olive oil
- ¼ teaspoon salt

Directions:

1. Combine honey, orange juice, grated rind, and ginger in a small bowl and set aside.
2. Toss the carrots, oil, and salt together to coat well and pour them into the air fryer oven.
3. Air-fry at 390°F for 5 minutes. Stir a little and air-fry for 4 minutes more, until carrots are barely tender.
4. Pour carrots into air fryer oven baking pan.
5. Stir the honey mixture to combine well, pour glaze over carrots, and stir to coat.

6. Air-fry at 360°F for 1 minute or just until heated through.

Classic Baked Potatoes

Servings: 4
Cooking Time: 50 Minutes
Ingredients:

- 4 medium baking potatoes,
- scrubbed and pierced with a fork

Directions:

1. Preheat the toaster oven to 450° F.
2. BAKE the potatoes on the oven rack for 50 minutes, or until tender when pierced with a fork.

Parmesan Asparagus

Servings: 2
Cooking Time: 5 Minutes
Ingredients:

- 1 bunch asparagus, stems trimmed
- 1 teaspoon olive oil
- salt and freshly ground black pepper
- ¼ cup coarsely grated Parmesan cheese
- ½ lemon

Directions:

1. Preheat the toaster oven to 400°F.
2. Toss the asparagus with the oil and season with salt and freshly ground black pepper.
3. Transfer the asparagus to the air fryer oven and air-fry at 400°F for 5 minutes, turn the asparagus once or twice during the cooking process.
4. When the asparagus is cooked to your liking, sprinkle the asparagus generously with the Parmesan cheese and close the air fryer oven again. Let the asparagus sit for 1 minute in the turned-off air fryer oven. Then, remove the asparagus, transfer it to a serving dish and finish with a grind of black pepper and a squeeze of lemon juice.

Salt And Pepper Baked Potatoes

Servings: 40
Cooking Time: 4 Minutes
Ingredients:

- 1 to 2 tablespoons olive oil
- 4 medium russet potatoes (about 9 to 10 ounces each)
- salt and coarsely ground black pepper
- butter, sour cream, chopped fresh chives, scallions or bacon bits (optional)

Directions:

1. Preheat the toaster oven to 400°F.
2. Rub the olive oil all over the potatoes and season them generously with salt and coarsely ground black pepper. Pierce all sides of the potatoes several times with the tines of a fork.
3. Air-fry for 40 minutes, turning the potatoes over halfway through the cooking time.
4. Serve the potatoes, split open with butter, sour cream, fresh chives, scallions or bacon bits.

Potato Shells With Cheese And Bacon

Servings: 4
Cooking Time: 8 Minutes
Ingredients:

- 4 tablespoons shredded reduced-fat cheddar cheese
- 4 slices lean turkey bacon, cooked and crumbled
- 4 potato shells
- 4 tablespoons nonfat sour cream
- 4 teaspoons chopped fresh or frozen chives
- Salt and freshly ground black pepper

Directions:

1. Sprinkle 1 tablespoon Cheddar cheese and 1 tablespoon crumbled bacon into each potato shell. Place the shells on a broiling rack with a pan underneath.
2. BROIL for 8 minutes, or until the cheese is melted and the shells lightly browned. Spoon 1 tablespoon sour cream into each shell and sprinkle with 1 teaspoon chives. Add salt and pepper to taste.

Honey-roasted Parsnips

Servings: 3
Cooking Time: 23 Minutes
Ingredients:

- 1½ pounds Medium parsnips, peeled
- Olive oil spray
- 1 tablespoon Honey
- 1½ teaspoons Water
- ¼ teaspoon Table salt

Directions:

1. Preheat the toaster oven to 350°F .
2. If the thick end of a parsnip is more than ½ inch in diameter, cut the parsnip just below where it swells to its large end, then slice the large section in half lengthwise. Generously coat the parsnips on all sides with olive oil spray.
3. When the machine is at temperature, set the parsnips in the air fryer oven with as much air space between them as possible. Air-fry undisturbed for 20 minutes.
4. Whisk the honey, water, and salt in a small bowl until smooth. Brush this mixture over the parsnips. Air-fry undisturbed for 3 minutes more, or until the glaze is lightly browned.
5. Use kitchen tongs to transfer the parsnips to a wire rack or a serving platter. Cool for a couple of minutes before serving.

Baked Stuffed Acorn Squash

Servings: 2
Cooking Time: 25 Minutes
Ingredients:

- Stuffing:
- ¼ cup multigrain bread crumbs
- 1 tablespoon olive oil
- ¼ cup canned or frozen thawed corn
- 2 tablespoons chopped onion
- 1 teaspoon capers
- 1 teaspoon garlic powder
- Salt and freshly ground black pepper
- 1 medium acorn squash, halved and seeds scooped out

Directions:

1. Preheat the toaster oven to 400° F.

2. Combine the stuffing ingredients and season to taste. Fill the squash cavities with the mixture and place in an oiled or nonstick 8½ × 8½ × 2-inch square baking (cake) pan.
3. BAKE for 25 minutes, or until the squash is tender and the stuffing is lightly browned.

Lentil "meat" Loaf

Servings: 4
Cooking Time: 55 Minutes
Ingredients:
- Oil spray (hand-pumped)
- 2 (14-ounce) cans low-sodium lentils, drained and rinsed
- ½ sweet onion, chopped
- 1 carrot, shredded
- 1 teaspoon minced garlic
- 1½ cups seasoned bread crumbs
- ½ cup vegetable broth
- 3 tablespoons tomato paste
- ¼ teaspoon sea salt
- ⅛ teaspoon freshly ground black pepper
- 3 tablespoons ketchup
- 2 tablespoons maple syrup
- 1 tablespoon apple cider vinegar

Directions:
1. Place the rack in position 1 and preheat oven to 375°F on BAKE for 5 minutes.
2. Lightly coat a 9-by-5-inch loaf pan with oil spray.
3. Place the lentils, onion, carrot, and garlic in a food processor and pulse until very well mixed. Transfer the mixture to a large bowl and add the bread crumbs, vegetable broth, tomato paste, salt, and pepper. Mix well. If the mixture doesn't hold together, add vegetable broth by tablespoons until it does.
4. Press the lentil mixture into the loaf pan.
5. In a small bowl, stir the ketchup, maple syrup, and vinegar together. Spread the glaze over the lentil loaf.
6. Bake for 55 minutes until lightly browned. Serve.

Zucchini Boats With Ham And Cheese

Servings: 4
Cooking Time: 12 Minutes
Ingredients:
- 2 6-inch-long zucchini
- 2 ounces Thinly sliced deli ham, any rind removed, meat roughly chopped
- 4 Dry-packed sun-dried tomatoes, chopped
- ⅓ cup Purchased pesto
- ¼ cup Packaged mini croutons
- ¼ cup (about 1 ounce) Shredded semi-firm mozzarella cheese

Directions:
1. Preheat the toaster oven to 375°F .
2. Split the zucchini in half lengthwise and use a flatware spoon or a serrated grapefruit spoon to scoop out the insides of the halves, leaving at least a ¼-inch border all around the zucchini half. (You can save the scooped out insides to add to soups and stews—or even freeze it for a much later use.)
3. Mix the ham, sun-dried tomatoes, pesto, croutons, and half the cheese in a bowl until well combined. Pack this mixture into the zucchini "shells." Top them with the remaining cheese.
4. Set them stuffing side up in the air fryer oven without touching (even a fraction of an inch between them is enough room). Air-fry undisturbed for 12 minutes, or until softened and browned, with the cheese melted on top.
5. Use a nonstick-safe spatula to transfer the zucchini boats stuffing side up on a wire rack. Cool for 5 or 10 minutes before serving.

Wilted Brussels Sprout Slaw

Servings: 4
Cooking Time: 18 Minutes
Ingredients:
- 2 Thick-cut bacon strip(s), halved widthwise (gluten-free, if a concern)
- 4½ cups (about 1 pound 2 ounces) Bagged shredded Brussels sprouts
- ¼ teaspoon Table salt
- 2 tablespoons White balsamic vinegar
- 2 teaspoons Worcestershire sauce (gluten-free, if a concern)
- 1 teaspoon Dijon mustard (gluten-free, if a concern)
- ¼ teaspoon Ground black pepper

Directions:
1. Preheat the toaster oven to 375°F .
2. When the machine is at temperature, lay the bacon strip halves in the air fryer oven in one layer and air-fry for 10 minutes, or until crisp.
3. Use kitchen tongs to transfer the bacon pieces to a wire rack. Put the shredded Brussels sprouts in a large bowl. Drain any fat from the pan or the tray under the pan onto the Brussels sprouts. Add the salt and toss well to coat.
4. Put the Brussels sprout shreds in the air fryer oven, spreading them out into as close to an even layer as you can. Air-fry for 8 minutes, tossing the air fryer oven's contents at least three times, until wilted and lightly browned.
5. Pour the contents of the air fryer oven into a serving bowl. Chop the bacon and add it to the Brussels sprouts. Add the vinegar, Worcestershire sauce, mustard, and pepper. Toss well to blend the dressing and coat the Brussels sprout shreds. Serve warm.

Mini Hasselback Potatoes

Servings: 25
Cooking Time: 4 Minutes
Ingredients:
- 1½ pounds baby Yukon Gold potatoes (about 10)
- 5 tablespoons butter, cut into very thin slices
- salt and freshly ground black pepper
- 1 tablespoon vegetable oil
- ¼ cup grated Parmesan cheese (optional)
- chopped fresh parsley or chives

Directions:
1. Preheat the toaster oven to 400°F.
2. Make six to eight deep vertical slits across the top of each potato about three quarters of the way down. Make sure

the slits are deep enough to allow the slices to spread apart a little, but don't cut all the way through the potato. Place a thin slice of butter between each of the slices and season generously with salt and pepper.

3. Transfer the potatoes to the air fryer oven. Pack them in next to each other. It's alright if some of the potatoes sit on top or rest on another potato. Air-fry for 20 minutes.

4. Spray or brush the potatoes with a little vegetable oil and sprinkle the Parmesan cheese on top. Air-fry for an additional 5 minutes. Garnish with chopped parsley or chives and serve hot.

Home Fries

Servings: 4
Cooking Time: 20 Minutes
Ingredients:

- 3 pounds potatoes, cut into 1-inch cubes
- ½ teaspoon oil
- salt and pepper

Directions:

1. In a large bowl, mix the potatoes and oil thoroughly.
2. Air-fry at 390°F for 10 minutes and redistribute potatoes.
3. Air-fry for an additional 10 minutes, until brown and crisp.
4. Season with salt and pepper to taste.

Roasted Corn Salad

Servings: 3
Cooking Time: 15 Minutes
Ingredients:

- 3 4-inch lengths husked and de-silked corn on the cob
- Olive oil spray
- 1 cup Packed baby arugula leaves
- 12 Cherry tomatoes, halved
- Up to 3 Medium scallion(s), trimmed and thinly sliced
- 2 tablespoons Lemon juice
- 1 tablespoon Olive oil
- 1½ teaspoons Honey
- ¼ teaspoon Mild paprika
- ¼ teaspoon Dried oregano
- ¼ teaspoon, plus more to taste Table salt
- ¼ teaspoon Ground black pepper

Directions:

1. Preheat the toaster oven to 400°F.
2. When the machine is at temperature, lightly coat the pieces of corn on the cob with olive oil spray. Set the pieces of corn in the air fryer oven with as much air space between them as possible. Air-fry undisturbed for 15 minutes, or until the corn is charred in a few spots.
3. Use kitchen tongs to transfer the corn to a wire rack. Cool for 15 minutes.
4. Cut the kernels off the ears by cutting the fat end off each piece so it will stand up straight on a cutting board, then running a knife down the corn. (Or you can save your fingers and buy a fancy tool to remove kernels from corn cobs. Check it out at online kitchenware stores.) Scoop the kernels into a serving bowl.
5. Chop the arugula into bite-size bits and add these to the kernels. Add the tomatoes and scallions, too. Whisk the lemon juice, olive oil, honey, paprika, oregano, salt, and pepper in a small bowl until the honey dissolves. Pour over the salad and toss well to coat, tasting for extra salt before serving.

Crisp Cajun Potato Wedges

Servings: 2
Cooking Time: 70 Minutes
Ingredients:

- 2 medium baking potatoes, scrubbed, halved, and cut lengthwise into ½-inch-wide wedges
- 1 tablespoon vegetable oil
- Cajun seasonings:
- ¼ teaspoon chili powder
- ⅛ teaspoon cayenne
- ⅛ teaspoon dry mustard
- ⅛ teaspoon salt
- ⅛ teaspoon cumin
- ¼ teaspoon onion powder
- ¼ teaspoon paprika

Directions:

1. Preheat the toaster oven to 450° F.
2. Soak the potato wedges in cold water for 10 minutes to crisp. Drain on paper towels. Brush with the oil.
3. Combine the Cajun seasonings in a small bowl, add the wedges, and toss to coat well. Transfer to an oiled or nonstick 8½ × 8½ × 2-inch square baking (cake) pan.
4. BAKE, covered, for 40 minutes, or until the potatoes are tender. Carefully remove the cover.
5. BROIL for 20 minutes to crisp, turning with a tongs every 5 minutes until the desired crispness is achieved.

Steakhouse Baked Potatoes

Servings: 3
Cooking Time: 55 Minutes
Ingredients:

- 3 10-ounce russet potatoes
- 2 tablespoons Olive oil
- 1 teaspoon Table salt

Directions:

1. Preheat the toaster oven to 375°F .
2. Poke holes all over each potato with a fork. Rub the skin of each potato with 2 teaspoons of the olive oil, then sprinkle ¼ teaspoon salt all over each potato.
3. When the machine is at temperature, set the potatoes in the air fryer oven in one layer with as much air space between them as possible. Air-fry for 50 minutes, turning once, or until soft to the touch but with crunchy skins. If the machine is at 360°F, you may need to add up to 5 minutes to the cooking time.
4. Use kitchen tongs to gently transfer the baked potatoes to a wire rack. Cool for 5 or 10 minutes before serving.

Baked Stuffed Potatoes With Vegetables

Servings: 2
Cooking Time: 30 Minutes
Ingredients:

- 2 large baking potatoes, baked, cooled, and pulp scooped out to make shells
- Stuffing:
- 1 carrot, shredded
- ½ bell pepper, seeded and shredded
- 2 tablespoons broccoli, shredded
- 2 tablespoons cauliflower, shredded
- 3 tablespoons fat-free half-and-half
- 1 teaspoon paprika
- ½ teaspoon garlic powder
- ½ teaspoon caraway seeds
- Salt and butcher's pepper to taste

Directions:

1. Preheat the toaster oven to 400° F.
2. Combine the stuffing mixture ingredients, mixing well. Fill the potato shells with the mixture and place the shells in an oiled 8½ × 8½ × 2-inch square baking (cake) pan.
3. BAKE for 25 minutes or until vegetables are cooked.
4. BROIL for 5 minutes, or until the tops are lightly browned.

Crispy, Cheesy Leeks

Servings: 4
Cooking Time: 15 Minutes
Ingredients:

- 2 Medium leek(s), about 9 ounces each
- Olive oil spray
- ¼ cup Seasoned Italian-style dried bread crumbs (gluten-free, if a concern)
- ¼ cup (about ¾ ounce) Finely grated Parmesan cheese
- 2 tablespoons Olive oil

Directions:

1. Preheat the toaster oven to 350°F .
2. Trim off the root end of the leek(s) as well as the dark green top(s), leaving about a 5-inch usable section. Split the leek section(s) in half lengthwise. Set the leek halves cut side up on your work surface. Pull out and remove in one piece the semicircles that make up the inner structure of the leek, about halfway down. Set the removed "inside" next to the outer leek "shells" on your cutting board. Generously coat them all on all sides (particularly the "bottoms") with olive oil spray.
3. Set the leeks and their insides cut side up in the air fryer oven with as much air space between them as possible. Air-fry undisturbed for 12 minutes.
4. Meanwhile, mix the bread crumbs, cheese, and olive oil in a small bowl until well combined.
5. After 12 minutes in the air fryer oven, sprinkle this mixture inside the leek shells and on top of the leek insides. Increase the machine's temperature to 375°F (or 380°F or 390°F, if one of these is the closest setting). Air-fry undisturbed for 3 minutes, or until the topping is lightly browned.
6. Use a nonstick-safe spatula to transfer the leeks to a serving platter. Cool for a few minutes before serving warm.

Ratatouille

Servings: 4
Cooking Time: 60 Minutes
Ingredients:

- Oil spray (hand-pumped)
- 1 eggplant, peeled and diced into ½-inch chunks
- 2 tomatoes, diced
- 1 zucchini, diced
- 2 bell peppers (any color), diced
- ½ red onion, chopped
- ½ cup tomato paste
- 2 teaspoons minced garlic
- 1 teaspoon dried basil
- ¼ teaspoon sea salt
- ⅛ teaspoon freshly ground black pepper
- Pinch red pepper flakes
- ½ cup low-sodium vegetable broth

Directions:

1. Place the rack in position 1 and preheat oven to 350°F on CONVECTION BAKE for 5 minutes.
2. Lightly coat a 1½-quart casserole dish with oil spray.
3. In a large bowl, toss the eggplant, tomatoes, zucchini, bell peppers, onion, tomato paste, garlic, basil, salt, black pepper, and red pepper flakes until well combined.
4. Transfer the vegetable mixture to the casserole dish, pour in the vegetable broth, and cover tightly with foil or a lid.
5. Convection bake for 1 hour, stirring once at the halfway mark, until the vegetables are very tender. Serve.

Zucchini Fries

Servings: 3
Cooking Time: 12 Minutes
Ingredients:

- 1 large Zucchini
- ½ cup All-purpose flour or tapioca flour
- 2 Large egg(s), well beaten
- 1 cup Seasoned Italian-style dried bread crumbs (gluten-free, if a concern)
- Olive oil spray

Directions:

1. Preheat the toaster oven to 400°F.
2. Trim the zucchini into a long rectangular block, taking off the ends and four "sides" to make this shape. Cut the block lengthwise into ½-inch-thick slices. Lay these slices flat and cut in half widthwise. Slice each of these pieces into ½-inch-thick batons.
3. Set up and fill three shallow soup plates or small pie plates on your counter: one for the flour, one for the beaten egg(s), and one for the bread crumbs.
4. Set a zucchini baton in the flour and turn it several times to coat all sides. Gently stir any excess flour, then dip it in the egg(s), turning it to coat. Let any excess egg slip back into the rest, then set the baton in the bread crumbs and turn it several times, pressing gently to coat all sides, even the

ends. Set aside on a cutting board and continue coating the remainder of the batons in the same way.

5. Lightly coat the batons on all sides with olive oil spray. Set them in two flat layers in the air fryer oven, the top layer at a 90-degree angle to the bottom one, with a little air space between the batons in each layer. In the end, the whole thing will look like a crosshatch pattern. Air-fry undisturbed for 6 minutes.

6. Use kitchen tongs to gently rearrange the batons so that any covered parts are now uncovered. The batons no longer need to be in a crosshatch pattern. Continue air-frying undisturbed for 6 minutes, or until lightly browned and crisp.

7. Gently pour the contents of the air fryer oven onto a wire rack. Spread the batons out and cool for only a minute or two before serving.

Roasted Fennel Salad

Servings: 3
Cooking Time: 20 Minutes

Ingredients:

- 3 cups (about ¾ pound) Trimmed fennel, roughly chopped
- 1½ tablespoons Olive oil
- ¼ teaspoon Table salt
- ¼ teaspoon Ground black pepper
- 1½ tablespoons White balsamic vinegar

Directions:

1. Preheat the toaster oven to 400°F.
2. Toss the fennel, olive oil, salt, and pepper in a large bowl until the fennel is well coated in the oil.
3. When the machine is at temperature, pour the fennel into the air fryer oven, spreading it out into as close to one layer as possible. Air-fry for 20 minutes, tossing and rearranging the fennel pieces twice so that any covered or touching parts get exposed to the air currents, until golden at the edges and softened.
4. Pour the fennel into a serving bowl. Add the vinegar while hot. Toss well, then cool a couple of minutes before serving. Or serve at room temperature.

Brown Rice And Goat Cheese Croquettes

Servings: 3
Cooking Time: 8 Minutes

Ingredients:

- ¾ cup Water
- 6 tablespoons Raw medium-grain brown rice, such as brown Arborio
- ½ cup Shredded carrot
- ¼ cup Walnut pieces
- 3 tablespoons (about 1½ ounces) Soft goat cheese
- 1 tablespoon Pasteurized egg substitute, such as Egg Beaters (gluten-free, if a concern)
- ¼ teaspoon Dried thyme
- ¼ teaspoon Table salt
- ¼ teaspoon Ground black pepper
- Olive oil spray

Directions:

1. Combine the water, rice, and carrots in a small saucepan set over medium-high heat. Bring to a boil, stirring occasionally. Cover, reduce the heat to very low, and simmer very slowly for 45 minutes, or until the water has been absorbed and the rice is tender. Set aside, covered, for 10 minutes.
2. Scrape the contents of the saucepan into a food processor. Cool for 10 minutes.
3. Preheat the toaster oven to 400°F.
4. Put the nuts, cheese, egg substitute, thyme, salt, and pepper into the food processor. Cover and pulse to a coarse paste, stopping the machine at least once to scrape down the inside of the canister.
5. Uncover the food processor; scrape down and remove the blade. Using wet, clean hands, form the mixture into two 4-inch-diameter patties for a small batch, three 4-inch-diameter patties for a medium batch, or four 4-inch-diameter patties for a large one. Generously coat both sides of the patties with olive oil spray.
6. Set the patties in the air fryer oven with as much air space between them as possible. Air-fry undisturbed for 8 minutes, or until brown and crisp.
7. Use a nonstick-safe spatula to transfer the croquettes to a wire rack. Cool for 5 minutes before serving.

Moroccan Cauliflower

Servings: 6
Cooking Time: 15 Minutes

Ingredients:

- 1 tablespoon curry powder
- 2 teaspoons smoky paprika
- ½ teaspoon ground cumin
- ½ teaspoon salt
- 1 head cauliflower, cut into bite-size pieces
- ¼ cup red wine vinegar
- 2 tablespoons extra-virgin olive oil
- 2 tablespoons chopped parsley

Directions:

1. Preheat the toaster oven to 370°F.
2. In a large bowl, mix the curry powder, paprika, cumin, and salt. Add the cauliflower and stir to coat. Pour the red wine vinegar over the top and continue stirring.
3. Place the cauliflower into the air fryer oven; drizzle olive oil over the top.
4. Cook the cauliflower for 5 minutes, toss, and cook another 5 minutes. Raise the temperature to 400°F and continue cooking for 4 to 6 minutes, or until crispy.

Asparagus Ronald

Servings: 4
Cooking Time: 25 Minutes

Ingredients:

- 20 asparagus spears, rinsed and hard stem ends cut off
- 1 tablespoon soy sauce
- 3 tablespoons lemon juice
- 3 tablespoons olive oil
- Salt and freshly ground black pepper
- 3 tablespoons crumbled feta cheese

Directions:

1. Preheat the toaster oven to 400° F.
2. Place the asparagus spears in a 1-quart 8½ × 8½ × 4-inch ovenproof baking dish.
3. Drizzle the soy sauce, lemon juice, and olive oil over the asparagus spears. Season to taste with salt and pepper. Cover the dish with aluminum foil.
4. BAKE for 25 minutes, or until tender. Sprinkle with the feta cheese before serving.

Sweet Potato Curly Fries

Servings: 4
Cooking Time: 10 Minutes
Ingredients:

- 2 medium sweet potatoes, washed
- 2 tablespoons avocado oil
- ¾ teaspoon salt, divided
- 1 medium avocado
- ½ teaspoon garlic powder
- ½ teaspoon paprika
- ¼ teaspoon black pepper
- ½ juice lime
- 3 tablespoons fresh cilantro

Directions:

1. Preheat the toaster oven to 400°F.
2. Using a spiralizer, create curly spirals with the sweet potatoes. Keep the pieces about 1½ inches long. Continue until all the potatoes are used.
3. In a large bowl, toss the curly sweet potatoes with the avocado oil and ½ teaspoon of the salt.
4. Place the potatoes in the air fryer oven and air-fry for 5 minutes; cook another 5 minutes.
5. While cooking, add the avocado, garlic, paprika, pepper, the remaining ¼ teaspoon of salt, lime juice, and cilantro to a blender and process until smooth. Set aside.
6. When cooking completes, remove the fries and serve warm with the lime avocado sauce.

Fingerling Potatoes

Servings: 4
Cooking Time: 15 Minutes
Ingredients:

- 1 pound fingerling potatoes
- 1 tablespoon light olive oil
- ½ teaspoon dried parsley
- ½ teaspoon lemon juice
- coarsely ground sea salt

Directions:

1. Cut potatoes in half lengthwise.
2. In a large bowl, combine potatoes, oil, parsley, and lemon juice. Stir well to coat potatoes.
3. Place potatoes in air fryer oven and air-fry at 360°F for 15 minutes or until lightly browned and tender inside.
4. Sprinkle with sea salt before serving.

Roasted Root Vegetables With Cinnamon

Servings: 4
Cooking Time: 20 Minutes
Ingredients:

- 1 small sweet potato, cut into 1-inch pieces
- 2 carrots, cut into 1-inch pieces
- 2 parsnips, cut into 1-inch pieces
- 2 tablespoons brown sugar (dark or light)
- 1 tablespoon olive oil
- ¼ teaspoon ground cinnamon
- Oil spray (hand-pumped)
- Sea salt, for seasoning

Directions:

1. Preheat the toaster oven to 350°F on AIR FRY for 5 minutes.
2. In a large bowl, toss the sweet potato, carrots, parsnips, brown sugar, oil, and cinnamon until well mixed.
3. Place the air-fryer basket in the baking tray and generously spray the mesh with oil.
4. Spread the vegetables in the basket and air fry in position 2 for 20 minutes, shaking the basket after 10 minutes, until the vegetables are tender and lightly caramelized.
5. Season with salt and serve.

Asparagus And Cherry Tomato Quiche

Servings: 4
Cooking Time: 50 Minutes
Ingredients:

- 6 asparagus spears, woody ends removed, cut into 1-inch pieces
- 1 premade unbaked pie crust
- 5 large eggs
- ½ cup half-and-half
- ¾ cup shredded Swiss cheese, divided
- Sea salt, for seasoning
- Freshly ground black pepper, for seasoning
- 10 cherry tomatoes, quartered
- 1 scallion, both white and green parts, finely chopped

Directions:

1. Place the rack in position 1 and preheat oven to 350°F on BAKE for 5 minutes.
2. Place a small saucepan three-quarters filled with water on high heat and bring to a boil. Blanch the asparagus until bright green, about 1 minute. Drain and set aside.
3. Line an 8-inch-round pie dish with the pie crust, then trim and flute the edges.
4. In a small bowl, beat the eggs, half-and-half, and ½ cup of the cheese until well blended; season with salt and pepper.
5. Arrange the asparagus, tomatoes, and scallion in the pie crust. Pour in the egg mixture and top with the remaining ¼ cup of cheese.
6. Bake for 45 to 50 minutes until the quiche is puffed and lightly browned, and a knife inserted in the center comes out clean.
7. Serve warm or cold.

Spicy Sweet Potatoes

Servings: 4
Cooking Time: 25 Minutes

Ingredients:

- 2 sweet potatoes, peeled and sliced into 1-inch rounds
- 1 tablespoon vegetable oil
- Seasonings:
- ½ teaspoon each: grated nutmeg, ground cinnamon, cardamom, and ginger
- Salt and freshly ground black pepper to taste

Directions:

1. Preheat the toaster oven to 400° F.
2. Brush the potato slices with oil and set aside.
3. Combine the seasonings in a 1-quart 8½ × 8½ × 4-inch ovenproof baking dish and add the potato slices. Toss to coat well and adjust the seasonings to taste. Cover the dish with aluminum foil.
4. BAKE for 25 minutes, or until the potatoes are tender.

Crispy Brussels Sprouts

Servings: 3
Cooking Time: 12 Minutes

Ingredients:

- 1¼ pounds Medium, 2-inch-in-length Brussels sprouts
- 1½ tablespoons Olive oil
- ¾ teaspoon Table salt

Directions:

1. Preheat the toaster oven to 400°F.
2. Halve each Brussels sprout through the stem end, pulling off and discarding any discolored outer leaves. Put the sprout halves in a large bowl, add the oil and salt, and stir well to coat evenly, until the Brussels sprouts are glistening.
3. When the machine is at temperature, scrape the contents of the bowl into the air fryer oven, gently spreading the Brussels sprout halves into as close to one layer as possible. Air-fry for 12 minutes, gently tossing and rearranging the vegetables twice to get all covered or touching parts exposed to the air currents, until crisp and browned at the edges.
4. Gently pour the contents of the air fryer oven onto a wire rack. Cool for a minute or two before serving.

Hasselback Garlic-and-butter Potatoes

Servings: 3
Cooking Time: 48 Minutes

Ingredients:

- 3 8-ounce russet potatoes
- 6 Brown button or Baby Bella mushrooms, very thinly sliced
- Olive oil spray
- 3 tablespoons Butter, melted and cooled
- 1 tablespoon Minced garlic
- ¾ teaspoon Table salt
- 3 tablespoons (about ½ ounce) Finely grated Parmesan cheese

Directions:

1. Preheat the toaster oven to 350°F .
2. Cut slits down the length of each potato, about three-quarters down into the potato and spaced about ¼ inch apart. Wedge a thin mushroom slice in each slit. Generously coat the potatoes on all sides with olive oil spray.
3. When the machine is at temperature, set the potatoes mushroom side up in the air fryer oven with as much air space between them as possible. Air-fry undisturbed for 45 minutes, or tender when pricked with a fork.
4. Increase the machine's temperature to 400°F. Use kitchen tongs, and perhaps a flatware fork for balance, to gently transfer the potatoes to a cutting board. Brush each evenly with butter, then sprinkle the minced garlic and salt over them. Sprinkle the cheese evenly over the potatoes.
5. Use those same tongs to gently transfer the potatoes cheese side up to the air fryer oven in one layer with some space for air flow between them. Air-fry undisturbed for 3 minutes, or until the cheese has melted and begun to brown.
6. Use those same tongs to gently transfer the potatoes back to the wire rack. Cool for 5 minutes before serving.

Cheesy Potato Skins

Servings: 6
Cooking Time: 54 Minutes

Ingredients:

- 3 6- to 8-ounce small russet potatoes
- 3 Thick-cut bacon strips, halved widthwise (gluten-free, if a concern)
- ¾ teaspoon Mild paprika
- ¼ teaspoon Garlic powder
- ¼ teaspoon Table salt
- ¼ teaspoon Ground black pepper
- ½ cup plus 1 tablespoon (a little over 2 ounces) Shredded Cheddar cheese
- 3 tablespoons Thinly sliced trimmed chives
- 6 tablespoons (a little over 1 ounce) Finely grated Parmesan cheese

Directions:

1. Preheat the toaster oven to 375°F .
2. Prick each potato in four places with a fork (not four places in a line but four places all around the potato). Set the potatoes in the air fryer oven with as much air space between them as possible. Air-fry undisturbed for 45 minutes, or until the potatoes are tender when pricked with a fork.
3. Use kitchen tongs to gently transfer the potatoes to a wire rack. Cool for 15 minutes. Maintain the machine's temperature.
4. Lay the bacon strip halves in the air fryer oven in one layer. They may touch but should not overlap. Air-fry undisturbed for 5 minutes, until crisp. Use those same tongs to transfer the bacon pieces to the wire rack. If there's a great deal of rendered bacon fat in the air fryer oven's bottom or on a tray under the pan attachment, pour this into a bowl, cool, and discard. Don't throw it down the drain!
5. Cut the potatoes in half lengthwise (not just slit them open but actually cut in half). Use a flatware spoon to scoop the hot, soft middles into a bowl, leaving ½ inch of potato all around the inside of the spud next to the skin. Sprinkle the inside of the potato "shells" evenly with paprika, garlic powder, salt, and pepper.
6. Chop the bacon pieces into small bits. Sprinkle these along with the Cheddar and chives evenly inside the potato

shells. Crumble 2 to 3 tablespoons of the soft potato insides over the filling mixture. Divide the grated Parmesan evenly over the tops of the potatoes.
7. Set the stuffed potatoes in the air fryer oven with as much air space between them as possible. Air-fry undisturbed for 4 minutes, until the cheese melts and lightly browns.
8. Use kitchen tongs to gently transfer the stuffed potato halves to a wire rack. Cool for 5 minutes before serving.

Tasty Golden Potatoes

Servings: 4
Cooking Time: 38 Minutes
Ingredients:

- 2 cups peeled and shredded potatoes
- ½ cup peeled and shredded carrots
- ¼ cup shredded onion
- 1 teaspoon salt
- 1 teaspoon dried rosemary
- 1 teaspoon dried cumin
- 3 tablespoons vegetable oil
- Salt and freshly ground black pepper to taste

Directions:
1. Preheat the toaster oven to 400° F.
2. Mix all the ingredients together in a 1-quart 8½ × 8½ × 2-inch ovenproof baking dish. Adjust the seasonings to taste. Cover the dish with aluminum foil.
3. BAKE, covered, for 30 minutes, or until tender. Remove the cover.
4. BROIL for 8 minutes, or until the top is browned.

Ranch Potatoes

Servings: 2
Cooking Time: 50 Minutes
Ingredients:

- 2 medium russet potatoes, scrubbed and cut lengthwise into ¼-inch strips
- 1 medium onion, chopped
- 2 tablespoons vegetable oil
- 2 tablespoons barbecue sauce
- ¼ teaspoon hot sauce
- Salt and freshly ground black pepper

Directions:
1. Preheat the toaster oven to 400° F.
2. Combine all the ingredients in a medium bowl, mixing well and adjusting the seasonings to taste.
3. Place equal portions of the potatoes on two 12 × 12-inch squares of heavy-duty aluminum foil. Fold up the edges of the foil to form a sealed packet and place on the oven rack.
4. BAKE for 40 minutes, or until the potatoes are tender. Carefully open the packet and fold back the foil.
5. BROIL 10 minutes, or until the potatoes are browned.

Fried Okra

Servings: 4
Cooking Time: 8 Minutes
Ingredients:

- 1 pound okra
- 1 large egg
- 1 tablespoon milk
- 1 teaspoon salt, divided
- ½ teaspoon black pepper, divided
- ¼ teaspoon paprika
- ¼ teaspoon thyme
- ½ cup cornmeal
- ½ cup all-purpose flour

Directions:
1. Preheat the toaster oven to 400°F.
2. Cut the okra into ½-inch rounds.
3. In a medium bowl, whisk together the egg, milk, ½ teaspoon of the salt, and ¼ teaspoon of black pepper. Place the okra into the egg mixture and toss until well coated.
4. In a separate bowl, mix together the remaining ½ teaspoon of salt, the remaining ¼ teaspoon of black pepper, the paprika, the thyme, the cornmeal, and the flour. Working in small batches, dredge the egg-coated okra in the cornmeal mixture until all the okra has been breaded.
5. Place a single layer of okra in the air fryer oven and spray with cooking spray. Air-fry for 4 minutes, toss to check for crispness, and cook another 4 minutes. Repeat in batches, as needed.

Crispy Herbed Potatoes

Servings: 6
Cooking Time: 20 Minutes
Ingredients:

- 3 medium baking potatoes, washed and cubed
- ½ teaspoon dried thyme
- 1 teaspoon minced dried rosemary
- ½ teaspoon garlic powder
- 1 teaspoon sea salt
- ½ teaspoon black pepper
- 2 tablespoons extra-virgin olive oil
- ¼ cup chopped parsley

Directions:
1. Preheat the toaster oven to 390°F.
2. Pat the potatoes dry. In a large bowl, mix together the cubed potatoes, thyme, rosemary, garlic powder, sea salt, and pepper. Drizzle and toss with olive oil.
3. Pour the herbed potatoes into the air fryer oven. Air-fry for 20 minutes, stirring every 5 minutes.
4. Toss the cooked potatoes with chopped parsley and serve immediately.
5. VARY IT! Potatoes are versatile — add any spice or seasoning mixture you prefer and create your own favorite side dish.

Roasted Vegetables

Servings: 4
Cooking Time: 20 Minutes
Ingredients:

- 1 1-pound package frozen vegetable mixture
- 1 tablespoon olive oil
- 1 tablespoon bread crumbs
- 1 teaspoon dried oregano
- 1 teaspoon ground cumin
- Salt and freshly ground black pepper to taste

- 1 tablespoon grated Parmesan cheese
- 1 tablespoon chopped walnuts

Directions:

1. Blend all the ingredients in an oiled or nonstick 8½ × 8½ × 2-inch square baking (cake) pan, tossing to coat the vegetable pieces with the oil, bread crumbs, and seasonings. Adjust the seasonings.
2. BROIL for 10 minutes. Remove the pan from the oven and turn the pieces with tongs. Add the cheese and walnuts. Broil for another 10 minutes, or until the vegetables are lightly browned. Adjust the seasonings and serve.

Roasted Cauliflower With Garlic And Capers

Servings: 3
Cooking Time: 10 Minutes

Ingredients:

- 3 cups (about 15 ounces) 1-inch cauliflower florets
- 2 tablespoons Olive oil
- 1½ tablespoons Drained and rinsed capers, chopped
- 2 teaspoons Minced garlic
- ¼ teaspoon Table salt
- Up to ¼ teaspoon Red pepper flakes

Directions:

1. Preheat the toaster oven to 375°F .
2. Stir the cauliflower florets, olive oil, capers, garlic, salt, and red pepper flakes in a large bowl until the florets are evenly coated.
3. When the machine is at temperature, put the florets in the pan, spreading them out to as close to one layer as you can. Air-fry for 10 minutes, tossing once to get any covered pieces exposed to the air currents, until tender and lightly browned.
4. Dump the contents of the air fryer oven into a serving bowl or onto a serving platter. Cool for a minute or two before serving.

Eggplant And Tomato Slices

Servings: 4
Cooking Time: 36 Minutes

Ingredients:

- 2 tablespoons olive oil
- ¼ teaspoon garlic powder
- 4½-inch-thick slices eggplant
- 4 ¼-inch-thick slices fresh tomato
- 2 tablespoons tomato sauce or salsa
- ½ cup shredded Parmesan cheese
- Salt and freshly ground black pepper to taste
- 2 tablespoons chopped fresh basil, cilantro, parsley, or oregano

Directions:

1. Whisk together the oil and garlic powder in a small bowl. Brush each eggplant slice with the mixture and place in an oiled or nonstick 8½ × 8½ × 2-inch square baking (cake) pan.
2. BROIL for 20 minutes. Remove the pan from the oven and turn the pieces with tongs. Top each with a slice of tomato and broil another 10 minutes, or until tender. Remove the pan from the oven, brush each slice with tomato sauce or salsa, and sprinkle generously with Parmesan cheese. Season to taste with salt and pepper. Broil again for 6 minutes, until the tops are browned.
3. Garnish with the fresh herb and serve.

Onions

Servings: 4
Cooking Time: 18 Minutes

Ingredients:

- 2 yellow onions (Vidalia or 1015 recommended)
- salt and pepper
- ¼ teaspoon ground thyme
- ¼ teaspoon smoked paprika
- 2 teaspoons olive oil
- 1 ounce Gruyère cheese, grated

Directions:

1. Peel onions and halve lengthwise (vertically).
2. Sprinkle cut sides of onions with salt, pepper, thyme, and paprika.
3. Place each onion half, cut-surface up, on a large square of aluminum foil. Pull sides of foil up to cup around onion. Drizzle cut surface of onions with oil.
4. Crimp foil at top to seal closed.
5. Place wrapped onions in air fryer oven and air-fry at 390°F for 18 minutes. When done, onions should be soft enough to pierce with fork but still slightly firm.
6. Open foil just enough to sprinkle each onion with grated cheese.
7. Air-fry for 30 seconds to 1 minute to melt cheese.

Pecan Parmesan Cauliflower

Servings: 4
Cooking Time: 35 Minutes

Ingredients:

- 2½ cups (frozen thawed or fresh) thinly sliced cauliflower florets
- Salt and freshly ground black pepper
- 3 tablespoons freshly grated Parmesan cheese
- ½ cup ground pecans

Directions:

1. Preheat the toaster oven to 400° F.
2. Combine the florets and oil in a 1-quart 8½ × 8½ × 4-inch ovenproof baking dish, tossing to coat well. Season to taste with salt and pepper. Cover the dish with aluminum foil.
3. BAKE for 25 minutes, or until tender. Uncover and sprinkle with the cheese and pecans.
4. BROIL for 10 minutes, or until lightly browned.

Crispy Noodle Salad

Servings: 3
Cooking Time: 22 Minutes

Ingredients:

- 6 ounces Fresh Chinese-style stir-fry or lo mein wheat noodles
- 1½ tablespoons Cornstarch
- ¾ cup Chopped stemmed and cored red bell pepper
- 2 Medium scallion(s), trimmed and thinly sliced

- 2 teaspoons Sambal oelek or other pulpy hot red pepper sauce
- 2 teaspoons Thai sweet chili sauce or red ketchup-like chili sauce, such as Heinz
- 2 teaspoons Regular or low-sodium soy sauce or tamari sauce
- 2 teaspoons Unseasoned rice vinegar
- 1 tablespoon White or black sesame seeds

Directions:

1. Bring a large saucepan of water to a boil over high heat. Add the noodles and boil for 2 minutes. Drain in a colander set in the sink. Rinse several times with cold water, shaking the colander to drain the noodles very well. Spread the noodles out on a large cutting board and air-dry for 10 minutes.
2. Preheat the toaster oven to 400°F.
3. Toss the noodles in a bowl with the cornstarch until well coated. Spread them out across the entire air fryer oven (although they will be touching and overlapping a bit). Air-fry for 6 minutes, then turn the solid mass of noodles over as one piece. If it cracks in half or smaller pieces, just fit these back together after turning. Continue air-frying for 6 minutes, or until golden brown and crisp.
4. As the noodles cook, stir the bell pepper, scallion(s), sambal oelek, red chili sauce, soy sauce, vinegar, and sesame seeds in a serving bowl until well combined.
5. Turn the air fryer oven of noodles out onto a cutting board and cool for a minute or two. Break the mass of noodles into individual noodles and/or small chunks and add to the dressing in the serving bowl. Toss well to serve.

Simple Roasted Sweet Potatoes

Servings: 2
Cooking Time: 45 Minutes

Ingredients:

- 2 10- to 12-ounce sweet potato(es)

Directions:

1. Preheat the toaster oven to 350°F .
2. Prick the sweet potato(es) in four or five different places with the tines of a flatware fork (not in a line but all around).
3. When the machine is at temperature, set the sweet potato(es) in the air fryer oven with as much air space between them as possible. Air-fry undisturbed for 45 minutes, or until soft when pricked with a fork.
4. Use kitchen tongs to transfer the sweet potato(es) to a wire rack. Cool for 5 minutes before serving.

Panzanella Salad With Crispy Croutons

Servings: 4
Cooking Time: 3 Minutes

Ingredients:

- ½ French baguette, sliced in half lengthwise
- 2 large cloves garlic
- 2 large ripe tomatoes, divided
- 2 small Persian cucumbers, quartered and diced
- ¼ cup Kalamata olives
- 1 tablespoon chopped, fresh oregano or 1 teaspoon dried oregano
- ¼ cup chopped fresh basil
- ¼ cup chopped fresh parsley
- ½ cup sliced red onion
- 2 tablespoons red wine vinegar
- ¼ cup extra-virgin olive oil
- Salt and pepper, to taste

Directions:

1. Preheat the toaster oven to 380°F.
2. Place the baguette into the air fryer oven and toast for 3 to 5 minutes or until lightly golden brown.
3. Remove the bread from air fryer oven and immediately rub 1 raw garlic clove firmly onto the inside portion of each piece of bread, scraping the garlic onto the bread.
4. Slice 1 of the tomatoes in half and rub the cut edge of one half of the tomato onto the toasted bread. Season the rubbed bread with sea salt to taste.
5. Cut the bread into cubes and place in a large bowl. Cube the remaining 1½ tomatoes and add to the bowl. Add the cucumbers, olives, oregano, basil, parsley, and onion; stir to mix. Drizzle the red wine vinegar into the bowl, and stir. Drizzle the olive oil over the top, stir, and adjust the seasonings with salt and pepper.
6. Serve immediately or allow to sit at room temperature up to 1 hour before serving.

Molasses Baked Beans

Servings: 4
Cooking Time: 60 Minutes

Ingredients:

- Oil spray (hand-pumped)
- 3 (15-ounce) cans low-sodium canned pinto beans, drained and rinsed
- ½ sweet onion, chopped
- ½ cup low-sodium vegetable broth
- ½ cup tomato paste
- ¼ cup blackstrap molasses
- 1 tablespoon stone-ground mustard
- 1 teaspoon garlic powder

Directions:

1. Place the rack on position 1 and preheat the toaster oven on BAKE to 350°F for 5 minutes.
2. Lightly coat a 1½-quart casserole dish with oil spray.
3. In the dish, combine the beans, onion, broth, tomato paste, molasses, mustard, and garlic powder.
4. Cover the dish with a lid or foil and bake until very tender and the sauce is thick, about 1 hour. Serve.

Salmon Salad With Steamboat Dressing

Servings: 4
Cooking Time: 18 Minutes

Ingredients:

- ¼ teaspoon salt
- 1½ teaspoons dried dill weed
- 1 tablespoon fresh lemon juice
- 8 ounces fresh or frozen salmon fillet (skin on)
- 8 cups shredded romaine, Boston, or other leaf lettuce
- 8 spears cooked asparagus, cut in 1-inch pieces
- 8 cherry tomatoes, halved or quartered

Directions:

1. Mix the salt and dill weed together. Rub the lemon juice over the salmon on both sides and sprinkle the dill and salt all over. Refrigerate for 15 to 20 minutes.
2. Make Steamboat Dressing and refrigerate while cooking salmon and preparing salad.
3. Cook salmon in air fryer oven at 330°F for 18 minutes. Cooking time will vary depending on thickness of fillets. When done, salmon should flake with fork but still be moist and tender.
4. Remove salmon from air fryer oven and cool slightly. At this point, the skin should slide off easily. Cut salmon into 4 pieces and discard skin.
5. Divide the lettuce among 4 plates. Scatter asparagus spears and tomato pieces evenly over the lettuce, allowing roughly 2 whole spears and 2 whole cherry tomatoes per plate.
6. Top each salad with one portion of the salmon and drizzle with a tablespoon of dressing. Serve with additional dressing to pass at the table.

Lemon-glazed Baby Carrots

Servings: 4
Cooking Time: 33 Minutes
Ingredients:

- Glaze:
- 1 tablespoon margarine
- 2 tablespoons lemon juice
- 1 tablespoon honey
- 1 teaspoon garlic powder
- Salt and freshly ground black pepper to taste
- 2 cups peeled baby carrots (approximately 1 pound)
- 1 tablespoon chopped fresh parsley or cilantro

Directions:

1. Place the glaze ingredients in a 1-quart 8½ × 8½ × 4-inch ovenproof baking dish and broil for 4 minutes, or until the margarine is melted. Remove from the oven and mix well. Add the carrots and toss to coat. Cover the dish with aluminum foil.
2. BAKE, covered, at 350° F. for 30 minutes, or until the carrots are tender. Garnish with chopped parsley or cilantro and serve immediately.

Green Peas With Mint

Servings: 4
Cooking Time: 5 Minutes
Ingredients:

- 1 cup shredded lettuce
- 1 10-ounce package frozen green peas, thawed
- 1 tablespoon fresh mint, shredded
- 1 teaspoon melted butter

Directions:

1. Lay the shredded lettuce in the air fryer oven.
2. Toss together the peas, mint, and melted butter and spoon over the lettuce.
3. Air-fry at 360°F for 5 minutes, until peas are warm and lettuce wilts.

Fried Cauliflowerwith Parmesan Lemon Dressing

Servings: 2
Cooking Time: 12 Minutes
Ingredients:

- 4 cups cauliflower florets (about half a large head)
- 1 tablespoon olive oil
- salt and freshly ground black pepper
- 1 teaspoon finely chopped lemon zest
- 1 tablespoon fresh lemon juice (about half a lemon)
- ¼ cup grated Parmigiano-Reggiano cheese
- 4 tablespoons extra virgin olive oil
- ¼ teaspoon salt
- lots of freshly ground black pepper
- 1 tablespoon chopped fresh parsley

Directions:

1. Preheat the toaster oven to 400°F.
2. Toss the cauliflower florets with the olive oil, salt and freshly ground black pepper. Air-fry for 12 minutes.
3. While the cauliflower is frying, make the dressing. Combine the lemon zest, lemon juice, Parmigiano-Reggiano cheese and olive oil in a small bowl. Season with salt and lots of freshly ground black pepper. Stir in the parsley.
4. Turn the fried cauliflower out onto a serving platter and drizzle the dressing over the top.

Mushrooms, Sautéed

Servings: 4
Cooking Time: 4 Minutes
Ingredients:

- 8 ounces sliced white mushrooms, rinsed and well drained
- ¼ teaspoon garlic powder
- 1 tablespoon Worcestershire sauce

Directions:

1. Place mushrooms in a large bowl and sprinkle with garlic powder and Worcestershire. Stir well to distribute seasonings evenly.
2. Place in air fryer oven and air-fry at 390°F for 4 minutes, until tender.

Roasted Garlic Potatoes

Servings: 2
Cooking Time: 40 Minutes
Ingredients:

- 2 medium potatoes, peeled and chopped
- 6 garlic cloves, roasted
- 1 tablespoon olive oil
- Salt and freshly ground black pepper
- 1 tablespoon chopped fresh parsley

Directions:

1. Preheat the toaster oven to 400° F.
2. Place the potatoes in an oiled or nonstick 8½ × 8½ × 2-inch square baking (cake) pan. Add the garlic, oil, and salt and pepper to taste. Toss to coat well. Cover the pan with aluminum foil.
3. BAKE, covered, for 40 minutes, or until the potatoes are tender. Remove the cover.

4. BROIL 10 minutes, or until lightly browned. Garnish with fresh parsley before serving.

Latkes

Servings: 12
Cooking Time: 13 Minutes
Ingredients:

- 1 russet potato
- ¼ onion
- 2 eggs, lightly beaten
- ⅓ cup flour
- ½ teaspoon baking powder
- 1 teaspoon salt
- freshly ground black pepper
- canola or vegetable oil, in a spray bottle
- chopped chives, for garnish
- apple sauce
- sour cream

Directions:

1. Shred the potato and onion with a coarse box grater or a food processor with the shredding blade. Place the shredded vegetables into a colander or mesh strainer and squeeze or press down firmly to remove the excess water.
2. Transfer the onion and potato to a large bowl and add the eggs, flour, baking powder, salt and black pepper. Mix to combine and then shape the mixture into patties, about ¼-cup of mixture each. Brush or spray both sides of the latkes with oil.
3. Preheat the toaster oven to 400°F.
4. Air-fry the latkes in batches. Transfer one layer of the latkes to the air fryer oven and air-fry at 400°F for 12 to 13 minutes, flipping them over halfway through the cooking time. Transfer the finished latkes to a platter and cover with aluminum foil, or place them in a warm oven to keep warm.
5. Garnish the latkes with chopped chives and serve with sour cream and applesauce.

Roasted Ratatouille Vegetables

Servings: 15
Cooking Time: 2 Minutes
Ingredients:

- 1 baby or Japanese eggplant, cut into 1½-inch cubes
- 1 red pepper, cut into 1-inch chunks
- 1 yellow pepper, cut into 1-inch chunks
- 1 zucchini, cut into 1-inch chunks
- 1 clove garlic, minced
- ½ teaspoon dried basil
- 1 tablespoon olive oil
- salt and freshly ground black pepper
- ¼ cup sliced sun-dried tomatoes in oil
- 2 tablespoons chopped fresh basil

Directions:

1. Preheat the toaster oven to 400°F.
2. Toss the eggplant, peppers and zucchini with the garlic, dried basil, olive oil, salt and freshly ground black pepper.
3. Air-fry the vegetables at 400°F for 15 minutes.
4. As soon as the vegetables are tender, toss them with the sliced sun-dried tomatoes and fresh basil and serve.

Homemade Potato Puffs

Servings: 4
Cooking Time: 15 Minutes
Ingredients:

- 1¾ cups Water
- 4 tablespoons (¼ cup/½ stick) Butter
- 2 cups plus 2 tablespoons Instant mashed potato flakes
- 1½ teaspoons Table salt
- ¾ teaspoon Ground black pepper
- ¼ teaspoon Mild paprika
- ¼ teaspoon Dried thyme
- 1¼ cups Seasoned Italian-style dried bread crumbs (gluten-free, if a concern)
- Olive oil spray

Directions:

1. Heat the water with the butter in a medium saucepan set over medium-low heat just until the butter melts. Do not bring to a boil.
2. Remove the saucepan from the heat and stir in the potato flakes, salt, pepper, paprika, and thyme until smooth. Set aside to cool for 5 minutes.
3. Preheat the toaster oven to 400°F. Spread the bread crumbs on a dinner plate.
4. Scrape up 2 tablespoons of the potato flake mixture and form it into a small, oblong puff, like a little cylinder about 1½ inches long. Gently roll the puff in the bread crumbs until coated on all sides. Set it aside and continue making more, about 12 for the small batch, 18 for the medium batch, or 24 for the large.
5. Coat the potato cylinders with olive oil spray on all sides, then arrange them in the air fryer oven in one layer with some air space between them. Air-fry undisturbed for 15 minutes, or until crisp and brown.
6. Gently dump the contents of the air fryer oven onto a wire rack. Cool for 5 minutes before serving.

Almond-crusted Spinach Soufflé

Servings: 4
Cooking Time: 25 Minutes
Ingredients:

- 2 tablespoons reduced-fat sour cream
- 1 tablespoon unbleached flour
- 2 cups fresh spinach, rinsed well, drained, and finely chopped, or 1 10-oz. package frozen spinach, thawed, drained, and blotted dry
- 1 egg, separated
- 1 teaspoon olive oil
- Salt and freshly ground black pepper
- Grated nutmeg
- ¼ cup finely chopped almonds

Directions:

1. Preheat the toaster oven to 350° F.
2. Stir together the sour cream and flour in a medium bowl until smooth. Add the spinach, egg yolk, and oil, mixing well and seasoning to taste with the salt, pepper, and nutmeg.
3. Beat the egg white until stiff and fold into the spinach mixture. Pour into a 1-quart 8½ × 8½ × 4-inch ovenproof baking dish. Sprinkle with the almonds.

4. BAKE, uncovered, for 25 minutes, or until firm and the topping is lightly browned.

Yellow Squash

Servings: 4
Cooking Time: 10 Minutes
Ingredients:

- 1 large yellow squash (about 1½ cups)
- 2 eggs
- ¼ cup buttermilk
- 1 cup panko breadcrumbs
- ¼ cup white cornmeal
- ½ teaspoon salt
- oil for misting or cooking spray

Directions:

1. Preheat the toaster oven to 390°F.
2. Cut the squash into ¼-inch slices.
3. In a shallow dish, beat together eggs and buttermilk.
4. In sealable plastic bag or container with lid, combine ¼ cup panko crumbs, white cornmeal, and salt. Shake to mix well.
5. Place the remaining ¾ cup panko crumbs in a separate shallow dish.
6. Dump all the squash slices into the egg/buttermilk mixture. Stir to coat.
7. Remove squash from buttermilk mixture with a slotted spoon, letting excess drip off, and transfer to the panko/cornmeal mixture. Close bag or container and shake well to coat.
8. Remove squash from crumb mixture, letting excess fall off. Return squash to egg/buttermilk mixture, stirring gently to coat. If you need more liquid to coat all the squash, add a little more buttermilk.
9. Remove each squash slice from egg wash and dip in a dish of ¾ cup panko crumbs.
10. Mist squash slices with oil or cooking spray and place in air fryer oven. Squash should be in a single layer, but it's okay if the slices crowd together and overlap a little.
11. Air-fry at 390°F for 5 minutes. Break up any that have stuck together. Mist again with oil or spray.
12. Cook 5 minutes longer and check. If necessary, mist again with oil and cook an additional two minutes, until squash slices are golden brown and crisp.

Mushrooms

Servings: 4
Cooking Time: 12 Minutes
Ingredients:

- 8 ounces whole white button mushrooms
- ½ teaspoon salt
- ⅛ teaspoon pepper
- ¼ teaspoon garlic powder
- ¼ teaspoon onion powder
- 5 tablespoons potato starch
- 1 egg, beaten
- ¾ cup panko breadcrumbs
- oil for misting or cooking spray

Directions:

1. Place mushrooms in a large bowl. Add the salt, pepper, garlic and onion powders, and stir well to distribute seasonings.
2. Add potato starch to mushrooms and toss in bowl until well coated.
3. Dip mushrooms in beaten egg, roll in panko crumbs, and mist with oil or cooking spray.
4. Place mushrooms in air fryer oven. You can cook them all at once, and it's okay if a few are stacked.
5. Air-fry at 390°F for 5 minutes. Rotate, then continue cooking for 7 more minutes, until golden brown and crispy.

Chilaquiles

Servings: 4
Cooking Time: 25 Minutes
Ingredients:

- Oil spray (hand-pumped)
- 1¼ cups store-bought salsa
- 1 (15-ounce) can low-sodium navy or black beans, drained and rinsed
- ½ cup corn kernels
- ¼ cup chicken broth
- ¼ sweet onion, chopped
- ½ teaspoon minced garlic
- 25 tortilla chips, broken up into 2-inch pieces
- 1½ cups queso fresco cheese, crumbled
- 1 avocado, chopped
- 1 scallion, white and green parts, chopped

Directions:

1. Place the rack in position 1 and preheat the toaster oven to 400°F on BAKE for 5 minutes.
2. Lightly coat an 8-inch-square baking dish with oil spray and set aside.
3. In a large bowl, stir the salsa, beans, corn, chicken broth, onion, and garlic until well mixed.
4. Add the tortilla chips and stir to combine. It is okay if the tortilla chips break up a little.
5. Transfer the mixture to the baking dish, top with the cheese, and cover tightly with foil.
6. Bake for 20 minutes until the chips are soft, the mixture is bubbly, and then uncover and bake until the cheese is golden and melted, about 5 minutes.
7. Serve topped with the avocado and scallion.

Roasted Veggie Kebabs

Servings: 4
Cooking Time: 45 Minutes
Ingredients:

- Brushing mixture:
- 3 tablespoons olive oil
- 1 tablespoon soy sauce
- 1 teaspoon garlic powder
- 1 teaspoon ground cumin
- 2 tablespoons balsamic vinegar
- Salt and freshly ground black pepper to taste
- Cauliflower, zucchini, onion, broccoli, bell pepper, mushrooms, celery, cabbage, beets, and the like, cut into approximately 2 × 2-inch pieces

Directions:

1. Preheat the toaster oven to 400° F.
2. Combine the brushing mixture ingredients in a small bowl, mixing well. Set aside.
3. Skewer the vegetable pieces on 4 9-inch metal skewers and place the skewers lengthwise on a broiling rack with a pan underneath.
4. BAKE for 40 minutes, or until the vegetables are tender, brushing with the mixture every 10 minutes.
5. BROIL for 5 minutes, or until lightly browned.

Desserts

Little Swedish Coffee Cakes

Servings: 4
Cooking Time: 30 Minutes
Ingredients:

- Cake batter:
- 1 cup unbleached flour
- 1 teaspoon baking powder
- ½ cup sugar
- ½ cup finely ground pecans
- ¾ cup low-fat buttermilk
- 1 tablespoon vegetable oil
- 1 egg, lightly beaten
- 1 teaspoon vanilla extract
- Salt to taste
- Sifted confectioners' sugar
- Canola oil for brushing pan

Directions:

1. Preheat the toaster oven to 350° F.
2. Combine the cake batter ingredients in a bowl, mixing well. Pour the batter into an oiled or nonstick 8½ × 8½ × 2-inch square baking (cake) pan.
3. BAKE for 30 minutes, or until a toothpick inserted in the center comes out clean. Run a knife around the edge of the pan, invert, and place on a rack to cool. Sprinkle the top with sifted confectioners' sugar and cut into small squares.

Blueberry Crumbles

Servings: 2
Cooking Time: 60 Minutes
Ingredients:

- 2 tablespoons granulated sugar
- 1½ teaspoons cornstarch
- ⅛ teaspoon table salt, divided
- 10 ounces (2 cups) blueberries
- ½ cup (1½ ounces) old-fashioned rolled oats
- ¼ cup (1¼ ounces) all-purpose flour
- ¼ cup packed (1¾ ounces) light brown sugar
- ¼ teaspoon ground cinnamon
- 4 tablespoons unsalted butter, melted and cooled

Directions:

1. Adjust toaster oven rack to lowest position and preheat the toaster oven to 375 degrees. Combine granulated sugar, cornstarch, and pinch salt in medium bowl. Gently toss blueberries in sugar mixture, then divide between two 12-ounce ramekins.
2. Combine oats, flour, brown sugar, cinnamon, and remaining pinch salt in now-empty bowl. Drizzle with melted butter and toss with fork until evenly moistened and mixture forms large chunks with some pea-size pieces throughout. Sprinkle topping evenly over blueberries, breaking up any large chunks.
3. Place ramekins on aluminum foil–lined small rimmed baking sheet and bake until filling is bubbling around edges and topping is deep golden brown, 25 to 30 minutes, rotating sheet halfway through baking. Let crumbles cool on wire rack for 15 minutes before serving.

Cranapple Crisp

Servings: 6
Cooking Time: 35 Minutes
Ingredients:

- 2 apples, peeled, cored, and diced
- 3 cups chopped fresh or thawed frozen cranberries
- ¼ cup brown sugar
- ¼ cup wheat germ
- 1 tablespoon margarine
- 1 tablespoon vegetable oil
- ½ cup brown sugar
- 1 teaspoon ground cinnamon
- ¼ teaspoon grated nutmeg
- Salt to taste

Directions:

1. Preheat the toaster oven to 350° F.
2. Combine the cranberries, apples, and sugar in a large bowl, mixing well. Transfer to an oiled or nonstick 8½ × 8½ × 2-inch square baking (cake) pan. Set aside.

3. Combine the topping ingredients in a medium bowl, stirring with a fork until crumbly. Sprinkle evenly on top of the cranberry/apple mixture.
4. BAKE for 35 minutes, or until the top is golden brown.

Chewy Brownies

Servings: 16
Cooking Time: 60 Minutes
Ingredients:

- 3 tablespoons Dutch-processed cocoa powder
- ¾ teaspoon espresso powder (optional)
- ⅓ cup boiling water
- 1 ounce unsweetened chocolate, chopped fine
- 5 tablespoons vegetable oil
- 2 tablespoons unsalted butter, melted and cooled
- 1¼ cups (8¾ ounces) sugar
- 1 large egg plus 1 large yolk
- 1 teaspoon vanilla extract
- ¾ cup (3¾ ounces) plus 2 tablespoons all-purpose flour
- 3 ounces bittersweet chocolate, cut into ½-inch pieces
- ½ teaspoon table salt

Directions:

1. Adjust toaster oven rack to middle position and preheat the toaster oven to 350 degrees. Make foil sling for 8-inch square baking pan by folding 2 long sheets of aluminum foil so each is 8 inches wide. Lay sheets of foil in pan perpendicular to each other, with extra foil hanging over edges of pan. Push foil into corners and up sides of pan, smoothing foil flush to pan. Spray foil with vegetable oil spray.
2. Whisk cocoa; espresso powder, if using; and boiling water together in large bowl until smooth. Add unsweetened chocolate and whisk until chocolate is melted. Whisk in oil and melted butter. (Mixture may look curdled.) Whisk in sugar, egg and yolk, and vanilla until smooth. Add flour, bittersweet chocolate, and salt and mix with rubber spatula until no dry flour remains.
3. Scrape batter into prepared pan, smooth top, and bake until toothpick inserted in center comes out with few moist crumbs attached, 25 to 30 minutes, rotating dish halfway through baking. Transfer pan to wire rack and cool for 1½ hours.
4. Using foil overhang, lift brownies from pan. Return brownies to wire rack and let cool completely, about 1 hour. Cut into 2-inch squares and serve.

Honey-roasted Mixed Nuts

Servings: 8
Cooking Time: 15 Minutes
Ingredients:

- ½ cup raw, shelled pistachios
- ½ cup raw almonds
- 1 cup raw walnuts
- 2 tablespoons filtered water
- 2 tablespoons honey
- 1 tablespoon vegetable oil
- 2 tablespoons sugar
- ½ teaspoon salt

Directions:

1. Preheat the toaster oven to 300°F.
2. Lightly spray an air-fryer-safe pan with olive oil; then place the pistachios, almonds, and walnuts inside the pan and place the pan inside the air fryer oven.
3. Air-fry for 15 minutes, every 5 minutes to rotate the nuts.
4. While the nuts are roasting, boil the water in a small pan and stir in the honey and oil. Continue to stir while cooking until the water begins to evaporate and a thick sauce is formed. The sauce should stick to the back of a wooden spoon when mixed. Turn off the heat.
5. Remove the nuts from the air fryer oven (cooking should have just completed) and spoon the nuts into the stovetop pan. Use a spatula to coat the nuts with the honey syrup.
6. Line a baking sheet with parchment paper and spoon the nuts onto the sheet. Lightly sprinkle the sugar and salt over the nuts and let cool in the refrigerator for at least 2 hours.
7. When the honey and sugar have hardened, store the nuts in an airtight container in the refrigerator.

Peanut Butter S'mores

Servings: 10
Cooking Time: 1 Minutes
Ingredients:

- 10 Graham crackers (full, double-square cookies as they come out of the package)
- 5 tablespoons Natural-style creamy or crunchy peanut butter
- ½ cup Milk chocolate chips
- 10 Standard-size marshmallows (not minis and not jumbo campfire ones)

Directions:

1. Preheat the toaster oven to 350°F.
2. Break the graham crackers in half widthwise at the marked place, so the rectangle is now in two squares. Set half of the squares flat side up on your work surface. Spread each with about 1½ teaspoons peanut butter, then set 10 to 12 chocolate chips point side up into the peanut butter on each, pressing gently so the chips stick.
3. Flatten a marshmallow between your clean, dry hands and set it atop the chips. Do the same with the remaining marshmallows on the other coated graham crackers. Do not set the other half of the graham crackers on top of these coated graham crackers.
4. When the machine is at temperature, set the treats graham cracker side down in a single layer in the air fryer oven. They may touch, but even a fraction of an inch between them will provide better air flow. Air-fry undisturbed for 45 seconds.
5. Use a nonstick-safe spatula to transfer the topped graham crackers to a wire rack. Set the other graham cracker squares flat side down over the marshmallows. Cool for a couple of minutes before serving.

Buttermilk Confetti Cake

Servings: 10-12
Cooking Time: 25 Minutes
Ingredients:
- 1 1/2 cups all purpose flour
- 1/2 teaspoon baking soda
- 1/4 teaspoon salt
- 1/2 cup butter, softened
- 1 cup sugar
- 1 teaspoon vanilla extract
- 2 large eggs
- 3/4 cup buttermilk
- 1/4 cup multi-colored sprinkle
- Cream Cheese Frosting
- Multi-colored sprinkles

Directions:
1. Preheat the toaster oven to 350°F. Grease two 8-inch cake pans and line with parchment paper.
2. Stir flour, baking soda and salt in small bowl. Set mixture aside.
3. Beat butter, sugar and vanilla extract on HIGH in large bowl until blended. Add eggs, one at a time, until well blended.
4. Alternately add flour mixture and buttermilk until combined. Stir in 1/4 cup sprinkles.
5. Divide batter evenly between prepared pans. Place one pan on bottom rack and one pan on top rack, rotate halfway through baking.
6. Bake 20 to 25 minutes or until a toothpick inserted in center of cakes comes out clean. Cool 10 minutes on wire rack.
7. Remove cakes from pans and cool completely on wire racks. Frost with Cream Cheese Frosting and top with sprinkles.

Orange Strawberry Flan

Servings: 4
Cooking Time: 45 Minutes
Ingredients:
- ¼ cup sugar
- ½ cup concentrated orange juice
- 1 12-ounce can low-fat evaporated milk
- 3 egg yolks
- 1 cup frozen strawberries, thawed and sliced, or 1 cup fresh strawberries, washed, stemmed, and sliced
- 4 fresh mint sprigs

Directions:
1. Preheat the toaster oven to 375° F.
2. Place the sugar in a baking pan and broil for 4 minutes, or until the sugar melts. Remove from the oven, stir briefly, and pour equal portions of the caramelized sugar into four 1-cup-size ovenproof dishes. Set aside.
3. Blend the orange juice, evaporated milk, and egg yolks in a food processor or blender until smooth. Transfer the mixture to a medium bowl and fold in the sliced strawberries. Pour the mixture in equal portions into the four dishes.
4. BAKE for 45 minutes, or until a knife inserted in the center comes out clean. Chill for several hours. The flan may be loosened by running a knife around the edge and inverted on individual plates or served in the dishes. Garnish with fresh mint sprigs.

Pineapple Tartlets

Servings: 4
Cooking Time: 20 Minutes
Ingredients:
- Vegetable oil
- 6 sheets phyllo pastry
- 1 8-ounce can crushed pineapple, drained
- 3 tablespoons low-fat cottage cheese
- 2 tablespoons orange or pineapple marmalade
- 6 teaspoons concentrated thawed frozen orange juice
- Vanilla frozen yogurt or nonfat whipped topping

Directions:
1. Preheat the toaster oven to 350° F.
2. Brush the pans of a 6-muffin tin with vegetable oil. Lay a phyllo sheet on a clean, flat surface and brush with oil. Fold the sheet into quarters to fit the muffin pan. Repeat the process for the remaining phyllo sheets and pans.
3. BAKE for 5 minutes, or until lightly browned. Remove from the oven and cool.
4. Combine the pineapple, cottage cheese, and marmalade in a small bowl, mixing well. Fill the phyllo shells (in the pans) with equal portions of the mixture. Drizzle 1 teaspoon orange juice concentrate over each.
5. BAKE at 400° F. for 15 minutes, or until the filling is cooked. Cool and remove the tartlets carefully from the muffin pans to dessert dishes. Top with vanilla frozen yogurt or nonfat whipped topping.

Black And Blue Clafoutis

Servings: 2
Cooking Time: 15 Minutes
Ingredients:
- 6-inch pie pan
- 3 large eggs
- ½ cup sugar
- 1 teaspoon vanilla extract
- 2 tablespoons butter, melted 1 cup milk
- ½ cup all-purpose flour
- 1 cup blackberries
- 1 cup blueberries
- 2 tablespoons confectioners' sugar

Directions:
1. Preheat the toaster oven to 320°F.
2. Combine the eggs and sugar in a bowl and whisk vigorously until smooth, lighter in color and well combined. Add the vanilla extract, butter and milk and whisk together well. Add the flour and whisk just until no lumps or streaks of white remain.
3. Scatter half the blueberries and blackberries in a greased (6-inch) pie pan or cake pan. Pour half of the batter (about 1¼ cups) on top of the berries and transfer the tart pan to the air fryer oven. You can use an aluminum foil sling to help with this by taking a long piece of aluminum foil, folding it in half lengthwise twice until it is roughly 26-inches by 3-inches. Place this under the pie dish and hold the ends of the

foil to move the pie dish in and out of the air fryer oven. Tuck the ends of the foil beside the pie dish while it cooks in the air fryer oven.
4. Air-fry at 320°F for 15 minutes or until the clafoutis has puffed up and is still a little jiggly in the center. Remove the clafoutis from the air fryer oven, invert it onto a plate and let it cool while you bake the second batch. Serve the clafoutis warm, dusted with confectioners' sugar on top.

Not Key Lime, Lime Pie

Servings: 3
Cooking Time: 27 Minutes
Ingredients:
- 1 tablespoon grated lime zest
- 3 large egg yolks
- 1 (14-ounce) can sweetened condensed milk
- ½ cup fresh lime juice
- 1 ¾ cups graham cracker crumbs (about 12 full graham crackers)
- ⅓ cup granulated sugar
- ⅛ teaspoon table salt
- ½ cup unsalted butter, melted
- Nonstick cooking spray
- WHIPPED CREAM
- 1 cup heavy cream
- ⅓ cup confectioners' sugar

Directions:
1. Preheat the toaster oven to 350°F.
2. Whisk the lime zest and egg yolks in a large bowl for 1 minute. Whisk in the sweetened condensed milk and lime juice. Set aside to thicken while you prepare the crust.
3. Stir the graham cracker crumbs, granulated sugar, and salt in a medium bowl. Pour the butter over the mixture and mix until combined and moist. Press the crust evenly into the bottom and up the sides of a 9-inch pie plate. Pack tightly using the back of a large spoon. Bake for 10 minutes. Let cool on a cooling rack.
4. When the crust is completely cool, pour the lime filling inside. Bake for 15 to 17 minutes, or until the center is set (it will still jiggle a bit). Allow the pie to cool completely at room temperature. Spray plastic wrap with nonstick cooking spray and place on the pie. Refrigerate for at least 3 hours or overnight.
5. Beat the cream in a large bowl with an electric mixer at medium-high speed until soft peaks form. Add the confectioners' sugar, one tablespoon at a time, and continue to beat until stiff peaks form. Dollop, pipe, or spread the whipped cream over the pie before serving. Refrigerate leftovers for up to 3 days.

Glazed Apple Crostata

Servings: 6
Cooking Time: 35 Minutes
Ingredients:
- PASTRY
- 1 ¼ cups all-purpose flour
- 3 tablespoons granulated sugar
- ¼ teaspoon table salt
- ½ cup unsalted butter, cut into 1-inch pieces
- 2 ½ to 3 ½ tablespoons ice water
- FILLING
- ¼ cup granulated sugar
- 3 tablespoons all-purpose flour
- ½ teaspoon ground cinnamon
- ¼ teaspoon ground nutmeg
- Dash table salt
- 3 large Granny Smith apples, peeled, cored, and thinly sliced
- 1 tablespoon unsalted butter, cut into small pieces
- 1 large egg
- Coarse white sugar
- GLAZE
- ¼ cup apricot preserves or apple jelly

Directions:
1. Place the flour, sugar, and salt in the work bowl of a food processor. Pulse to combine. Add the butter and pulse until it forms coarse crumbs. With the motor running, drizzle in enough cold water that the mixture comes together and forms a dough. Shape the dough into a disk, wrap in plastic wrap, and refrigerate for at least 1 hour or until chilled.
2. Make the filling: Stir the sugar, flour, cinnamon, nutmeg, and salt in a large bowl. Add the apples and stir to coat; set aside.
3. Preheat the toaster oven to 400°F. Line a 12-inch pizza pan or 12 x 12-inch baking pan with parchment paper.
4. Roll the pastry into a 12-inch circle on a lightly floured board. Gently fold the dough into quarters and transfer to the prepared pan. Unfold the dough. Pile the filling in the center of the pastry, leaving a 1- to 2-inch border around the edges. Dot the apples with the butter. Fold the edges of the crust up around the outer edge of the apples. Whisk the egg in a small bowl, then brush the edges of the crust with the egg. Sprinkle the crust with coarse sugar.
5. Bake for 30 to 35 minutes or until golden brown and the apples are tender.
6. Set on a wire rack. For the glaze, microwave the preserves in a small, microwave-safe glass bowl on High (100 percent) power for 30 seconds or until melted. Pour the preserves through a fine mesh strainer. Brush the warm preserves over the apples (but not over the crust). Serve warm.

Campfire Banana Boats

Servings: 4
Cooking Time: 20 Minutes
Ingredients:
- 4 medium, unpeeled ripe bananas
- ¼ cup dark chocolate chips
- 4 teaspoons shredded, unsweetened coconut
- ½ cup mini marshmallows
- 4 graham crackers, chopped

Directions:
1. Preheat the toaster oven to 400°F on BAKE for 5 minutes.
2. Cut the bananas lengthwise through the skin about halfway through. Open the pocket to create a space for the other ingredients.

3. Evenly divide the chocolate, coconut, marshmallows, and graham crackers among the bananas.
4. Tear off four 12-inch squares of foil and place the bananas in the center of each. Crimp the foil around the banana to form a boat.
5. Place the bananas on the baking tray, two at a time, and in position 2, bake for 10 minutes until the fillings are gooey and the banana is warmed through.
6. Repeat with the remaining two bananas and serve.

Mini Gingerbread Bundt Cakes

Servings: 16
Cooking Time: 24 Minutes

Ingredients:

- 3 cups all-purpose flour
- 1/4 cup baking cocoa
- 1 tablespoon baking soda
- 1 teaspoon ground cinnamon
- 1 teaspoon ground ginger
- 1 teaspoon salt
- 1/4 teaspoon ground cloves
- 1/4 teaspoon ground nutmeg
- 1 cup butter, softened
- 1 1/4 cups milk
- 1 cup packed dark brown sugar
- 1 cup molasses
- 2 large eggs
- 1 cup mini chocolate chips Glaze: 1 package (12 oz.) semi-sweet chocolate chips
- 1/3 cup heavy cream
- 2 tablespoons butter
- 2 tablespoons light corn syrup
- Chopped crystallized ginger

Directions:

1. Preheat the toaster oven to 350°F. Spray mini bundt pans with nonstick cooking spray. Dust with flour.
2. In a medium bowl, stir together flour, cocoa, baking soda, cinnamon, ginger, salt, cloves and nutmeg.
3. In a large mixer bowl, beat butter until creamy. Gradually beat in milk, brown sugar, molasses and eggs until well blended.
4. Reduce speed to LOW. Slowly add flour mixture until blended. Stir in chocolate chips.
5. Pour into prepared bundt pans.
6. Bake 20 to 24 minutes or until toothpick inserted in center comes out clean.
7. Cool on wire rack 10 minutes. Invert onto cooling rack and cool completely.
8. In a microwavable bowl, stir together 1 cup chocolate chips, heavy cream, butter and corn syrup.
9. Microwave on MEDIUM power 1 minute or until chips are shiny. Stir until mixture is smooth.
10. Spread glaze over top of each mini bundt and sprinkle with crystallized ginger.

Pear And Almond Biscotti Crumble

Servings: 6
Cooking Time: 65 Minutes

Ingredients:

- 7-inch cake pan or ceramic dish
- 3 pears, peeled, cored and sliced
- ½ cup brown sugar
- ¼ teaspoon ground ginger
- 1 teaspoon ground cinnamon
- ⅛ teaspoon ground nutmeg
- 2 tablespoons cornstarch
- 1¼ cups (4 to 5) almond biscotti, coarsely crushed
- ¼ cup all-purpose flour
- ¼ cup sliced almonds
- ¼ cup butter, melted

Directions:

1. Combine the pears, brown sugar, ginger, cinnamon, nutmeg and cornstarch in a bowl. Toss to combine and then pour the pear mixture into a greased 7-inch cake pan or ceramic dish.
2. Combine the crushed biscotti, flour, almonds and melted butter in a medium bowl. Toss with a fork until the mixture resembles large crumbles. Sprinkle the biscotti crumble over the pears and cover the pan with aluminum foil.
3. Preheat the toaster oven to 350°F.
4. Air-fry at 350°F for 60 minutes. Remove the aluminum foil and air-fry for an additional 5 minutes to brown the crumble layer.
5. Serve warm.

Triple Chocolate Brownies

Servings: 16
Cooking Time: 25 Minutes

Ingredients:

- ⅓ cup salted butter, room temperature, plus extra for greasing the baking dish
- ¾ cup brown sugar
- 2 large eggs
- 1 teaspoon vanilla extract
- ½ cup all-purpose flour
- ¼ cup cocoa powder
- ¼ teaspoon baking powder
- ⅛ teaspoon salt
- ½ cup dark chocolate chips
- ¼ cup white chocolate chips

Directions:

1. Place the rack in position 1 and preheat the oven to 325°F on BAKE for 5 minutes.
2. Lightly grease a 6-inch-square baking dish with butter.
3. In a large bowl, beat together the butter and sugar with an electric hand beater or a whisk until combined. Add the eggs and vanilla and beat to combine.
4. Beat in the flour, cocoa powder, baking powder, and salt until just combined.
5. Stir in dark chocolate and white chocolate chips, then spoon the batter into the prepared dish.
6. Bake for 25 minutes or until a knife inserted in the center comes out mostly clean.
7. Cool in the baking dish and serve.

Chewy Coconut Cake

Servings: 6

Cooking Time: 22 Minutes

Ingredients:

- ¾ cup plus 2½ tablespoons All-purpose flour
- ¾ teaspoon Baking powder
- ⅛ teaspoon Table salt
- 7½ tablespoons (1 stick minus ½ tablespoon) Butter, at room temperature
- ⅓ cup plus 1 tablespoon Granulated white sugar
- 5 tablespoons Packed light brown sugar
- 5 tablespoons Pasteurized egg substitute, such as Egg Beaters
- 2 teaspoons Vanilla extract
- ½ cup Unsweetened shredded coconut
- Baking spray

Directions:

1. Preheat the toaster oven to 325°F.
2. Mix the flour, baking powder, and salt in a small bowl until well combined.
3. Using an electric hand mixer at medium speed , beat the butter, granulated white sugar, and brown sugar in a medium bowl until creamy and smooth, about 3 minutes, occasionally scraping down the inside of the bowl. Beat in the egg substitute or egg and vanilla until smooth.
4. Scrape down and remove the beaters. Fold in the flour mixture with a rubber spatula just until all the flour is moistened. Fold in the coconut until the mixture is a uniform color.
5. Use the baking spray to generously coat the inside of a 6-inch round cake pan for a small batch, a 7-inch round cake pan for a medium batch, or an 8-inch round cake pan for a large batch. Scrape and spread the batter into the pan, smoothing the batter out to an even layer.
6. Set the pan in the toaster oven and air-fry for 18 minutes for a 6-inch layer, 20 minutes for a 7-inch layer, or 22 minutes for an 8-inch layer, or until the cake is well browned and set even if there's a little soft give right at the center. Start checking it at the 16-minute mark to know where you are.
7. Use hot pads or silicone baking mitts to transfer the cake pan to a wire rack. Cool for at least 1 hour or up to 4 hours. Use a nonstick-safe knife to slice the cake into wedges right in the pan, lifting them out one by one.

Rum-glazed Roasted Pineapple

Servings: 4

Cooking Time: 45 Minutes

Ingredients:

- ½ pineapple, peeled, cored, and cut lengthwise into 4 wedges
- 2 tablespoons unsalted butter, melted
- 3 tablespoons packed dark brown sugar
- 1 tablespoon lime juice
- ½ teaspoon vanilla extract
- Pinch table salt
- 1 tablespoon white or aged rum
- 2 tablespoons unsweetened shredded coconut, toasted

Directions:

1. Adjust toaster oven rack to lowest position and preheat the toaster oven to 450 degrees. Toss pineapple with melted butter in 8-inch square baking dish or pan, then arrange in single layer. Roast until bottoms of wedges are deep golden brown and fork slips easily in and out of pineapple, 25 to 35 minutes, rotating dish halfway through roasting.
2. Remove pan from oven and transfer pineapple to serving dish. Whisk sugar, lime juice, vanilla, and salt into butter and juice in pan, scraping up any browned bits, until well combined. Return pineapple wedges to pan, browned side up, along with any accumulated juices. Roast until sauce is reduced to syrupy consistency, 3 to 5 minutes.
3. Remove pan from oven and transfer pineapple to serving dish. Whisk rum into sauce in pan until smooth, then spoon sauce over pineapple. Sprinkle with coconut and serve.

Sour Cream Pound Cake

Servings: 6

Cooking Time: 60 Minutes

Ingredients:

- ¾ cup unsalted butter, plus extra for greasing the baking pan
- 2½ cups all-purpose flour, sifted, plus extra for dusting the baking pan
- 1½ cups granulated sugar
- 4 large eggs
- 2 teaspoons pure vanilla extract
- ½ teaspoon baking soda
- ¾ cup sour cream

Directions:

1. Place the rack in position 1 and preheat the toaster oven to 350°F on BAKE for 5 minutes.
2. Lightly grease and dust a 9-by-5-inch loaf pan.
3. In a large bowl, cream the butter and sugar with an electric hand beater until very light and fluffy, about 4 minutes.
4. Beat in the eggs one at a time, scraping down the sides of the bowl after each addition.
5. Beat in the vanilla.
6. In a medium bowl, stir the flour and baking soda.
7. Fold the flour mixture and sour cream into the butter mixture, alternating two times each, until well combined.
8. Spoon the batter into the loaf pan and bake for 1 hour, or until a toothpick inserted in the center comes out clean.
9. Let cool completely in the pan and serve.

Individual Peach Crisps

Servings: 2

Cooking Time: 60 Minutes

Ingredients:

- 2 tablespoons granulated sugar, divided
- 1 teaspoon lemon juice
- ¼ teaspoon cornstarch
- ⅛ teaspoon table salt, divided
- 1 pound frozen sliced peaches, thawed
- ⅓ cup whole almonds or pecans, chopped fine
- ¼ cup (1¼ ounces) all-purpose flour
- 2 tablespoons packed light brown sugar

- ⅛ teaspoon ground cinnamon
- Pinch ground nutmeg
- 3 tablespoons unsalted butter, melted and cooled

Directions:

1. Adjust toaster oven rack to lowest position and preheat the toaster oven to 425 degrees. Combine 1 tablespoon granulated sugar, lemon juice, cornstarch, and pinch salt in medium bowl. Gently toss peaches with sugar mixture and divide evenly between two 12-ounce ramekins.
2. Combine almonds, flour, brown sugar, cinnamon, nutmeg, remaining pinch salt, and remaining 1 tablespoon granulated sugar in now-empty bowl. Drizzle with melted butter and toss with fork until evenly moistened and mixture forms large chunks with some pea-size pieces throughout. Sprinkle topping evenly over peaches, breaking up any large chunks.
3. Place ramekins on aluminum foil–lined small rimmed baking sheet and bake until filling is bubbling around edges and topping is deep golden brown, 25 to 30 minutes, rotating sheet halfway through baking. Let crisps cool on wire rack for 15 minutes before serving.

Scones

Servings: 8
Cooking Time: 20 Minutes

Ingredients:

- Scone mixture:
- 1 cup unbleached flour
- 1 teaspoon baking powder
- 2 ¼ cup brown sugar
- 3 tablespoons vegetable oil
- 4 ¼ cup low-fat buttermilk
- 5 ½ teaspoon vanilla extract
- Topping mixture:
- 1 tablespoon granulated sugar
- 1 tablespoon margarine
- 1 teaspoon ground cinnamon

Directions:

1. Preheat the toaster oven to 425° F.
2. Combine the scone mixture ingredients in a medium bowl, cutting to blend with 2 butter knives or a pastry blender. Add a little more buttermilk, if necessary, so that the dough is moist enough to stay together when pinched.
3. KNEAD the dough on a lightly floured surface for 2 minutes, then place the dough in an oiled or nonstick 9¾-inch round cake pan and pat down to spread out evenly to the edges of the pan. Cut into 8 wedges.
4. Combine the topping mixture in a small bowl, mixing well, and sprinkle evenly on the dough.
5. BAKE for 20 minutes, or until golden brown.

Cowboy Cookies

Servings: 3
Cooking Time: 14 Minutes

Ingredients:

- Recommended Hamilton Beach® Product: Stand Mixers
- 1 cup butter
- 1 cup sugar
- 1 cup light brown sugar
- 2 eggs
- 2 cups flour
- 1 teaspoon baking soda
- ½ teaspoon baking powder
- ½ teaspoon salt
- 2 cups oatmeal
- 1 tablespoon vanilla
- 12 ounces chocolate chips
- 1 ½ cups coconut

Directions:

1. Preheat the toaster oven to 350°F.
2. With flat beater attachment, cream together butter, sugar, and brown sugar at a medium setting until well blended. Mix in vanilla and eggs. Reduce speed and gradually add flour, baking soda, baking powder, and salt mix until smooth.
3. On a low setting, mix in oatmeal, chocolate chips, and coconut until well mixed. Drop rounded spoon full onto ungreased cookie sheet.
4. Bake on middle rack of oven for 12 to 14 minutes.

Coconut Cake

Servings: 6
Cooking Time: 25 Minutes

Ingredients:

- 2 cups unbleached flour
- 2 teaspoons baking powder
- 1 cup skim or low-fat soy milk
- 2 tablespoons vegetable oil
- 3 1 teaspoon vanilla extract
- 1 egg, beaten
- ¾ cup sugar
- Salt to taste
- Creamy Frosting (recipe follows)

Directions:

1. Preheat the toaster oven to 350° F.
2. Combine all the ingredients in a large bowl, mixing well.
3. Pour the cake batter into an oiled or nonstick 8½ × 8½ × 2-inch square baking (cake) pan.
4. BAKE for 25 minutes, or until a toothpick inserted in the center comes out clean. Ice with Creamy Frosting and sprinkle with coconut.

Almond Amaretto Bundt Cake

Servings: 8
Cooking Time: 37 Minutes

Ingredients:

- Nonstick baking spray with flour
- 1 (15.25- to 18-ounce) box yellow cake mix
- 1 (3.9-ounce) box vanilla instant pudding
- 1 cup sour cream
- ½ cup canola or vegetable oil
- ¼ cup amaretto or almond liqueur
- 4 large eggs
- ¼ teaspoon pure almond extract
- GLAZE
- 2 ½ cups confectioners' sugar

- 2 tablespoons amaretto
- 1 teaspoon pure vanilla extract
- 1 to 2 tablespoons milk
- Sliced almonds, toasted

Directions:

1. Preheat the toaster oven to 350°F. Spray a 12-cup Bundt pan with nonstick baking spray with flour.
2. Beat the cake mix, instant pudding, sour cream, oil, ¼ cup water, the amaretto, eggs, and almond extract in a large bowl with a handheld mixer at low speed for 30 seconds to combine the ingredients. Scrape the sides of the bowl with a rubber scraper. Beat on medium-high speed for 2 minutes.
3. Pour the batter into the prepared pan. Bake for 30 to 35 minutes, or until a wooden pick inserted into the center comes out clean.
4. Place the pan on a wire rack to cool for 10 minutes. Invert the cake onto the rack and let cool completely.
5. Meanwhile, make the glaze: Whisk the sugar, amaretto, vanilla, and 1 tablespoon milk in a small bowl. If needed, stir in the additional milk to make the desired consistency. Pour over the cake. Garnish with the sliced almonds.

Warm Chocolate Fudge Cakes

Servings: 2
Cooking Time: 35 Minutes
Ingredients:

- 6 tablespoons (1¾ ounces) all-purpose flour
- ¼ teaspoon baking powder
- ⅛ teaspoon baking soda
- ⅛ teaspoon table salt
- 2½ ounces bittersweet chocolate (2 ounces chopped, ½ ounce cut into ½-inch pieces)
- ¼ cup whole milk, room temperature
- 3 tablespoons packed light brown sugar
- 2 tablespoons vegetable oil
- 1 large egg, lightly beaten
- ¼ teaspoon vanilla extract

Directions:

1. Adjust toaster oven rack to middle position and preheat the toaster oven to 350 degrees. Grease and flour two 6-ounce ramekins. Whisk flour, baking powder, baking soda, and salt together in bowl.
2. Microwave chopped chocolate and milk in medium bowl at 50 percent power, stirring occasionally, until chocolate is melted and mixture is smooth, 1 to 3 minutes. Stir in sugar until dissolved; let cool slightly. Whisk in oil, egg, and vanilla until combined. Gently whisk in flour mixture until just combined.
3. Divide batter evenly between prepared ramekins and gently tap each ramekin on counter to release air bubbles. Wipe any drops of batter off sides of ramekins. Gently press chocolate pieces evenly into center of each ramekin to submerge in batter. Place ramekins on small rimmed baking sheet and bake cakes until tops are just firm to touch and center is gooey when pierced with toothpick, 10 to 15 minutes. Let cool for 2 to 3 minutes before serving.

Bourbon Bread Pudding

Servings: 2
Cooking Time: 120 Minutes
Ingredients:

- 6 ounces baguette, torn into 1-inch pieces (4 cups)
- ¼ cup raisins
- 2 tablespoons bourbon
- ¾ cup heavy cream
- ⅓ cup packed (2⅓ ounces) light brown sugar
- ¼ cup whole milk
- 2 large egg yolks
- 1 teaspoon vanilla extract
- ½ teaspoon ground cinnamon, divided
- ⅛ teaspoon table salt
- Pinch ground nutmeg
- 2 tablespoons unsalted butter, cut into ¼-inch pieces
- 1 tablespoon granulated sugar

Directions:

1. Adjust toaster oven rack to middle position and preheat the toaster oven to 375 degrees. Spread bread in single layer on small rimmed baking sheet and bake until golden brown and crisp, 10 to 20 minutes, tossing halfway through baking. Let bread cool completely.
2. Meanwhile, microwave raisins and bourbon in covered bowl until bubbling, 30 to 60 seconds. Let sit until softened, about 15 minutes.
3. Whisk cream, brown sugar, milk, egg yolks, vanilla, ¼ teaspoon cinnamon, salt, and nutmeg together in large bowl. Add bread and raisin mixture and toss until evenly coated. Let mixture sit, tossing occasionally, until bread begins to absorb custard and is softened, about 20 minutes.
4. Grease two 12-ounce ramekins. Divide bread mixture evenly between prepared ramekins and sprinkle with butter, granulated sugar, and remaining ¼ teaspoon cinnamon. Cover each ramekin with aluminum foil, place on small rimmed baking sheet, and bake for 30 minutes.
5. Remove foil from bread puddings and continue to bake until tops are crisp and golden brown, 10 to 15 minutes. Let bread puddings cool for 15 minutes before serving.

Mississippi Mud Brownies

Servings: 16
Cooking Time: 34 Minutes
Ingredients:

- Nonstick cooking spray
- 3 tablespoons unsweetened cocoa powder
- ¼ cup canola or vegetable oil
- ¼ cup unsalted butter, softened
- 1 cup granulated sugar
- 2 large eggs
- 1 teaspoon pure vanilla extract
- ¾ cup all-purpose flour
- ½ teaspoon table salt
- ½ cup pecan pieces, toasted
- 2 cups mini marshmallows
- FROSTING
- ¼ cup unsalted butter, melted
- 3 tablespoons unsweetened cocoa powder
- ½ teaspoon pure vanilla extract
- 2 cups confectioners' sugar

- 2 to 3 tablespoons whole milk

Directions:

1. Preheat the toaster oven to 350°F. Spray an 8-inch square baking pan with nonstick cooking spray.
2. Beat the cocoa and oil in a large bowl with a handheld mixer at medium speed. Add the butter and mix until smooth. Beat in the granulated sugar. Add the eggs, one at a time, mixing after each addition. Add the vanilla and mix. On low speed, blend in the flour and salt. Stir in the pecans.
3. Pour the batter into the prepared pan. Bake for 28 to 32 minutes, or until a wooden pick inserted into the center comes out clean.
4. Remove the brownies from the oven and sprinkle the marshmallows over the top. Return to the oven and bake for about 2 minutes or until the marshmallows are puffed. Place on a wire rack and let cool completely.
5. Meanwhile, make the frosting: Combine the butter, cocoa, vanilla, confectioners' sugar, and 2 tablespoons milk in a large bowl. Beat until smooth. If needed for the desired consistency, add additional milk. Frost the cooled brownies.

Goat Cheese–stuffed Nectarines

Servings: 4

Cooking Time: 10 Minutes

Ingredients:

- 4 ripe nectarines, halved and pitted
- 1 tablespoon olive oil
- 1 cup soft goat cheese, room temperature
- 1 tablespoon maple syrup
- ¼ teaspoon vanilla extract
- ¼ teaspoon ground cinnamon
- 2 tablespoons pecans, chopped

Directions:

1. Preheat the toaster oven to 350°F on AIR FRY for 5 minutes.
2. Place the air-fryer basket in the baking tray and place the nectarines in the basket, hollow-side up. Brush the tops and hollow of the fruit with the olive oil.
3. In position 2, air fry for 5 minutes to soften and lightly brown the fruit.
4. While the fruit is air frying, in a small bowl, stir the goat cheese, maple syrup, vanilla, and cinnamon until well blended.
5. Take the fruit out and evenly divide the cheese filling between the halves. Air fry for 5 minutes until the filling is heated through and a little melted.
6. Serve topped with pecans.

Easy Churros

Servings: 12

Cooking Time: 10 Minutes

Ingredients:

- ½ cup Water
- 4 tablespoons (¼ cup/½ stick) Butter
- ¼ teaspoon Table salt
- ½ cup All-purpose flour
- 2 Large egg(s)
- ¼ cup Granulated white sugar
- 2 teaspoons Ground cinnamon

Directions:

1. Bring the water, butter, and salt to a boil in a small saucepan set over high heat, stirring occasionally.
2. When the butter has fully melted, reduce the heat to medium and stir in the flour to form a dough. Continue cooking, stirring constantly, to dry out the dough until it coats the bottom and sides of the pan with a film, even a crust. Remove the pan from the heat, scrape the dough into a bowl, and cool for 15 minutes.
3. Using an electric hand mixer at medium speed, beat in the egg, or eggs one at a time, until the dough is smooth and firm enough to hold its shape.
4. Mix the sugar and cinnamon in a small bowl. Scoop up 1 tablespoon of the dough and roll it in the sugar mixture to form a small, coated tube about ½ inch in diameter and 2 inches long. Set it aside and make 5 more tubes for the small batch or 11 more for the large one.
5. Set the tubes on a plate and freeze for 20 minutes. Meanwhile, preheat the toaster oven to 375°F.
6. Set 3 frozen tubes in the air fryer oven for a small batch or 6 for a large one with as much air space between them as possible. Air-fry undisturbed for 10 minutes, or until puffed, brown, and set.
7. Use kitchen tongs to transfer the churros to a wire rack to cool for at least 5 minutes. Meanwhile, air-fry and cool the second batch of churros in the same way.

Wild Blueberry Sweet Empanadas

Servings: 12

Cooking Time: 8 Minutes

Ingredients:

- 2 cups frozen wild blueberries
- 5 tablespoons chia seeds
- ¼ cup honey
- 1 tablespoon lemon or lime juice
- ¼ cup water
- 1½ cups all-purpose flour
- 1 cup whole-wheat flour
- ½ teaspoon salt
- 1 tablespoon sugar
- ½ cup cold unsalted butter
- 1 egg
- ½ cup plus 2 tablespoons milk, divided
- 1 cup powdered sugar
- 1 teaspoon vanilla extract

Directions:

1. To make the wild blueberry chia jam, place the blueberries, chia seeds, honey, lemon or lime juice, and water into a blender and pulse for 2 minutes. Pour the chia jam into a glass jar or bowl and cover. Store in the refrigerator at least 4 to 8 hours or until the jam is thickened.
2. In a food processor, place the all-purpose flour, whole-wheat flour, salt, sugar, and butter and process for 2 minutes, scraping down the sides of the food processor every 30 seconds. Add in the egg and blend for 30 seconds. Using the pulse button, add in ½ cup of the milk 1 tablespoon at a time or until the dough is moist enough to handle and be rolled into a ball. Let the dough rest at room temperature for 30 minutes.

3. On a floured surface, cut the dough in half; then form a ball and cut each ball into 6 equal pieces, totaling 12 equal pieces. Work with one piece at a time, and cover the remaining dough with a towel. Roll out the dough into a 6-inch round, much like a tortilla, with ¼ inch thickness. Place 4 tablespoons of filling in the center of round, fold over to form a half-circle. Using a fork, crimp the edges together and pierce the top with a fork for air holes. Repeat with the remaining dough and filling.
4. Preheat the toaster oven to 350°F.
5. Working in batches, place 3 to 4 empanadas in the air fryer oven and spray with cooking spray. Air-fry for 8 minutes. Repeat in batches, as needed. Allow the sweet empanadas to cool for 15 minutes. Meanwhile, in a small bowl, whisk together the powdered sugar, the remaining 2 tablespoons of milk, and the vanilla extract. Then drizzle the glaze over the surface and serve.

Fresh Strawberry Bars

Servings: 16
Cooking Time: 55 Minutes
Ingredients:

- 1 cup unsalted butter, softened
- 2 cups all-purpose flour
- ½ teaspoon table salt
- 1 ⅓ cups sugar
- 2 ½ cups sliced fresh strawberries
- 2 teaspoons fresh lemon juice
- 2 tablespoons cornstarch

Directions:

1. Preheat the toaster oven to 375°F. Line an 8-inch square pan with nonstick aluminum foil.
2. Beat the butter, flour, salt, and 1 cup of the sugar in a large bowl with a handheld mixer at medium speed, until the mixture is combined and resembles crumbles. Place half of the mixture in the prepared pan. Press down evenly to form a crust.
3. Combine the remaining ⅓ cup sugar, the strawberries, lemon juice, and cornstarch in a medium bowl. Spread evenly over the crust. Sprinkle the remaining crumb mixture over the strawberries. Bake for 50 to 55 minutes or until bubbly and light brown. Let cool completely on a wire rack. They are best served at room temperature.

Coconut Rice Cake

Servings: 8
Cooking Time: 30 Minutes
Ingredients:

- 1 cup all-natural coconut water
- 1 cup unsweetened coconut milk
- 1 teaspoon almond extract
- ¼ teaspoon salt
- 4 tablespoons honey
- cooking spray
- ¾ cup raw jasmine rice
- 2 cups sliced or cubed fruit

Directions:

1. In a medium bowl, mix together the coconut water, coconut milk, almond extract, salt, and honey.
2. Spray air fryer oven baking pan with cooking spray and add the rice.
3. Pour liquid mixture over rice.
4. Preheat the toaster oven to 360°F and air-fry for 15 minutes. Stir and air-fry for 15 minutes longer or until rice grains are tender.
5. Allow cake to cool slightly. Run a dull knife around edge of cake, inside the pan. Turn the cake out onto a platter and garnish with fruit.

Fried Snickers Bars

Servings: 8
Cooking Time: 4 Minutes
Ingredients:

- ⅓ cup All-purpose flour
- 1 Large egg white(s), beaten until foamy
- 1½ cups (6 ounces) Vanilla wafer cookie crumbs
- 8 Fun-size (0.6-ounce/17-gram) Snickers bars, frozen
- Vegetable oil spray

Directions:

1. Preheat the toaster oven to 400°F.
2. Set up and fill three shallow soup plates or small pie plates on your counter: one for the flour, one for the beaten egg white(s), and one for the cookie crumbs.
3. Unwrap the frozen candy bars. Dip one in the flour, turning it to coat on all sides. Gently stir any excess, then set it in the beaten egg white(s). Turn it to coat all sides, even the ends, then let any excess egg white slip back into the rest. Set the candy bar in the cookie crumbs. Turn to coat on all sides, even the ends. Dip the candy bar back in the egg white(s) a second time, then into the cookie crumbs a second time, making sure you have an even coating all around. Coat the covered candy bar all over with vegetable oil spray. Set aside so you can dip and coat the remaining candy bars.
4. Set the coated candy bars in the pan with as much air space between them as possible. Air-fry undisturbed for 4 minutes, or until golden brown.
5. Remove the pan from the machine and let the candy bars cool in the pan for 10 minutes. Use a nonstick-safe spatula to transfer them to a wire rack and cool for 5 minutes more before chowing down.

Orange-glazed Brownies

Servings: 12
Cooking Time: 30 Minutes
Ingredients:

- 3 squares unsweetened chocolate
- 3 tablespoons margarine
- 1 cup sugar
- ½ cup orange juice
- 2 eggs
- 1½ cups unbleached flour
- 1 teaspoon baking powder
- Salt to taste
- 1 tablespoon grated orange zest
- Orange Glaze (recipe follows)

Directions:

1. BROIL the chocolate and margarine in an oiled or nonstick 8½ × 8½ × 2-inch square baking (cake) pan for 3

minutes, or until almost melted. Remove from the oven and stir until completely melted. Transfer the chocolate/margarine mixture to a medium bowl.
2. Beat in the sugar, orange juice, and eggs with an electric mixer. Stir in the flour, baking powder, salt, and orange zest and mix until well blended. Pour into the oiled or nonstick square cake pan.
3. BAKE at 350° F. for 30 minutes, or until a toothpick inserted in the center comes out clean. Make holes over the entire top by piercing with a fork or toothpick. Paint with Orange Glaze and cut into squares.

Make-ahead Oatmeal-raisin Cookies

Servings: 8
Cooking Time: 45 Minutes
Ingredients:
- 1 cup (5 ounces) all-purpose flour
- ¾ teaspoon table salt
- ½ teaspoon baking soda
- ¼ teaspoon ground cinnamon
- ¾ cup (5¼ ounces) dark brown sugar
- ½ cup (3½ ounces) granulated sugar
- ½ cup vegetable oil
- 4 tablespoons unsalted butter, melted and cooled
- 1 large egg plus 1 large yolk
- 1 teaspoon vanilla extract
- 3 cups (9 ounces) old-fashioned rolled oats
- ½ cup raisins

Directions:
1. Adjust toaster oven rack to middle position and preheat the toaster oven to 350 degrees. Line large and small rimmed baking sheets with parchment paper. Whisk flour, salt, baking soda, and cinnamon together in bowl.
2. Whisk brown sugar and granulated sugar together in medium bowl. Whisk in oil and melted butter until combined. Whisk in egg and yolk and vanilla until smooth. Gently stir in flour mixture with rubber spatula until soft dough forms. Fold in oats and raisins until evenly distributed (mixture will be stiff).
3. Working with 3 tablespoons dough at a time, roll into balls. Space desired number of dough balls at least 1½ inches apart on prepared small sheet; space remaining dough balls evenly on prepared large sheet. Using bottom of greased dry measuring cup, press each ball until 2½ inches in diameter.
4. Bake small sheet of cookies until edges are just beginning to brown and centers are still soft but not wet, 10 to 15 minutes. Let cookies cool slightly on sheet. Serve warm or at room temperature.
5. Freeze remaining large sheet of cookies until firm, about 1 hour. Transfer cookies to 1-gallon zipper-lock bag and freeze for up to 1 month. Bake frozen cookies as directed; do not thaw.

Freezer-to-oven Chocolate Chip Cookies

Servings: 6
Cooking Time: 15 Minutes
Ingredients:
- 2 ½ cups all-purpose flour
- 1 teaspoon baking soda
- ½ teaspoon table salt
- ¼ teaspoon baking powder
- 1 cup unsalted butter, softened
- 1 cup packed dark brown sugar
- ¾ cup granulated sugar
- 2 large eggs
- 2 teaspoons pure vanilla extract
- 1 (12-ounce) package semisweet chocolate chips

Directions:
1. Preheat the toaster oven to 375°F. Line a 12 x 12-inch baking sheet with parchment paper.
2. Whisk the flour, baking soda, salt, and baking powder in a medium bowl; set aside.
3. Beat the butter, brown sugar, and granulated sugar in a large bowl with a handheld mixer at medium-high speed for 2 minutes or until creamy. Beat in the eggs, one at a time, beating well after each addition. Beat in the vanilla. Mix in the dry ingredients until blended. Stir in the chocolate chips.
4. Using a 2-tablespoon scoop, shape the batter into balls about 1 ½ inches in diameter. Arrange the cookies 1 inch apart on the prepared baking sheet. Bake for 13 to 15 minutes or until golden brown. Remove from the oven and let cool for 1 minute, then transfer the cookies to a wire rack.

Soft Peanut Butter Cookies

Servings: 12
Cooking Time: 20 Minutes
Ingredients:
- 1/2 cup vegetable shortening
- 1/2 cup peanut butter
- 1 1/4 cups light brown sugar
- 1 egg
- 1 teaspoon vanilla
- 1/2 teaspoon salt
- 1 1/2 cups flour
- 1 teaspoon baking soda
- Sugar crystals

Directions:
1. Preheat the toaster oven to 275°F.
2. Using the flat beater attachment, beat shortening, peanut butter, brown sugar, egg, and vanilla at a medium setting until well blended.
3. Reduce speed to low and gradually add dry ingredients until blended. Dough will be crumbly.
4. Roll 3 tablespoon-size portions of the dough into a ball. Place on ungreased cookie sheet.
5. Press to 1/2-inch thick. Sprinkle with sugar crystals.
6. Bake 18 to 20 minutes. Do not overcook.

White Chocolate Cranberry Blondies

Servings: 6
Cooking Time: 18 Minutes
Ingredients:

- ⅓ cup butter
- ½ cup sugar
- 1 teaspoon vanilla extract
- 1 large egg
- 1 cup all-purpose flour
- ½ teaspoon baking powder
- ⅛ teaspoon salt
- ¼ cup dried cranberries
- ¼ cup white chocolate chips

Directions:

1. Preheat the toaster oven to 320°F.
2. In a large bowl, cream the butter with the sugar and vanilla extract. Whisk in the egg and set aside.
3. In a separate bowl, mix the flour with the baking powder and salt. Then gently mix the dry ingredients into the wet. Fold in the cranberries and chocolate chips.
4. Liberally spray an oven-safe 7-inch springform pan with olive oil and pour the batter into the pan.
5. Air-fry for 17 minutes or until a toothpick inserted in the center comes out clean.
6. Remove and let cool 5 minutes before serving.

Cheese Blintzes

Servings: 6
Cooking Time: 10 Minutes
Ingredients:

- 1½ 7½-ounce package(s) farmer cheese
- 3 tablespoons Regular or low-fat cream cheese (not fat-free)
- 3 tablespoons Granulated white sugar
- ¼ teaspoon Vanilla extract
- 6 Egg roll wrappers
- 3 tablespoons Butter, melted and cooled

Directions:

1. Preheat the toaster oven to 375°F.
2. Use a flatware fork to mash the farmer cheese, cream cheese, sugar, and vanilla in a small bowl until smooth.
3. Set one egg roll wrapper on a clean, dry work surface. Place ¼ cup of the filling at the edge closest to you, leaving a ½-inch gap before the edge of the wrapper. Dip your clean finger in water and wet the edges of the wrapper. Fold the perpendicular sides over the filling, then roll the wrapper closed with the filling inside. Set it aside seam side down and continue filling the remainder of the wrappers.
4. Brush the wrappers on all sides with the melted butter. Be generous. Set them seam side down in the air fryer oven with as much space between them as possible. Air-fry undisturbed for 10 minutes, or until lightly browned.
5. Use a nonstick-safe spatula to transfer the blintzes to a wire rack. Cool for at least 5 minutes or up to 20 minutes before serving.

Maple-glazed Pumpkin Pie

Servings: 2
Cooking Time: 10 Minutes
Ingredients:

- Filling:
- 1 15-ounce can pumpkin pie filling
- 1 12-ounce can low-fat evaporated milk
- 1 egg
- 3 tablespoons maple syrup
- ½ teaspoon grated nutmeg
- ½ teaspoon ground ginger
- 1 teaspoon ground cinnamon
- Salt to taste
- 1 Apple Juice Piecrust, baked (recipe follows)
- Dark glaze:
- 3 tablespoons maple syrup
- 2 tablespoons dark brown sugar

Directions:

1. Preheat the toaster oven to 400° F.
2. Combine all the filling ingredients in a large bowl and beat with an electric mixer until smooth. Pour into the piecrust shell.
3. BAKE for 40 minutes, or until a knife inserted in the center comes out clean.
4. Combine the dark glaze ingredients in a baking pan.
5. BROIL for 5 minutes, or until bubbling. Remove from the oven and stir to dissolve the sugar. Broil again for 3 minutes, or until the liquid is thickened and the sugar is dissolved. Spoon on top of the cooled pumpkin pie, spreading evenly, then chill for at least 1 hour before serving.

Frozen Brazo De Mercedes

Servings: 8
Cooking Time: 15 Minutes
Ingredients:

- 1 pint vanilla ice cream, softened to room temperature
- 1 (8 inch) premade graham cracker crust
- 6 large eggs, yolks and whites separated
- 7 ounces condensed milk
- ½ teaspoon vanilla extract
- ¼ teaspoon cream of tartar
- ⅓ cup granulated sugar

Directions:

1. Spread the ice cream on the bottom of the graham cracker crust in an even layer, cover with plastic wrap, and place in the freezer for 8 hours or overnight.
2. Whisk egg yolks and condensed milk over a double boiler continuously for 15 minutes or until the mixture becomes thick.
3. Whisk the vanilla extract into the egg mixture until fully combined.
4. Pass the custard through a fine sieve to remove any clumps.
5. Remove the ice cream and top with the egg yolk mixture, cover with plastic wrap, and place back into the freezer for 2 hours.
6. Beat the egg whites and cream of tartar in a stand mixer on high speed.
7. Add the sugar in slowly once the egg whites begin to foam.

8. Beat the egg whites for two minutes or until they form stiff peaks.
9. Remove the plastic wrap from the pie and top with the beaten egg whites.
10. Preheat the toaster Oven to 350°F.
11. Place the pie on the wire rack, then insert the rack at mid position in the preheated air fryer.
12. Select the Bake and Shake functions, adjust time to 15 minutes, and press Start/Pause.
13. Rotate the pie halfway through cooking for even browning. The Shake Reminder will let you know when.
14. Remove when done and place in the fridge for 1 hour, uncovered.
15. Cover the pie, then place in the freezer for 6 hours or overnight.
16. Remove the pie and allow it to rest at room temperature for 10 minutes, then slice and serve.

Blackberry Pie

Servings: 6
Cooking Time: 30 Minutes
Ingredients:
- Filling:
- 2 16-ounce bags frozen blackberries, thawed, or 2 cups fresh blackberries, washed and well drained
- 1 4-ounce jar baby food prunes
- 2 tablespoons cornstarch
- 3 ¼ cup brown sugar
- 1 tablespoon lemon juice
- Salt to taste
- 1 Graham Cracker Crust, baked (recipe follows)
- Meringue Topping (recipe follows)

Directions:
1. Preheat the toaster oven to 350° F.
2. Combine the filling ingredients in a large bowl, mixing well. Spoon the filling into the baked Graham Cracker Crust and spread evenly.
3. BAKE for 30 minutes. When cool, top with the Meringue Topping.

Cheesecake Wontons

Servings: 6
Cooking Time: 16 Minutes
Ingredients:
- ¼ cup Regular or low-fat cream cheese (not fat-free)
- 2 tablespoons Granulated white sugar
- 1½ tablespoons Egg yolk
- ¼ teaspoon Vanilla extract
- ⅛ teaspoon Table salt
- 1½ tablespoons All-purpose flour
- 16 Wonton wrappers (vegetarian, if a concern)
- Vegetable oil spray

Directions:
1. Preheat the toaster oven to 400°F.
2. Using a flatware fork, mash the cream cheese, sugar, egg yolk, and vanilla in a small bowl until smooth. Add the salt and flour and continue mashing until evenly combined.
3. Set a wonton wrapper on a clean, dry work surface so that one corner faces you (so that it looks like a diamond on your work surface). Set 1 teaspoon of the cream cheese mixture in the middle of the wrapper but just above a horizontal line that would divide the wrapper in half. Dip your clean finger in water and run it along the edges of the wrapper. Fold the corner closest to you up and over the filling, lining it up with the corner farthest from you, thereby making a stuffed triangle. Press gently to seal. Wet the two triangle tips nearest you, then fold them up and together over the filling. Gently press together to seal and fuse. Set aside and continue making more stuffed wontons, 11 more for the small batch, 15 more for the medium batch, or 23 more for the large one.
4. Lightly coat the stuffed wrappers on all sides with vegetable oil spray. Set them with the fused corners up in the air fryer oven with as much air space between them as possible. Air-fry undisturbed for 6 minutes, or until golden brown and crisp.
5. Gently dump the contents of the air fryer oven onto a wire rack. Cool for at least 5 minutes before serving.

Green Grape Meringues

Servings: 4
Cooking Time: 40 Minutes
Ingredients:
- 1 cup sugar
- 3 egg whites, beaten until stiff
- ½ teaspoon lemon juice
- Vanilla frozen yogurt
- 1 cup sliced fresh green grapes
- 2 squares unsweetened baking chocolate, shaved
- Nonfat whipped topping

Directions:
1. Preheat the toaster oven to 250° F.
2. Add the sugar slowly to the egg white mixture and continue to beat. Add the lemon juice. With a tablespoon, drop on an oiled or nonstick 6½ × 10-inch baking sheet to make a mound of meringue approximately 2 inches across. Make a slight depression in the center of each one.
3. BAKE for 40 minutes, or until crusty and browned. Cool and fill each meringue shell with a scoop of vanilla frozen yogurt. Top with equal portions of green grapes, chocolate shavings, and nonfat whipped topping. The meringues may be stored in an airtight container until ready to use.

Spice Cake

Servings: 6
Cooking Time: 25 Minutes
Ingredients:
- 1 cup applesauce or 2 4-ounce jars baby food prunes
- ¼ cup skim milk or low-fat soy milk
- 1 tablespoon vegetable oil
- ½ cup brown sugar
- 1 egg
- 1½ cups unbleached flour
- 1 teaspoon baking powder
- ½ teaspoon baking soda
- ¼ teaspoon grated nutmeg
- ½ teaspoon ground cinnamon

- ½ teaspoon grated orange zest
- Salt to taste
- Creamy Frosting

Directions:

1. Preheat the toaster oven to 350° F.
2. Stir together the applesauce, milk, oil, sugar, and egg in a small bowl. Set aside.
3. Combine the flour, baking powder, nutmeg, cinnamon, orange zest, and salt in a medium bowl. Add the applesauce mixture and stir to mix well. Pour the batter into an oiled or nonstick 8½ × 8½ × 2-inch square baking (cake) pan.
4. BAKE for 25 minutes, or until a toothpick inserted in the center comes out clean. Frost with Creamy Frosting.

Lime Cheesecake

Servings: 6
Cooking Time: 30 Minutes
Ingredients:

- Oil spray (hand-pumped)
- ½ cup graham cracker crumbs
- 24 ounces cream cheese, room temperature
- 1½ cups granulated sugar
- 4 large eggs
- ¼ cup sour cream
- Juice and zest of 1 lime
- 2 teaspoons vanilla extract

Directions:

1. Place the rack in position 1 and preheat the oven to 350°F on BAKE for 5 minutes.
2. Lightly spray an 8-inch springform pan with the oil and spread the graham cracker crumbs in the bottom.
3. Bake for 10 minutes, then remove the crust from the air fryer and set it aside.
4. In a large bowl, beat the cream cheese until very smooth with an electric hand beater. Add the sugar by ½-cup measures, beating very well after each addition and scraping down the sides of the bowl.
5. Add the eggs one at a time, beating well after each addition and scraping down the sides of the bowl.
6. Beat in the sour cream, lime juice, lime zest, and vanilla until very well blended and fluffy, about 4 minutes.
7. Transfer the batter to the pan and smooth the top.
8. Bake for 30 minutes or until set.
9. Let the cheesecake cool in the oven for 30 minutes and then transfer to the refrigerator to cool completely. Serve.

Baked Apple

Servings: 4
Cooking Time: 20 Minutes
Ingredients:

- 3 small Honey Crisp or other baking apples
- 3 tablespoons maple syrup
- 3 tablespoons chopped pecans
- 1 tablespoon firm butter, cut into 6 pieces

Directions:

1. Put ½ cup water in the drawer of the air fryer oven.
2. Wash apples well and dry them.
3. Split apples in half. Remove core and a little of the flesh to make a cavity for the pecans.
4. Place apple halves in air fryer oven, cut side up.
5. Spoon 1½ teaspoons pecans into each cavity.
6. Spoon ½ tablespoon maple syrup over pecans in each apple.
7. Top each apple with ½ teaspoon butter.
8. Preheat the toaster oven to 360°F and air-fry for 20 minutes, until apples are tender.

Heritage Chocolate Chip Cookies

Servings: 16-18
Cooking Time: 12 Minutes
Ingredients:

- 1 1/2 cups all-purpose flour
- 1 teaspoon baking powder
- 1/2 teaspoon salt
- 1 large egg, unbeaten
- 1/2 cup shortening
- 1/2 cup packed dark brown sugar
- 1/4 cup granulated sugar
- 2 teaspoons vanilla extract
- 1 tablespoon milk
- 1 cup chocolate chips

Directions:

1. Preheat the toaster oven to 375°F.
2. Place all ingredients except chocolate chips in large mixer bowl. With electric mixer on low speed, beat until ingredients are mixed. Gradually increase speed to medium and beat 3 minutes, stopping to scrape bowl as needed.
3. Add chocolate chips and beat on low until blended.
4. Line cookie sheets with parchment paper. Using a small scoop, place 12 scoops of cookie dough about 1-inch apart on parchment.
5. Bake 10 to 12 minutes or until cookies are browned. Slide parchment with baked cookies onto rack to cool. Repeat with remaining dough.

Peach Cobbler

Servings: 4
Cooking Time: 35 Minutes
Ingredients:

- FOR THE FILLING
- 4 cups chopped fresh peaches
- ½ cup sugar
- 2 tablespoons cornstarch
- 1 teaspoon vanilla extract
- FOR THE COBBLER
- 1 cup all-purpose flour
- ¼ cup sugar
- ¾ teaspoon baking powder
- Pinch of sea salt
- 3 tablespoons cold salted butter, cut into ½-inch cubes
- ½ cup buttermilk

Directions:

1. To make the filling
2. In a medium bowl, toss together the peaches, sugar, cornstarch, and vanilla.
3. Transfer to an 8-inch-square baking dish. Set aside.
4. To make the cobbler

5. Place the rack in position 1 and preheat the toaster oven to 350°F on BAKE for 5 minutes.
6. In a large bowl, stir the flour, sugar, baking powder, and sea salt.
7. Using your fingertips, rub the butter into the flour mixture until the mixture resembles coarse crumbs.
8. Add the buttermilk in a thin stream to the flour crumbs, tossing with a fork until a sticky dough forms.
9. Scoop the batter by tablespoons and dollop it on the peaches, spacing the mounds out evenly and leaving gaps for the steam to escape.
10. Bake for 35 minutes, or until the cobbler is golden brown and the filling is bubbly.
11. Serve warm.

Dark Chocolate Banana Bread

Servings: 8
Cooking Time: 60 Minutes
Ingredients:

- ½ cup salted butter, melted, plus extra for greasing the pan
- 1 cup all-purpose flour, plus extra for dusting the pan
- ¾ cup dark brown sugar
- ¼ cup cocoa powder
- 2 teaspoons baking powder
- ¼ teaspoon sea salt
- 2 large bananas, mashed
- 1 large egg
- 1½ teaspoons vanilla extract
- ½ cup dark chocolate chips

Directions:

1. Place the rack in position 1 and preheat the oven to 325°F on BAKE for 5 minutes.
2. Grease a 9-by-5-inch loaf pan with melted butter and dust with all-purpose flour. Set aside.
3. In a medium bowl, stir the flour, brown sugar, cocoa powder, baking powder, and salt together until well combined.
4. In a medium bowl, whisk the butter, bananas, egg, and vanilla until well blended.
5. Add the wet ingredients to the dry ingredients and stir until combined. Add the chocolate chips and stir until incorporated.
6. Bake for 1 hour, or until a toothpick inserted into the center of the bread comes out mostly clean. If the bread starts to get too dark, cover the top with foil and bake until done.
7. Let the bread cool for 10 minutes and then run a knife around the edge and remove the bread from the loaf pan to cool completely on a rack.
8. Serve when cool.

Lemon Torte

Servings: 6
Cooking Time: 16 Minutes
Ingredients:

- First mixture:
- ¼ cup margarine, at room temperature
- ½ teaspoon grated lemon zest
- 3 egg yolks
- ¼ cup sugar
- ⅓ cup unbleached flour
- 3 tablespoons cornstarch
- Second mixture:
- 3 egg whites
- 2 tablespoons sugar
- Cream Cheese Frosting (recipe follows)

Directions:

1. Beat together the first mixture ingredients in a medium bowl with an electric mixer until the mixture is smooth. Set aside. Clean the electric mixer beaters.
2. Beat the second mixture together: Beat the egg whites into soft peaks in a medium bowl, gradually adding the sugar, and continue beating until the peaks are stiff. Fold the first mixture into the second mixture to make the torte batter.
3. Pour ½ cup torte batter into a small oiled or nonstick 3½ × 7½ × 2¼-inch loaf pan.
4. BROIL for 1 or 2 minutes, or until lightly browned. Remove from the oven.
5. Pour and spread evenly another ½ cup batter on top of the first layer. Broil again for 1 or 2 minutes, or until lightly browned. Repeat the process until all the batter is used up. When cool, run a knife around the sides to loosen and invert onto a plate. Chill. Frost with Cream Cheese Frosting and serve chilled.

Orange Almond Ricotta Cookies

Servings: 24
Cooking Time: 15 Minutes
Ingredients:

- Cookie Ingredients
- ½ stick unsalted butter, room temperature
- 1 cup sugar
- 1 large egg
- 1 cup ricotta cheese, drained
- 1½ tablespoons orange juice
- 1 orange, zested
- ¼ teaspoon almond extract
- 1¼ cups all purpose flour
- ½ teaspoon baking powder
- ½ teaspoon salt
- Glaze Ingredients
- 1 cup powdered sugar
- 1½ tablespoons orange juice
- ½ orange, zested

Directions:

1. Beat together the butter and sugar for 3 minutes or until light and fluffy.
2. Add the egg, ricotta, orange juice, orange zest, and almond extract and beat until well combined. Add the flour, baking powder, and salt, then fold gently to combine. Don't overmix.
3. Preheat the toaster Oven to 350°F.
4. Line the food tray with parchment paper, then divide the dough into 1½-tablespoon pieces and place on the tray.
5. Insert the tray at mid position in the preheated oven.

6. Select the Bake function, adjust time to 15 minutes, and press Start/Pause.
7. Remove when done and allow cookies to cool completely before glazing.
8. Make the glaze by stirring together the powdered sugar, orange juice, and zest until smooth. According to your preference, add more powdered sugar to make the glaze thicker, or more orange juice to make the glaze thinner.
9. Spoon about ½-teaspoon of the glaze on each cookie and spread gently. Allow the glaze to harden before serving

Almond-roasted Pears

Servings: 4
Cooking Time: 15 Minutes

Ingredients:

- Yogurt Topping
- 1 container vanilla Greek yogurt (5–6 ounces)
- ¼ teaspoon almond flavoring
- 2 whole pears
- ¼ cup crushed Biscoff cookies (approx. 4 cookies)
- 1 tablespoon sliced almonds
- 1 tablespoon butter

Directions:

1. Stir almond flavoring into yogurt and set aside while preparing pears.
2. Halve each pear and spoon out the core.
3. Place pear halves in air fryer oven.
4. Stir together the cookie crumbs and almonds. Place a quarter of this mixture into the hollow of each pear half.
5. Cut butter into 4 pieces and place one piece on top of crumb mixture in each pear.
6. Preheat the toaster oven to 400°F and air-fry for 15 minutes or until pears have cooked through but are still slightly firm.
7. Serve pears warm with a dollop of yogurt topping.

Peanut Butter Cup Doughnut Holes

Servings: 24
Cooking Time: 4 Minutes

Ingredients:

- 1½ cups bread flour
- 1 teaspoon active dry yeast
- 1 tablespoon sugar
- ¼ teaspoon salt
- ½ cup warm milk
- ½ teaspoon vanilla extract
- 2 egg yolks
- 2 tablespoons melted butter
- 24 miniature peanut butter cups, plus a few more for garnish
- vegetable oil, in a spray bottle
- Doughnut Topping
- 1 cup chocolate chips
- 2 tablespoons milk

Directions:

1. Combine the flour, yeast, sugar and salt in a bowl. Add the milk, vanilla, egg yolks and butter. Mix well until the dough starts to come together. Transfer the dough to a floured surface and knead by hand for 2 minutes. Shape the dough into a ball and transfer it to a large oiled bowl. Cover the bowl with a towel and let the dough rise in a warm place for 1 to 1½ hours, until the dough has doubled in size.
2. When the dough has risen, punch it down and roll it into a 24-inch long log. Cut the dough into 24 pieces. Push a peanut butter cup into the center of each piece of dough, pinch the dough shut and roll it into a ball. Place the dough balls on a cookie sheet and let them rise in a warm place for 30 minutes.
3. Preheat the toaster oven to 400°F.
4. Spray or brush the dough balls lightly with vegetable oil. Air-fry eight at a time, at 400°F for 4 minutes, turning them over halfway through the cooking process.
5. While the doughnuts are air frying, prepare the topping. Place the chocolate chips and milk in a microwave safe bowl. Microwave on high for 1 minute. Stir and microwave for an additional 30 seconds if necessary to get all the chips to melt. Stir until the chips are melted and smooth.
6. Dip the top half of the doughnut holes into the melted chocolate. Place them on a rack to set up for just a few minutes and watch them disappear.

Key Lime Pie

Servings: 8
Cooking Time: 60 Minutes

Ingredients:

- FILLING
- 1 (14-ounce) can sweetened condensed milk
- 4 large egg yolks
- 4 teaspoons grated lime zest plus ½ cup juice (5 limes)
- CRUST
- 11 whole graham crackers, broken into 1-inch pieces
- 3 tablespoons granulated sugar
- 5 tablespoons unsalted butter, melted and cooled
- TOPPING
- ¾ cup heavy cream
- ¼ cup (1 ounce) confectioners' sugar

Directions:

1. FOR THE FILLING: Whisk condensed milk, egg yolks, and lime zest and juice together in bowl until smooth. Cover mixture and let sit at room temperature until thickened, about 30 minutes.
2. FOR THE CRUST: Adjust toaster oven rack to middle position and preheat the toaster oven to 325 degrees. Process graham cracker pieces and sugar in food processor to fine, even crumbs, about 30 seconds. Sprinkle melted butter over crumbs and pulse to incorporate, about 5 pulses.
3. Sprinkle mixture into 9-inch pie plate. Using bottom of dry measuring cup, press crumbs into even layer on bottom and up sides of pie plate. Bake until crust is fragrant and beginning to brown, 10 to 15 minutes. Transfer to wire rack and let cool slightly, about 10 minutes.
4. Pour thickened filling into warm crust and smooth top. Bake pie until center is firm but jiggles slightly when shaken, 12 to 17 minutes. Let pie cool slightly on wire rack, about 1 hour. Cover pie loosely with plastic wrap and refrigerate until filling is chilled and set, at least 3 hours or up to 24 hours.

5. For the topping Using stand mixer fitted with whisk attachment, whip cream and sugar on medium-low speed until foamy, about 1 minute. Increase speed to high and whip until soft peaks form, 1 to 3 minutes. (Topping can be refrigerated in fine-mesh strainer set over small bowl and covered with plastic wrap for up to 8 hours.) Spread whipped cream attractively over pie. Serve.

Almost Sinless Pear Banana Bread Pudding

Servings: 4
Cooking Time: 40 Minutes
Ingredients:

- 1 cup peeled and sliced fresh pears or 1 cup sliced canned pears, well drained
- 1 banana
- 1 cup skim milk
- 1 egg
- 2 tablespoons light brown sugar
- ¼ teaspoon salt ½ teaspoon ground cinnamon
- 2 cups toast, cut into 1 × 1-inch cubes or pieces

Directions:

1. Preheat the toaster oven to 400° F.
2. Blend the pears, banana, milk, egg, sugar, salt, and cinnamon in a food processor or blender until smooth. Transfer to an 8½ × 8½ × 4-inch ovenproof baking dish. Add the toast and mix well.
3. BAKE for 40 minutes, or until the center is firm and lightly browned. Cool and top with whipped cream, ice cream, nuts, or fresh or canned berries.

Brownie Cookies

Servings: 3
Cooking Time: 9 Minutes
Ingredients:

- 2/3 cup shortening
- 1 1/2 cups brown sugar, packed
- 1 tablespoon water
- 1 teaspoon vanilla
- 2 eggs
- 1 1/3 cups flour
- 1/3 cup unsweetened baking cocoa
- 1/4 teaspoon baking soda
- 1/2 teaspoon salt
- 12 ounces semi-sweet chocolate chips

Directions:

1. Preheat the toaster oven to 375°F.
2. With flat beater, cream shortening and brown sugar on medium setting until blended.
3. Add water, vanilla, and eggs and mix. Add flour, cocoa, baking soda, and salt and beat at a medium setting until thoroughly mixed.
4. Stir in chocolate chips on low setting.
5. Drop tablespoons of dough on ungreased baking sheets.
6. Bake 7 to 9 minutes. Do not overcook.

Blueberry Cookies

Servings: 4
Cooking Time: 12 Minutes
Ingredients:

- 1 egg
- 1 tablespoon margarine, at room temperature
- ⅓ cup sugar
- 1¼ cups unbleached flour
- Salt to taste
- 1 teaspoon baking powder
- 1 10-ounce package frozen blueberries, well drained, or
- 1½ cups fresh blueberries, rinsed and drained

Directions:

1. Preheat the toaster oven to 400° F.
2. Beat together the egg, margarine, and sugar in a medium bowl with an electric mixer until smooth. Add the flour, salt, and baking powder, mixing thoroughly. Gently stir in the blueberries just to blend. Do not overmix.
3. Drop by teaspoonfuls on an oiled or nonstick 6½ × 10-inch baking sheet or an oiled or nonstick 8½ × 8½ × 2-inch square baking (cake) pan.
4. BAKE for 12 minutes, or until the cookies are golden brown.

Coconut Rice Pudding

Servings: 6
Cooking Time: 55 Minutes
Ingredients:

- ½ cup short-grain brown rice
- Pudding mixture:
- 1 egg, beaten
- 1 tablespoon cornstarch
- ½ cup fat-free half-and-half
- ½ cup chopped raisins
- 1 teaspoon vanilla extract
- ½ teaspoon ground cinnamon
- ½ teaspoon grated nutmeg
- Salt to taste
- ¼ cup shredded sweetened coconut
- Fat-free whipped topping

Directions:

1. Preheat the toaster oven to 400° F.
2. Combine the rice and 1½ cups water in a 1-quart 8½ × 8½ × 4-inch ovenproof baking dish. Cover with aluminum foil.
3. BAKE, covered, for 45 minutes, or until the rice is tender. Remove from the oven and add the pudding mixture ingredients, mixing well.
4. BAKE, uncovered, for 10 minutes, or until the top is lightly browned. Sprinkle the top with coconut and chill before serving. Top with fat-free whipped topping.

Dark Chocolate Peanut Butter S'mores

Servings: 4
Cooking Time: 6 Minutes

Ingredients:

- 4 graham cracker sheets
- 4 marshmallows
- 4 teaspoons chunky peanut butter
- 4 ounces dark chocolate
- ½ teaspoon ground cinnamon

Directions:

1. Preheat the toaster oven to 390°F. Break the graham crackers in half so you have 8 pieces.
2. Place 4 pieces of graham cracker on the bottom of the air fryer oven. Top each with one of the marshmallows and bake for 6 or 7 minutes, or until the marshmallows have a golden brown center.
3. While cooking, slather each of the remaining graham crackers with 1 teaspoon peanut butter.
4. When baking completes, carefully remove each of the graham crackers, add 1 ounce of dark chocolate on top of the marshmallow, and lightly sprinkle with cinnamon. Top with the remaining peanut butter graham cracker to make the sandwich. Serve immediately.

INDEX

C

T

V

W

Y

Z

Lightning Source UK Ltd.
Milton Keynes UK
UKHW050809070922
408438UK00002B/46